The theory of natural monopoly

The theory of natural monopoly

WILLIAM W. SHARKEY

Bell Laboratories
Murray Hill, New Jersey

CAMBRIDGE UNIVERSITY PRESS

Cambridge
London   New York   New Rochelle
Melbourne   Sidney

Published by the Press Syndicate of the University of Cambridge
The Pitt Building, Trumpington Street, Cambridge CB2 1RP
32 East 57th Street, New York, NY 10022, USA
296 Beaconsfield Parade, Middle Park, Melbourne 3206, Australia

First published 1982

Printed in the United States of America

Library of Congress Cataloging in Publication Data
Sharkey, William W.
The theory of natural monopoly.
Bibliography: p.
Includes index.
1. Monopolies.   I. Title.   II. Title:
Natural monopoly.
HD2757.2.S47   338.8′2′01   82–1136
ISBN 0 521 24394 7   hard covers   AACR2
ISBN 0 521 27194 0   paperback

The type for this book was prepared and output at Bell Laboratories, Murray Hill, New Jersey, using the UNIX ™ system and the Autologic APS-5 typesetting machine.

Contents

Preface

This study was begun in the fall of 1978 following the publication in several major economics journals of results that cast the "theory of natural monopoly" in a new light. The traditional viewpoint had generally been that certain industries, primarily the regulated public utilities, might by nature be monopolies but that assuredly no theory was required to account for the natural monopoly status of any given industry.

Recently this viewpoint has been questioned by a number of sources. From a policy-making perspective the last decade has witnessed the transformation of many industries from a regime of pervasive regulation to one of substantial competition. From a theoretical perspective it has been observed that the proper definition of natural monopoly depends on the more elusive property known as subadditivity of costs, rather than on the simple and easily measured condition of economies of scale. Therefore it is no longer obvious, or self-evident, whether or not a given industry satisfies the conditions of natural monopoly.

The purpose of this book is to provide a comprehensive theory that will help those who wish to investigate natural monopoly from either a theoretical or a policy-making perspective. The mathematical level of presentation varies greatly from chapter to chapter, depending on the subject matter. However, at no point is the technical exposition more advanced than is necessary to convey the essential aspects of the theory. Thus, although the potential audience for this study is primarily the professional economist and the student of industrial organization, hopefully other sufficiently interested and motivated individuals, with some mathematical background, can gain a basic understanding of the essential ideas that are developed in this volume.

It is a pleasure to acknowledge the substantial support that an organization within AT&T, managed by Tim Stewart, provided during the preparation of an early draft of this book, consisting of Chapters 2, 3, 4, and 9. Michael Kennedy and Carl Inouye were particularly helpful during this phase of the research.

A number of individuals from Bell Laboratories have also contributed greatly to the development of this study. In particular,

John Panzar, whose own work is frequently cited in the following pages, and Ed Zajac have read the entire manuscript and offered valuable suggestions. In addition, Richard Spady was most helpful in instructing me on some of the material described in Chapter 2; Don Topkis contributed an example discussed in Chapter 6; and Asher Wolinsky offered useful suggestions on Chapter 8. In discussing the cost characteristics of telecommunications networks in Chapter 9, I was able to draw on the considerable expertise of Ron Skoog and others in his organization at Bell Laboratories.

In addition to Bell Laboratories staff, I am indebted to Gerry Faulhaber, Richard Gilbert, Carl Inouye, Michael Kennedy, Charlotte Kuh, Robert Rohr, Lester Telser, and Bobby Willig for their helpful suggestions and comments on various portions of the book.

I am especially grateful to Carmela Patuto, Geraldine Moore, Donna Manganelli and other members of the Text Processing Department of Bell Laboratories for the speed, accuracy, and good humor that they displayed while typing this manuscript.

Finally, I wish to express a sincere debt of gratitude to my wife, Rose, whose constant support and encouragement made *The Theory of Natural Monopoly* possible.

W. W. S.

CHAPTER 1

Introduction and overview

The purpose of this study is to define in substantial detail the conditions under which monopoly — production by a single firm — is a desirable form of market organization. In this chapter I will briefly describe many of the results that will be discussed at greater length later in the book.

The "theory of natural monopoly," which will be developed in the following chapters, should be considered as a part of a larger theory of "market organization" or "industrial organization." In the theory of industrial organization the concept of a "market" and of a "firm" in a market are fundamental. Although it will be assumed that the reader is familiar with the way in which these terms are used in economic theory, a brief discussion of each will help to lay the groundwork for the results that follow.[1] Throughout this book the term "market" will refer to any collection of buyers and sellers and to the outputs that are produced and sold. A market is a competitive market if there are a large number of sellers and no seller is able to influence the market price by a unilateral change in output. Consequently, in a competitive market there is no strategic interaction among sellers. None of them can increase their profits by taking account of the behavior of other sellers.

A market is an "oligopoly" if the number of sellers is small, but greater than one, and if strategic interactions among sellers are important. The profit of any one seller in an oligopoly market depends on his or her own price and quantity decision, as well as on the price-quantity choices of other individual sellers in the market. Furthermore, a change in the strategy of any one seller is likely to induce a change in the strategy of every other seller.

---

[1] Chapter 3 will contain a more extensive review of these and other concepts used in the book.

Finally, a market is a "monopoly" if there is only one active seller in the market, although there may or may not be other potential sellers who are ready and willing to take the place of the monopolist. If there are no inactive sellers in a monopoly market, then a monopolist, unless he or she is regulated, is free to make price and output choices so as to obtain the maximum profit. However, if there are inactive sellers, then a monopolist must take their behavior into account, just as a seller in an oligopoly market must consider the behavior of other active or inactive sellers.

Having described a market in terms of buyers, sellers, and outputs, I will now discuss somewhat more fully a seller, or firm in the market. A "firm" is an organizational structure in which a centralized planning authority replaces the decentralized, impersonal forces of a market. Fundamentally, this book is about the "theory of the firm." I do not intend, however, to develop a theory of the internal organization of firms.[2] Instead, I will use the concept of a cost of output function for a single firm in a market. Then if $q = (q_1, \cdots, q_n)$ represents a vector of outputs in a particular market, I let $C(q)$ represent the monetary value of both physical and organization inputs that are required if q is to be produced by a single firm. In this book the trade-off between a centralized firm and a decentralized market will be expressed in terms of the relative cost of producing an output q with a single firm or with many firms. Thus if $q^1, \cdots, q^k$ are output vectors that sum to q, then a single firm is more efficient than a multifirm market if

$$C(q) < C(q^1) + \cdots + C(q^k) \tag{1.1}$$

assuming, of course, that all firms in the market have the cost function C. If inequality (1.1) holds for any possible disaggregation of an output vector q, then C is said to be subadditive at q and the market is said to be a natural monopoly at q. Subadditivity is the central theme of this book. Each chapter will focus in some way on a particular characteristic of markets in which the cost function is subadditive.

The scope of a market in which one may apply the conclusions of later chapters depends on the definition of the output vector q, which may be a single output or many outputs. There may be close substitutes for particular outputs in other markets that are not explicitly studied; or alternatively q may be a complete listing of all

---

[2] For examples of theories and accounts of the internal organization of firms the reader may consult Simon (1957; 1976), Williamson (1975), Marschak and Radner (1972), or Chandler (1977).

outputs in an entire economy. Thus there are several levels at which the results of this study may be construed. If q is taken to represent a vector of outputs that describe in some sense a single industry (e.g., various grades of steel in the United States), then inequality (1.1) would hold if and only if that industry is a natural monopoly. On the other hand, if q is defined more narrowly (e.g., as a special type of steel to be used in a particular region of the United States), then inequality (1.1) may be used to define the firm itself. That is, one may say that a firm is defined by the largest q such that inequality (1.1) holds.

The theory of natural monopoly has a long history. The present form of that theory, however, is of more recent origin. In the early 1970s concern with the theoretical issues associated with pricing in regulated industries led to several new and surprising results specifically related to multiple output production. For example, both Zajac (1972) and Faulhaber (1972; 1975) developed models that exposed some of the inherent contradictions involved in setting prices that are both "optimal" and "subsidy-free" in a regulated natural monopoly market. These papers quickly led to a more precise characterization of multiple output natural monopoly in terms of cost subadditivity, as in inequality (1.1). These results became more widely known in the economics profession through the work of Baumol (1977), Baumol, Bailey, and Willig (1977), and Panzar and Willig (1977b). Since these publications many more have followed, and the "theory of natural monopoly" now has a secure position in economics literature.

Section 2.1 will be concerned with the intellectual history of the concept of natural monopoly. Then in Section 2.2, I will consider the relationship between the theory of natural monopoly and the attempt to measure the degree of scale economies in the railroad industry. The purpose of Section 2.2 is twofold: (1) to justify the formal approach to cost subadditivity that follows in Chapter 4, by examining in some detail the difficulties inherent in measuring economies of scale and in deriving policy conclusions from the findings; and (2) to enable nontechnical readers to gain some preliminary understanding of the basic elements of the theory of natural monopoly since Chapter 2 is largely free of technical notation. Similarly, Section 2.3, on natural monopoly and destructive competition, serves as an introduction to and justification for the concepts of market stability and market equilibrium, which will be considered in further detail in Chapters 5 through 8.

Chapter 3 is also preliminary in that it is intended primarily for readers who are not professional economists. In this chapter I will briefly survey some basic results from microeconomic theory that will be used later in the book.

Finally, in Chapter 4, I will begin to describe the formal theory of natural monopoly. As shown in inequality (1.1), a given market is a natural monopoly if and only if the cost function for a representative firm in that market satisfies a condition known as subadditivity.

Subadditivity in a single output market is closely related to the more familiar concept of economies of scale. Given a cost function C, scale economies are said to exist at an output q if

$$C(\lambda q) < \lambda C(q) \qquad (1.2)$$

for all λ such that $1 < \lambda \leq 1 + \epsilon$, where ϵ is a small positive number. Thus scale economies depend only on the behavior of C in the neighborhood of the output q. Dividing both sides of the inequality (1.2) by λq gives

$$\frac{C(\lambda q)}{\lambda q} < \frac{C(q)}{q} \qquad (1.3)$$

so that average costs are declining in the neighborhood of q if there are economies of scale at q.

Suppose that the average cost function $C(q)/q$ has the form as in Figure 1.1, in which average cost is uniformly falling to the output q_0 of minimum average cost and then rising uniformly thereafter. There are economies of scale at every output $q < q_0$ and diseconomies of scale at every $q > q_0$.

Now suppose that there are two firms in the market with cost function C. In Figure 1.2 the function $C(q)/q$ is reproduced from Figure 1.1, showing the minimum average cost possible with only one firm operating in the market. In addition, there is a second function indicating the minimum possible average cost in the market if both firms are allowed to produce. At the output $q = 2q_0$ it is most efficient for each firm to produce at the minimum average cost output q_0 and so costs are clearly lower with two firms than with one. In fact, for all outputs $q > q_1$, where q_1 defines the intersection of the two functions, two firms are more efficient than one. If $q < q_1$ there is subadditivity, so that

$$C(q) < C(x) + C(q-x)$$

for any x such that $0 < x < q$. A specific cost function having the shape of Figure 1.1 is the function $C(q) = 1 + q^2$. For this function it may be readily calculated that $q_0 = 1$ and $q_1 = \sqrt{2}$.

In the case of single output production it may be concluded that subadditivity adds a new dimension to, but is not a radical departure from, the traditional association of natural monopoly and economies of scale. Subadditivity is an essential concept, however, for the understanding of multiple output natural monopoly. In this case economies of scale are neither necessary nor sufficient for natural monopoly. Consider the cost function $C(q_1,q_2) = q_1 + q_2 + (q_1 q_2)^{1/3}$,

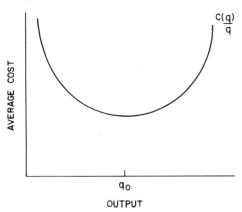

FIGURE 1.1

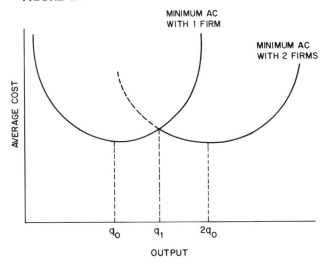

FIGURE 1.2

which is illustrated in Figure 1.3. The definition of economies of scale is the same as for a single output cost function. Since

$$\lambda C(q_1, q_2) = \lambda q_1 + \lambda q_2 + \lambda (q_1 q_2)^{1/3}$$

$$> \lambda q_1 + \lambda q_2 + \lambda^{2/3}(q_1 q_2)^{1/3}$$

$$= C(\lambda q_1, \lambda q_2)$$

whenever $\lambda > 1$, then the preceding function has economies of scale at every output q. However, this cost function is nowhere subadditive, because it may easily be seen that

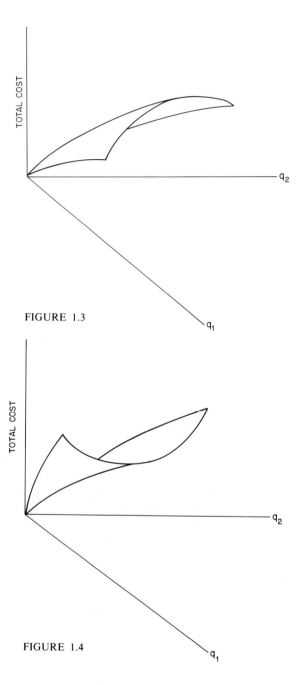

FIGURE 1.3

FIGURE 1.4

$$C(q_1,0) + C(0,q_2) = q_1 + q_2 < C(q_1,q_2)$$

whenever $q_1 > 0$ and $q_2 > 0$. This cost function has what is now known as a diseconomy of scope,[3] in which production of a given output is more efficient when carried out by speciality firms producing only one output than by a multiproduct firm.

Multiple output natural monopoly requires both economies of scope and economies of scale. For example, the cost function $C(q_1,q_2) = q_1^{1/4} + q_2^{1/4} - (q_1 q_2)^{1/4}$, which is illustrated in Figure 1.4, has economies of scope at every output, since

$$C(q_1,0) + C(0,q_2) = q_1^{1/4} + q_2^{1/4} > C(q_1,q_2)$$

Furthermore, this function has economies of scale at every output, since

$$\lambda C(q_1,q_2) = \lambda q_1^{1/4} + \lambda q_2^{1/4} - \lambda(q_1 q_2)^{1/4}$$

$$> \lambda^{1/2} q_1^{1/4} + \lambda^{1/2} q_2^{1/4} - \lambda^{1/2}(q_1 q_2)^{1/4}$$

$$> \lambda^{1/4} q_1^{1/4} + \lambda^{1/4} q_2^{1/4} - \lambda^{1/2}(q_1 q_2)^{1/4}$$

$$= C(\lambda q_1, \lambda q_2)$$

In addition, although it does not follow from these arguments, this cost function is subadditive at every output.

A different example of multiple output subadditivity is the cost function $C(q_1,q_2) = 1 + (q_1 + q_2)^2$ in which there is a fixed cost attributable to both outputs. For this function it may be readily calculated that there are economies of scale at an output q if and only if $q_1 + q_2 < 1$. There are economies of scope at q if and only if $q_1 q_2 < 1/2$. Finally it may also be demonstrated that this cost function is subadditive if and only if $q_1 q_2 < 1/2$. These constraints are illustrated in Figure 1.5. For this cost function subadditivity corresponds exactly to economies of scope. It is interesting to observe that for output vectors sufficiently close to one of the coordinate axes the cost function is necessarily subadditive even if there are substantial diseconomies of scale.

Chapter 4 will confirm and extend the preceding comments on subadditivity in both single output and multiple output markets. In addition to economies of scope, a number of other measures of the economies of joint production will be derived and discussed. Generally speaking, "cost complementarity" in any one of several possible forms is sufficient, when combined with economies of scale, to guarantee subadditivity of a multiple output cost function.

---

[3] Economies and diseconomies of scope are discussed in Panzar and Willig (1981).

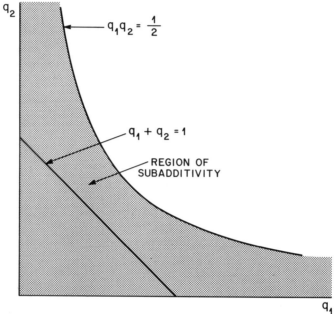

$$q_1 q_2 = \frac{1}{2}$$

$$q_1 + q_2 = 1$$

REGION OF
SUBADDITIVITY

FIGURE 1.5

The relationship between plant subadditivity and firm subadditivity will also be discussed in Chapter 4. Plant subadditivity is due strictly to technological aspects of production. For example, efficient production technique may require the use of factors of production that are suitable only for large-scale output. If such inputs are not divisible into smaller units for a smaller scale of operation, then a portion of total costs is independent of output, and as previously shown, costs may be subadditive.

An alternative form of subadditivity is due to the planning processes that are carried out within the firm. A single firm may be able to coordinate production or distribution of the industry outputs more efficiently than two or more competing firms. I will use the terms "firm subadditivity" to denote any such cost advantage that is not strictly technological in character. It has been argued[4] that plant subadditivity is generally insufficient to justify the existence of a firm and that firms exist only because of the relative advantages of a firm over a market in organizing or coordinating inputs into production. Indeed, plant subadditivity does not imply the existence of firm subadditivity. At the same time, however, firm subadditivity may exist in the absence of plant subadditivity. In any case, the

[4]   See, for example, Williamson (1975).

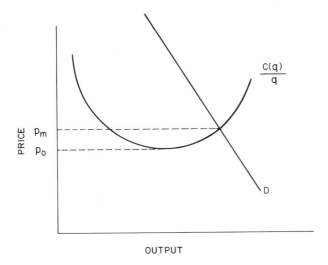

FIGURE 1.6

distinction between the two forms of subadditivity is more semantic than real, for an econometric estimate of a cost function must necessarily measure the combined effects of both plant and firm subadditivity.

The distinction between subadditivity and economies of scale has also led to a new and surprising result concerning the stability of natural monopoly in a market with open entry. Even if monopoly is natural, there may not be a price at which (1) total market demand is satisfied, (2) revenues cover total cost of production, (3) and entry by rival firms is unattractive. The paradox is illustrated for the case of single output natural monopoly in Figure 1.6. In order to satisfy the first two objectives, a monopolist must set a price $p \geq p_m$, but to satisfy the third objective, he or she must set $p = p_0 < p_m$. Because natural monopoly is by definition the most efficient form of production, entry into the market can only raise the total costs of production or reduce consumer welfare by restricting output to a suboptimal level. A natural monopoly in which an entry deterring price exists is known as a sustainable natural monopoly.[5] Chapter 5 will describe the conditions under which both single output and multiple output natural monopoly can be sustainable.

[5] The concept of sustainable natural monopoly was first defined in Baumol, Bailey, and Willig (1977) and Panzar and Willig (1977b).

Chapter 6 will consider a somewhat different approach to the stability of natural monopoly firms in which the buyers in a market are viewed as players in a cooperative game. The object of the game is to form coalitions in which production and distribution of outputs occur under the most favorable terms. In this approach there is a natural monopoly if the coalition of all buyers can achieve a better outcome than a partitioning of the buyers into disjoint subcoalitions. In the terminology of cooperative game theory there is a natural monopoly if and only if the characteristic function (which describes the outcomes that coalitions can achieve) is superadditive.

The core of a cooperative game describes outcomes that are feasible for the coalition of all buyers and which cannot be improved upon by any other coalition. Thus the core of a game defines outcomes that have a particular kind of stability with respect to defections from the coalition of all buyers. A natural monopoly market, in which a core exists in the underlying game, is a stable natural monopoly.

One of the advantages of the cooperative game approach is that it can easily be extended to the case of markets that are not natural monopolies. In Chapter 6 I will prove several theorems that guarantee the existence of stable markets and present several examples of unstable markets, in which competition is inherently destructive.

Chapters 7 and 8 will consider a third approach to the question of entry and exit in natural monopoly and natural oligopoly markets. After a brief discussion of the rationale for regulation in a natural monopoly or natural oligopoly market, I will focus in Chapter 7 on the extent to which competition can be a substitute for regulation, considering first the nature of barriers to entry and of contestable markets, markets in which there are no barriers to entry or exit. Then, I will treat the implications of the use of limit pricing and predatory pricing by incumbent firms in a market.

A noncooperative game theoretic model of a contestable market will be analyzed in Chapter 8. The major conclusion of this analysis is that if firms compete using only price as a strategic variable, then given sufficient potential competition, a contestable market equilibrium necessarily exists.

Chapter 9 will attempt to apply much of the theory in previous chapters to the specific technology and market conditions in the telecommunications industry. The primary focus of this chapter will be the existence of multiple output plant subadditivity and firm subadditivity.

Taken together the following eight chapters provide a comprehensive account of the most important issues associated with natural monopoly. However, this account is necessarily a personal one and not all issues that are conceivably of interest have been examined in detail. In particular, a number of traditional results on regulation of natural monopoly, including the so-called Averch-Johnson (1962) effect, are not considered. The cost functions assumed in the remainder of this book are minimum cost functions, which do not allow for distortions because of regulation or any other source. However, it should also be pointed out that in the discussion of sustainability and open entry, a firm must produce each output at minimum possible cost, even if there is an incentive for the distortion of inputs due to rate of return regulation. In a market with open entry, firms that did not minimize costs would quickly be replaced by more efficient rivals.[6]

Because this book is intended for a diverse audience, most readers will not be equally interested in all sections. Professional economists, concerned with industrial organization or related fields, may wish to concentrate on Chapters 4 through 9. Students in similar fields and policy-oriented readers may also read portions of Chapters 2 and 3 while omitting most of Chapters 6 and 8.

Primarily a technical exercise in economic theory, this book has many portions that use mathematical notation, and results are generally stated in the form of mathematical theorems. However, with the exception of some portions of Chapter 6, no advanced mathematics is used. Professional economists should have no difficulty with any of the results and most sections are accessible to noneconomists such as lawyers, engineers, or accountants, who may find the information helpful. As an aid to the lay reader, I have attempted, at the beginning of every technical chapter, to summarize without using jargon or mathematical notation the most important results to be found in that chapter. Furthermore, in setting forth technical material, I have sacrificed mathematical elegance in order to keep the discussion relatively informal.

Ultimately, the style of presentation is a compromise between rigor and readability. Professional economists will find a concise statement of a large number of results, which in my opinion comprise a theory of natural monopoly. In order to gain an understanding of as much of that theory as possible, nontechnical readers should proceed slowly and patiently.

[6] This finding follows as a simple corollary to the results in Chapter 5 on sustainable natural monopoly.

CHAPTER 2

Historical survey of natural monopoly

As previously mentioned, the theory of natural monopoly has a long history. Before proceeding to set out in mathematical terms the conditions for that theory, I will survey part of that history in Section 2.1. The purpose of such a survey is twofold. First, it will enable readers to place the present effort in the proper context. Although the theory to be developed in this book is more formal and mathematical than work that has preceded it, many of the important ideas were originally suggested by earlier writers. Second, the literature survey will help those readers who are unfamiliar with the mathematical approach used throughout the volume to understand the most significant concepts.

In addition to the survey, this chapter contains, in Section 2.2, an examination of some recent empirical work that has attempted to test for natural monopoly conditions — primarily economies of scale — in the railroad industry. The major implication of these studies is that the railroad industry is inherently a multiple output industry and that simple measures such as economies of scale are not adequate to answer the relevant policy questions. Much of the complexity in later chapters is due to the need to develop a theory of natural monopoly that is relevant to multiple output firms and markets.

Finally, I will briefly discuss in Section 2.3 the interrelationship between the theory of natural monopoly and the possibility of destructive competition. The works that are cited here indicate that there has been a persistent belief among business people and policy makers that competition is at times destructive. At the same time, economists have traditionally viewed the threat of destructive competition with great skepticism because of the absence of a coherent theory to explain it. Chapter 6 will present one approach to such a theory. More generally, Section 2.3 serves as an introduction to the discussion of market structure and performance in Chapters 5 through 8.

2.1   Evolution of the theory of natural monopoly

In the writings of economists of the preindustrial age the concept of monopoly was rarely mentioned, and for good reason. Of course, monopolies existed, typically when a government granted the exclusive right to engage in a particular type of business. But by and large, the economic life of the times was characterized by the conditions of laissez faire competition. For example, Schumpeter (1954; pp. 345-6) describes the thinking of the times as follows:

Economists, wishing to serve their time and countries, took for granted — and reasoned in terms of — the institutions of their time and countries ... They envisioned the legal institutions ... of a private-property economy that left so much room for free contracting as almost to justify the practice of economists to leave limitations out of consideration ...

The unit of that private-property economy was the firm of medium size. Its typical legal form was the private partnership ... The facts and problems of large scale production and, in connection with them, those of joint stock companies were recognized by economists (only) after everybody else had recognized them ...

In the normal case, these firms were supposed to work under what the "classics" called Free Competition. With them, this competition was an institutional assumption rather than the result of certain market conditions. And so firmly were they convinced that the competitive case was the obvious case, familiar to all, that they did not bother to analyze its logical content. In fact, the concept was usually not even defined. It just meant the absence of monopoly — which was considered as abnormal and was vigorously condemned, but was not properly defined either!

Augustin Cournot (1838) was the first to define monopoly correctly in terms of the downward-sloping demand curve facing a seller, implying that monopolists are free to choose their prices rather than accept the prevailing market rates. Cournot's example was bucolic — a landowner with a mineral spring discovers that he can sell the water from the spring but that larger quantities can be sold only by lowering the price. Cournot calculated the optimal pricing strategy for the seller, which led to the familiar profit-maximization formula — marginal revenue equals marginal cost.

At approximately the same time Jules Dupuit (1844), a French inspector of bridges and highways, was making another important contribution to the theory of monopoly. While seeking to quantify a measure of the benefits to society from the public works under his jurisdiction, he discovered that a monopolist who is able to price discriminate — to charge different prices to different customers — is led to choose an output that maximizes the social welfare. This insight implied that some sectors of the economy may be better served by a profit-maximizing monopolist than by a competitive industry. Dupuit's analysis was immensely important, but one hundred years passed before his idea became well known to economists, when it was discussed in a paper on taxation and utility rates by Harold Hotelling (1938). Hotelling developed Dupuit's example in the case of multiple commodities and showed that consumer welfare will be highest when prices are set equal to the marginal costs of production, with revenue shortfalls paid for by a system of fixed charges or by subsidies from general taxation.

John Stuart Mill, in 1848, was the first economist of note to speak of natural monopolies. Mill observed that certain public utilities in London could not be supplied competitively (Mill 1926; p. 143).

It is obvious, for example, how great an economy of labor would be obtained if London were supplied by a single gas or water company instead of the existing plurality ... Were there only one establishment, it could make lower charges consistently with obtaining the rate of profit now realized.

After Cournot and Dupuit, the next theoretical advance in the theory of monopoly was made by Marshall (1927). Cournot's example of the mineral spring was a clear instance of the allocative inefficiency of simple monopoly. Because water from the spring is costless and assumed to be inexhaustible, the socially optimal price for the water is zero. The monopoly price is greater than zero and therefore entails a loss in consumer satisfaction. Marshall, however, recognized that the likelihood of monopoly is related to the type of cost and production conditions in a given industry. Industries with increasing average cost will probably be competitive, whereas decreasing-cost industries, are likely to be monopolistic. Furthermore, Marshall realized that in decreasing cost industries monopoly may be socially desirable so that price may be lower and output higher than would be the case in a competitive industry.

Following Marshall, a number of eminent economists attempted to clarify the theory of monopoly and its relationship to the theory of pure competition. Essentially, competition and monopoly came to be seen as fundamental structures that could be analyzed with simple but powerful techniques. Although it was recognized that real industries might generally fall between the polar cases, little in the way of formal analysis, was thought necessary. Two prominent exceptions   are   the   theories   of   monopolistic   competition

(Chamberlain, 1936) and imperfect competition (Robinson, 1934).

The remainder of this section will be concerned with the specific treatment of natural monopoly by recent generations of economists.[1] Most of the discussions of natural monopoly have been contained in textbooks on public utility economics, regulatory theory, and antitrust economics. One of the first endeavors to identify natural monopoly by its economic characteristics was made by Thomas Farrer (1902). Farrer classified as natural monopolies those industries in which competition had never been tried, or in which competition had been attempted and failed. Five characteristics of these industries were enumerated, and all were deemed necessary for a true natural monopoly to exist. (1) The industry must supply an essential product or service. (2) The industry must occupy a favorable location for production. (3) The outputs of the industry must be nonstorable. (4) Production must be characterized by economies of scale. (5) The customers of the industry must require a "certainty and a well-defined harmonious arrangement" of supply, which can only be attained by a single supplier.[2]

In 1887 Henry Carter Adams discussed natural monopoly in *Relation of the State to Industrial Action*.[3] Industries were classified into three types according to whether they had constant, decreasing, or increasing returns to scale. Although competition is workable in the first two classes, industries with increasing returns require regulation by the state.

[W]here the law of increasing returns works with any degree of intensity, the principle of free competition is powerless to exercise a healthy regulating influence. This is true, because it is easier for an established business to extend its facilities for satisfactorily meeting a new demand than for a new industry to spring into competitive existence ... The control of the state over industries should be coextensive with the application of the law of increasing returns in industries ... Such businesses are by nature monopolies ... If it is for the interest of men to combine, no law can make them compete.[4]

Adams simplifies the definition of natural monopoly to the purely technical condition of scale economies in the industry. In addition, he is one of the first to suggest direct regulation of natural monopoly

[1] A recent survey of the evolution of the concept of natural monopoly may be found in Lowry (1973). Much of the following discussion is based on Lowry's study.

[2] Lowry (1973; p. 2), quoting from Farrer (1902).

[3] Reprinted in Dorfman (1969).

[4] Lowry (1973; p. 3) quoting from Dorfman (1969).

as a means of maximizing the social welfare. Regulation was viewed by Adams as a device that would allow a single firm to secure all the advantages of larger scale production but which would protect consumers from the abuse of monopoly power.

A fundamentally different view of natural monopoly is presented by Richard T. Ely (1937). Ely identified three classes of natural monopoly. (1) Those dependent on unique sources of supply (such as Cournot's mineral spring); (2) Those based on secrecy or special privilege (patents); (3) Those arising from "peculiar properties" inherent in the business. Ely considered the most important natural monopolies, such as the railroad industry and public utilities, to be of the third class. He explained this class in more detail as follows:

Natural monopolies of this third class are, however, more often rooted in conditions that make competition self-destructive. These conditions are three in number, and the presence of all three is generally necessary to create monopoly: (1) The commodity or service rendered must be of such a nature that a small difference in price will lead buyers to purchase from one producer rather than from another. (2) The business must be of such a nature as to make the creation of a large number of competitive plants impossible. Either because the business is one in which special advantages attach to large-scale production or because there are actual physical difficulties in the way of the multiplication of competing plants, there must be fairly definite limits to the possible increase of the number of plants among which the business might be divided. (3) The proportion of fixed to variable expenses of production must be high.[5]

Thus, for Ely, natural monopoly is defined as the "unsuitability of competition." The unsuitability of competition may arise from conditions of economies of scale in production; but Ely believed that there may also be other conditions — those that make competition self-destructive. Here there appears for the first time a second major trend of thought in the theory of natural monopoly. Monopoly may be a superior source of supply because it is more stable as well as more efficient.

Although Adams and Ely are not the only, or even the most prominent, economists to develop a theory of natural monopoly, together they managed to establish the most important characteristics of natural monopoly industries.[6] Later economists worked primarily to clarify and extend the basic results. One

[5] Lowry (1973, p. 3), quoting from Ely (1937).
[6] In addition to the references cited in the text, the interested reader should consult Burns (1936), Clark (1939; 1940), Knight (1921b), and Stigler (1968).

important extension is the realization that simple economies of scale are neither necessary nor sufficient for a natural monopoly. For example, James Bonbright (1961, pp. 14-15) argues that the association of natural monopoly with decreasing costs "ignores the point that even if the unit cost of supplying a given area with a given type of public utility service must increase with an enhanced rate of output, any specified required rate of output can be supplied most economically by a single firm or single system."

Posner (1969, p. 548) states that natural monopoly "does not refer to the actual number of sellers in a market but to the relationship between demand and the technology of supply." Kahn (1971, p. 123) argues that caution must be exercised in interpreting the condition of declining average costs, or economies of scale.

These are cases of natural monopoly that would seem at first blush not explicable in terms of long-run decreasing costs. We have already observed, for example, that as the number of telephone subscribers goes up, the number of possible connections among them grows more rapidly; local exchange service is therefore generally believed to be subject to increasing, not decreasing unit costs, when the unit of output is the number of subscribers. And yet, it seems clear that this service is a natural monopoly: if there were two telephone systems serving a community, each subscriber would have to have two instruments, two lines into his home, two bills if he wanted to be able to call everyone else. Despite the apparent presence of increasing costs, in short, monopoly is still natural because one company can serve any given number of subscribers (for example, all in a community) at lower cost than two.

Kaysen and Turner (1959, p. 189-90) describe natural monopoly as one of several situations in which competition may be unworkable.

For clarity of analysis, it is important to distinguish among the following three kinds of situations that may make departures from antitrust policy either necessary or desirable:

(a) Situations in which competition, as a practical matter, cannot exist or survive for long, and in which, therefore an unregulated market will not produce competitive results.

(b) Situations in which active competition exists, but where, because of imperfections in the market, competition does not produce one or more competitive results.

(c) Situations in which competition exists, or could exist, and has produced or may be expected to produce competitive results, but where in light of other policy considerations competitive results are unsatisfactory in one or more respects.

We draw these distinctions because they suggest different kinds of regulatory approaches to meet the different problems they pose ... .

Kaysen and Turner (1959, p. 191) include in the class of inherently noncompetitive markets both natural monopoly and natural oligopoly.

In the economic sense, natural monopoly is monopoly resulting from economies of scale, a relationship between the size of the market and the size of the most efficient firm such that one firm of efficient size can produce all or more than the market can take at a remunerative price, and can continually expand its capacity at less cost than that of a new firm entering the business. In this situation, competition may exist for a time but only until bankruptcy or merger leaves the field to one firm; in a meaningful sense, competition here is self-destructive.

The authors warn, however, that the existence of economies of scale depends critically on the correct definition of the market (1959, p. 191).

As noted, economies of scale is a relative concept. Natural monopoly may exist in the market as large as the entire country, as seems probably the case in the telephone industry. In the past, high transportation costs created many local natural monopolies which have since been largely eradicated. In today's underdeveloped countries there are many markets so thin that industries which are highly competitive in more industrialized countries are natural monopolies there. In the United States and similar countries, however, few industries now fall in the natural monopoly category. The list of significant industries of this type is largely exhausted by the telephone industry; distribution of power gas, and water; electric power production (in most areas); and railroads (in some).

Kaysen and Turner (1959, pp. 195-6) also discuss destructive competition as an example of a competitive market that fails to achieve competitive results.

In most instances, apart from natural monopoly situations, ruinous competition simply reflects a commitment to the industry of factors of production in excess of current demand. Usually excess capacity is thought of in the investment sense, i.e., fixed factors like plant and equipment. Ruinous competition may well be prolonged in an industry characterized by a fairly high ratio of fixed to variable costs. Given slack demand, or overexpansion of capacity, the incremental cost of production may fall far below total unit cost. Fixed factors are not being fully utilized; they can be more fully utilized at little or no extra cost, and thus the cost of higher output is only the cost of those factors (labor, materials, etc.) needed in additional amounts. In a competitive industry, this generates strong pressures toward price cutting, and price may be expected to fall to incremental cost. As price drops below the incremental cost of less efficient producers, their capacity will be withdrawn from production. But if inefficient capacity is relatively small, or the excess capacity relatively great, prices may settle at a level unprofitable to all or most producers and persist there for fairly long periods of time, until all excess capacity is worn out or withdrawn. In short, the losses may be severe and the process of adjustment a long, painful one.

The authors, however, view destructive competition as a transitory phenomenon and caution against any intervention. Kahn (1971, pp. 119, 173) discusses both natural monopoly and destructive competition in virtually the same terms as Kaysen and Turner.

The critical and — if properly defined — all embracing characteristic of natural monopoly is an inherent tendency to decreasing unit costs over the entire extent of the market. This is so only when the economies achievable by a larger output are internal to the individual firm — if, that is to say, it is only as more output is concentrated in a single supplier that unit cost will decline.

The major prerequisites for competition to be destructive are fixed or sunk costs that bulk large as a percentage of total cost; and long-sustained and recurrent periods of excess capacity. These two circumstances describe a condition in which marginal costs may for long periods of time be far below average total costs. If in these circumstances the structure of the industry is unconcentrated — that is, its sellers are too small in relation to the total size of the market to perceive and to act on the basis of their joint interest in avoiding competition that drives price down to marginal cost — the possibility arises that the industry as a whole, or at least the majority of its firms, may find themselves operating at a loss for extended periods of time.

Kahn (1971, pp. 119-13) notes, however, that the same forces — the need to assemble a large capital-intensive plant in order to meet a highly variable demand — may generate either a natural monopoly or a condition of destructive competition.

The principal source of this tendency is the necessity of making a large investment merely in order to be in a position to serve customers on demand ... .

Clearly, these tendencies are related to the fact that fixed or capacity costs bulk unusually large among total costs in most public utility industries. And it is these fixed costs that might be wastefully duplicated if two companies tried to serve the same markets. But heavy fixed costs do not themselves necessarily make for natural monopoly. An industry's technology might be such that all of its costs were fixed — its output produced in fully automated plants, drawing their energy from the sun and their raw materials from the air — yet in the absence of internal economies of scale over a sufficient range of supply, it might be equally efficient to have that production carried on by a large number of separate firms, each with its own wholly automatic, completely fixed-cost plant. The tendency of agriculture to suffer wide fluctuations in prices is correctly attributed in part to the importance of fixed costs in that industry, a large proportion of a farmer's costs being the return of his own investment in the land and its improvements, in his equipment, and on his own labor. This has the effect of making supply highly inelastic, so that even slight changes in demand result in sharp fluctuations in price. But since economies of scale in agriculture are very limited relative to the size of the market, the industry is clearly not a natural monopoly.

An additional source of these potential economies of scale is to be found not on the supply but on the demand side. We have mentioned the effect of variability in demand in imposing on a public utility company the burden of maintaining capacity sufficient to supply however much service is demanded at the peak. This variability tends, other things being equal, to make it more efficient to supply many customers and regions than few; that is to say, it gives rise to economies of scale when the dimension along which output is measured is not the quantities taken by some given number of customers but the number and diversity of customers and markets served. The greater the latter, the greater is the likelihood that the variations in their separate demands will tend to cancel one another out; the more diverse the market the greater possibility that the maximum requirements of some will fall at times different from the maximum requirements of others. In consequence, the firm that covers the entire market is likely to have a better relationship (that is, a lower ratio) between total investment costs (which are determined by the total demand placed on it at the system peak) and total dollar sales over the year, hence lower average costs, than two or more separate firms, each supplying some portion of the total market.

This survey may be summarized as follows.

1. All authors agree that natural monopolies are primarily industries in which there are pervasive economies of scale. Some have noted that there can be natural monopoly if a single firm can produce more efficiently than two or more firms even in the absence of economies of scale.

2. Most authors have recognized that competition may be unstable and that the conditions for destructive competition are related to the conditions for natural monopoly (although there is no agreement on the precise relationship).

3. Most authors would agree that it is difficult or impossible to label a given industry a natural monopoly by a simple measure of economies of scale (or any other easily quantified measure). Instead, account must be taken of other relevant conditions such as definition of the market and the nature of demand in the industry.

2.2   Natural monopoly and economies of scale

It is evident from the preceding general literature survey that the existence or nonexistence of economies of scale is of importance in determining whether any given industry is a natural monopoly. Although the test for economies of scale is an incomplete test of natural monopoly (as shown by some of the previous sources and as will be explained more fully in Chapter 4), it will be illuminating to examine the application of this test in a particular industry. The obvious candidate for such an investigation is the railroad industry. Throughout most of the nineteenth century, when the basic ideas of natural monopoly were being developed, railroads were the most rapidly growing and most capital-intensive industry in the United States. They are characterized by large fixed costs and highly variable demand — conditions that we have seen are conducive to both natural monopoly and destructive competition. Thus railroads are a natural candidate for natural monopoly. In this section I will survey several empirical studies of the railroad industry, in order to gain some insight into the practical and theoretical issues that a theory of natural monopoly should address.

All empirical studies of the railroad industry begin by choosing the "output" to be measured. It is possible to specify a single output production function or a multiple output function and to measure output in physical units, such as train-car miles or ton-miles of traffic, or in monetary units, such as total revenue or net revenue (also referred to as value added). None of these measures, however, adequately describe the real output in the industry, which consists of a large number of distinct kinds of traffic carried over a network of great complexity. Because of limitations in the available data, most studies have been based on one, or at most two types of output, generally freight ton-miles and passenger-miles.

Whether one or two outputs are used, the primary object of investigation, particularly in the earlier studies, has been the degree of scale economies in the industry. In this literature, scale economies have generally been measured by the elasticity of cost with respect to output, which is the ratio of marginal cost to average cost. If the elasticity of cost is less than one, then there are economies of scale in the industry and marginal cost is less than average cost. A finding of economies of scale was considered to be evidence of natural monopoly and perhaps justification for a subsidy to allow for efficient marginal cost pricing.

Early studies of the industry tended to find overwhelming evidence of scale economies. Ripley (1912), for example, calculated a cost elasticity, then known as the percentage of variable cost, of 0.33. This estimate may have seemed plausible at the time, given the large share of total railroad costs that are insensitive to increases in traffic. Over the long run, however, even the "fixed" expenses such as track, tunnels, and switches, must increase with traffic.

Clark (1923) attempted to correct for the short-run bias in estimates of the cost elasticity by measuring a cost function reflecting long-run growth in the industry. This led to an elasticity of cost in the neighborhood of 0.8 to 0.9. Clark also observed that the magnitude of economies of scale depends on the size of the railroad being measured. Small railroads were found to have substantially larger scale economies than larger railroads. Finally, Clark observed that aggregation of outputs raised some troublesome issues. For example, railroads in different parts of the country carried traffic over different kinds of terrain. Some transported primarily bulk commodities such as coal or agricultural goods, whereas others conveyed only manufactured goods. When outputs were disaggregated into more homogeneous groupings it was found that the economies of scale were less pronounced. "In other words, part of the downward trend of costs per ton-mile [was] due to more favorable topography or larger percentages of cheap low-grade freight, or both" (Clark 1923, p. 269).

In a more modern study Griliches (1972) verified most of Clark's observations. Using a single, aggregate measure of output (gross ton-miles) and data from the Interstate Commerce Commission (ICC) for the period 1957-61, Griliches separated carriers into two groups, depending on the size of their total network (in terms of miles of track). For the larger railroads the cost elasticity was shown to be greater than 0.9 and not significantly different from unity. Thus although admitting that there may be decreasing average costs for some types of traffic, Griliches concludes that overall the industry is best characterized by constant returns to scale.

The studies of Griliches and others have more recently been criticized by Harris (1977). According to Harris, the principal defect of the earlier studies is the confusion between economies of scale and economies of density in railroad traffic. In his attempt to correct the ICC measure of output (gross ton-miles per mile of track) in order to avoid comparing small railroads and large railroads in the same sample, Griliches ensured that his estimate of scale economies would not capture the effect on cost of a change in output over a given route system. For the question of natural monopoly in the industry the distinction between scale and density is quite important. For example, it may follow that a merger of two railroads that increases the size of the network and the total traffic carried in the same proportion would leave average cost unchanged, whereas a consolidation of two railroads that allows for a higher traffic density on the combined road would have lower average costs.

Harris (1977) also notes that the omission of the average length of haul in most previous studies results in a serious specification error. "By using only ton-miles as a measure of output, we implicitly assume that one ton carried 1000 miles is equivalent to 1000 tons carried one mile" (Harris 1977, p. 558). Thus an end-to-end merger of two railroads would be likely to reduce total costs by increasing the average length of haul and eliminating a stage in switching. On the other hand, a parallel merger would enjoy no such advantage. Therefore again we see that it is the network configuration rather than the network size that is relevant in the determination of natural monopoly characteristics in the industry.

A different dimension to the aggregation problem was noted by Hasenkamp (1976a; 1976b), who used a multiple output production function with passenger miles and freight ton-miles as outputs. Using data from an earlier study of Klein (1953), he found increasing returns to scale, and more interestingly, that the isocost contour was convex rather than concave. In a later study Brown, Caves, and Christensen (1979) reached substantially the same result, employing a more general cost function. This result is important because it suggests that profit-maximizing firms would prefer to specialize in freight or passenger traffic rather than provide a combination of outputs. Thus in addition to the degree of economies of scale, natural monopoly in the railroad industry depends on the advantages of joint production of multiple outputs, which we will later describe in terms of economies of scope. Hasenkamp's results suggest that there are diseconomies of scope, but the general issue of multiproduct economies of scope in the industry is by no means settled. For example, it would be useful to know if both manufactured and bulk goods could be carried more efficiently on one rail network or on two speciality networks. Also, switching and line haul are distinctly different outputs of railroad firm, and it would be desirable to know more precisely the cost characteristics of each.

Many of the preceding issues are accounted for, at least in part, in the recent work of Spady (1979). Spady estimates a multiple output cost function with passenger miles and revenue ton-miles as outputs. In addition, average length of haul, passenger average travel length, freight traffic mix (ratio of manufactured to nonmanufactured ton-miles), and the number of low-density route-miles in the network are included as arguments. Overall, Spady finds evidence of moderate economies of scale, with a cost elasticity of 0.87. As he notes, this finding does not preclude the existence of constant returns to scale for the larger railroads. However, some of his other results lead to more definite conclusions. An increase in average length of haul, holding other arguments constant, reduces costs, whereas an increase in low-density route mileage and in the proportion of manufactured goods increases costs. An increase in traffic with constant network size, average length of haul, and low-density route mileage is subject to economies of scale as previously reported. However, a uniform increase in traffic, network size, and low-density route mileage is subject to diseconomies of scale. Thus for large railroads Spady concludes that there are managerial diseconomies of scale. Mergers would therefore be unlikely to succeed unless accompanied by either a more favorable length of haul or the abandonment of low-density routes.

In conclusion, it should be emphasized that many of the results obtained in studies of the railroad industry are directly relevant for the theory to be developed in Chapter 4. A large part of that chapter will be devoted to specifying conditions on a multiple output cost function that guarantee the existence of natural monopoly. As seen in the earlier studies, an economy of scale is much too ambiguous a concept to settle the question of natural monopoly satisfactorily for the railroad industry. Chapter 4 will show that, indeed, scale economies are neither necessary nor sufficient for natural monopoly in a multiple output industry. However, by considering, in addition, the important concept of cost complementarity among multiple outputs, one can generate conditions that are sufficient (but not necessary) for natural monopoly. Also, Chapter 4 will attempt to address the economies of organization or coordination within a firm that transcend the purely technological measures of economies of scale or scope. All the preceding empirical studies suggest that there is an optimal railroad network of some size and scope. The remaining chapters may be seen as an attempt to describe abstractly, but precisely, the dimensions of the optimal firm in the railroad or any other industry.

2.3   Natural monopoly and destructive competition

In the previous section it was shown that the natural monopoly status of the railroad industry is unclear from available evidence. Even if the railroads are not natural monopolies, however, it does not follow that the industry can be characterized as competitive. Indeed, for most of its history, the industry has been characterized by pervasive regulations governing maximum and minimum rates and both entry and exit of firms. This section will consider the extent to which competition in the railroad and other related sectors of the transportation industry may validly be described as "destructive."[7]

Before the invention of the steam locomotive, railroads were operated much like toll highways. Cars were pulled over rails by horsepower and shippers generally provided their own equipment. The powered locomotive, however, and other specialized equipment made continued toll operation technically infeasible. Rail carriers were then given a monopoly in the transportation of goods along their own roads and it was recognized that competition in the industry would have to be among railroad systems rather than among different carriers on the same system of track.

The second half of the nineteenth century was a period of rapid growth in the industry. In 1865 there were 35,085 miles of track in the United States, whereas in 1887 there were 149,214 miles in operation.[8] Largely, this expansion was fostered by generous financial aid from the U.S. government and from state and local governments. The period after the Civil War was also one of attempted cartellization of the industry. By pooling either traffic or revenues, the railroads tried to set rates at the monopoly level.

Entry into the industry, however, was relatively easy, despite the heavy investment required. The net effect of government subsidization and the prospect of monopoly profits in the industry was, not surprisingly, a substantial amount of overbuilding and excess capacity. This is the classic formula for destructive competition.[9] When there is excess capacity it is to be expected that incremental costs are less than average costs because the production of an incremental unit of output does not require an incremental unit of capacity. Furthermore, a railroad, once constructed, is an extremely durable investment, without any alternative uses. Consequently, competition in the industry could not be expected to lead to a rapid adjustment of capacity to demand. Rather, competition in these circumstances led to rate wars, secret rebates, and favoritism to particular shippers, all of which were highly unpopular with most shippers and the public at large.

---

[7] Additional material on regulation and destructive competition in the transportation section may be found in Hilton (1966), Boies (1968), Friedlaender (1969), Kahn (1971), and Friedlaender and Spady (1981).

[8] Friedlaender (1969, p. 9).

[9] See Kahn (1971, p. 173) and Chapter 6 for additional discussion of destructive competition.

Another unpopular feature of railroad rates in this period arose from the nature of demand. Railroads were quickly able to learn that the profits of price-discriminating monopoly exceed those of ordinary monopoly. The correct method of price discrimination, which came to be known as "value of service pricing," involves charging a higher price for goods whose demand is relatively less elastic. Because transportation costs are generally lower, as a fraction of the total, for manufactured goods than for agricultural goods, their demand for transportation is less elastic. Consequently, rates for bulk commodities were set lower relative to their costs than were rates for manufactured goods. This, in itself, posed no problem, for the agricultural interests were politically powerful at the time. However, later growth of the motor trucking industry drastically changed the nature of railroad demand. Then manufactured goods could generally be carried on the highways at a total cost that was not substantially different from the incremental cost of the railroads. In addition, the economic development of the West tended to reduce the demand for westbound shipment of manufactured goods relative to eastbound shipment of bulk goods. For these two reasons the demand for carrying manufactured goods by railroad became more elastic.

It was clearly a time to reevaluate the traditional rate structures. However, the regulation of railroad rates was now deeply entrenched, and political coalitions operating through the regulatory process were able to prevent a restructuring of railroad rates. Another round of apparently destructive competition followed as demand shifted to motor carriers, and in addition, total market demand fell substantially due to the Depression of the 1930s.

The financial viability of the railroads was seriously threatened during this period. As a result, the U.S. Congress passed the Emergency Transportation Act in 1933. Previous regulation in the industry, which began with the creation of the Interstate Commerce Commission (ICC) in 1887, had been directed primarily toward preventing abuses in railroad pricing and favoring competition in the industry by restrictions on pools. After 1933, however, the ICC was directed also to set minimum rates, consistent with the cost of providing service.

Two years later in the Motor Carrier Act, regulation was extended to the entire transportation industry. Now entry into trucking, as well as into the other sectors of the transportation industry, was restricted and both minimum and maximum trucking rates came under ICC jurisdiction. Initially, regulation by the ICC attempted to satisfy two objectives (Friedlaender 1969, p. 43): (1) to maintain the traditional value of service rate structures that favored agricultural and bulk commodities over manufactured commodities and (2) to maintain adequate levels of profits in the railroad industry, because the transportation of bulk commodities at low rates desired by shippers required a viable rail system. Thus trucking rates were initially set according to the same value of service structure that had historically prevailed in the rail industry; and these rates were raised by the ICC whenever the financial viability of the railroads was threatened.

Ultimately, the ICC was perceived by economists as an agency whose primary function was to protect all carriers in the transportation industry from the rigors of competition. However, the management of a regime of regulated competition proved to be a formidable task. Changing technology, primarily in the development of the interstate highway system, gave the trucking industry a competitive advantage in the transportation of high value or perishable commodities. Attempts by the railroads to compete by lowering selected rates were repeatedly blocked by the ICC. By the 1960s it was the trucking industry, rather than the railroads, that demanded regulatory protection from the evils of destructive competition.

The primary conclusion to be drawn from the preceding discussion is that competition in the transportation industry has throughout its history been periodically unstable. It would be accurate to say that competition has been "destructive," in a transitory sense, during the periods in which excess capacity has been greatest. However, any instability that may be inherent in the competitive process may have been confounded by an artificially induced instability due to the regulatory process. For example, government subsidization of early railroad expansion was in part responsible for the first episode of destructive competition. Later, the inflexibility of the ICC may have intensified episodes of instability by preventing a rational restructuring of rates and the consequent flow of capital into the most productive sectors of the industry. Thus from historical evidence alone it is difficult to argue a persuasive case that competition has been truly destructive.

There is, however, a case to be made on a more theoretical level, and here the contrast between railroads and trucking is instructive.[10] Recently, a number of studies, both theoretical and applied, have

---

[10] See, for example, Kahn (1971) and Friedlaender and Spady (1981). See also, Bailey and Panzar (1981) for a similar argument in favor of competition in the airline industry.

concluded that unrestricted competition in trucking would be stable and efficient, because fixed costs in the trucking industry are low, or nonexistent. Econometric studies by Friedlaender and Spady (1981) and others suggest that the trucking industry is characterized by diseconomies of scale, although there are perhaps some network economies similar to those that exist in railroading. More importantly, costs in the trucking industry are not sunk costs to any significant degree. Trucks may be freely and costlessly transferred, in the absence of regulation, from one market to another, and so the industry as a whole can respond quickly to unforeseen changes in demand. Prolonged excess capacity should not be a problem in the trucking industry.

Railroads, on the other hand, have a different cost structure. There are substantial economies of scale in the industry, although it is likely that the largest existing railroads operate under constant, or even increasing costs. Furthermore, the track, right-of-way, and much of the other capital stock in a typical railroad is a sunk cost that cannot be easily transferred to alternative markets. Thus given uncertain, or rapidly fluctuating, demand in the industry it is possible that capacity will never adjust to an equilibrium level. In this industry destructive competition may be a long-run as well as a transitory problem.

In four subsequent chapters I will describe some theoretical results that are relevant in a theory of destructive competition. Chapter 5 will consider a potential instability that may result when there is asymmetric competition involving a dominant firm natural monopoly and a large number of small potential or actual competitors in a market with free entry. Chapter 6 will use some of the tools of cooperative game theory to determine when and if competition in an ideal state, representing costless coalition formation, is unstable. Finally, Chapters 7 and 8 will consider the nature of equilibrium among firms in markets with free entry and in markets with various barriers to entry.

2.4   Concluding comments

In this chapter a portion of the economics literature that pertains to natural monopoly has been surveyed. The reader should now have a basic understanding of what natural monopoly is and how a formal theory might be constructed. The following chapter will review a number of important economic concepts that will be useful in building that theory.

CHAPTER 3

Natural monopoly and economic theory: some basic results

Although most of the theory to be developed in Chapters 4 through 8 is of recent origin, the concept of natural monopoly is not new. In this chapter I will review some of the tools that have traditionally been available to economists who studied natural monopoly. The first two sections describe the basic methodology common to almost all of microeconomic theory. The reader who is unfamiliar with this presentation may wish to review a standard economics text such as Samuelson (1980). The remaining sections describe more specialized results that will be used, or assumed, elsewhere in the book. References will be given when appropriate for a more detailed discussion of these conclusions. The primary function in collecting these results is to define a basic set of ideas upon which the remainder of the book will be built, rather than to teach the reader who is totally unacquainted with the material that is presented in this chapter.

3.1 Competitive equilibrium and monopoly equilibrium

One of the earliest formal models of competitive equilibrium is the analysis of supply and demand, due to Alfred Marshall (1927). Suppose that there are a large number of both potential buyers and potential sellers for a single well-defined product. On the supply side, each seller is assumed to have a cost curve defining the marginal cost of all possible units of output. Marginal cost for each seller is assumed to be an upward-sloping function of output. Industry supply is determined by the horizontal summation of individual marginal cost curves and is therefore an upward-sloping function of output. That is, if the market price is p, then each seller would be willing to supply units up to the point that his or her marginal cost exceeds p. If q_i is the output corresponding to p for each seller, then industry supply at p is equal to the summation of the outputs q_i over all sellers in the market.

Similarly, every potential buyer is assumed to have a demand function reflecting the number of units of output desired at every possible price. The inverse demand function reflects the marginal price that a buyer is willing to pay for each unit of output. Demand is assumed to be a downward-sloping function of output. Market demand is the horizontal summation of individual demands.

The competitive equilibrium is determined by the intersection of the market demand and supply curves as in Figure 3.1. This intersection determines the price p and output q. It is an equilibrium because at price equal to p, buyers in the aggregate wish to consume exactly q units, whereas sellers are willing to supply exactly q. For an equilibrium of supply and demand to be competitive it is necessary that the following conditions hold. No suppliers are so large that a change in their output could cause a change in the equilibrium price. Similarly, no buyers are so large that a change in their purchases would result in a different price. Both buyers and sellers are required to be price takers.

The determination of the number of firms in a competitive equilibrium requires some additional information about the set of potential suppliers in the industry. If the marginal cost function for every firm passes through the origin, as shown in Figure 3.1, and there are no additional costs, then each firm would make a positive profit in a competitive equilibrium. For example, the profit of firm 1 is shown by the shaded area in Figure 3.1, representing the difference of total revenue (which is equal to $p \cdot q_1$) and total cost (which is equal to the area under MC_1).

Firms, however, have fixed as well as variable costs. If fixed costs are less than the excess of total revenue over variable cost, then the firm makes a profit. If fixed costs are greater than total revenue minus variable cost, then profits are negative and the firm will go out of business in the long run.

In mathematical terms, a cost function with fixed costs is characterized by the fact that cost does not go to zero as output falls to zero. This is shown in Figure 3.2 by a total cost function, which is the vertical summation of a fixed and a variable cost. Marginal cost is merely the change in total (and variable) cost accompanying a unit change in output. With cost curves as drawn in Figure 3.2, the marginal cost assumes its usual upward-sloping shape, as in Figure 3.1. Whenever there are fixed costs, it is obvious that average cost is falling for levels of output close to zero. In Figure 3.3 the marginal cost is shown to intersect average cost at the point at which the latter function is at a minimum. This is a necessary condition

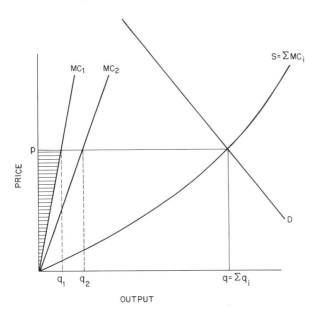

FIGURE 3.1

that can be seen to follow easily from the definitions of the two functions.[1]

Figure 3.2 also illustrates the condition for long-run competitive equilibrium. At the price p_c' positive profits can be made because price (or average revenue) is greater than average cost. At p_c profits are equal to zero and at any price less than p_c the firm would incur a loss. In a competitive equilibrium all active firms in an industry must earn profits that are greater than or equal to zero, and all inactive firms must earn profits that are less than or equal to zero.[2] Thus a competitive equilibrium determines the price, the quantity, and the collection of active firms in a market.

---

[1] Whenever average cost is at a minimum, its derivative with respect to output must be zero. That is,

$$\frac{d\left[\dfrac{C(x)}{x}\right]}{dx} = \frac{x\,\dfrac{dC}{dx} - C(x)}{x^2} = 0$$

and therefore $dC/dx = C(x)/x$.

[2] Additional discussion of entry and exit may be found in Chapter 7.

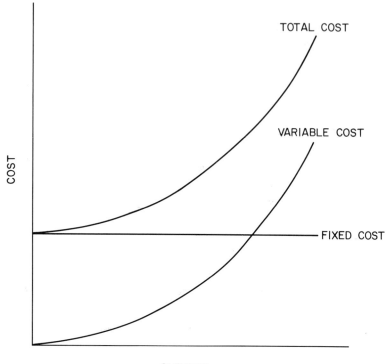

FIGURE 3.2

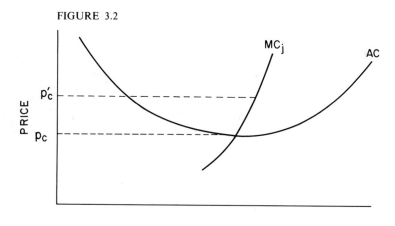

FIGURE 3.3

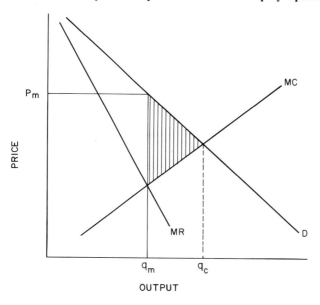

FIGURE 3.4

Now consider the monopoly equilibrium in which there is only one firm in the market. Like a competitive firm, a monopolist has a marginal cost function and it may be assumed for the present that marginal costs rise with output. The monopolist wishes to maximize profits and, unlike a competitive firm, a monopolist is able to choose the industry price so as to satisfy this objective. That is, the monopolist chooses a price p to maximize total revenue minus total cost. Because price and quantity are related through the market demand function, it is also accurate to say that the monopolist chooses the quantity q so as to maximize profits. That is, the monopoly output q_m is the output that maximizes

$$p(q) \cdot q - C(q)$$

where $p(q)$ is the inverse demand function and $C(q)$ is the total cost function. Solving the first-order conditions leads to the result that at $q = q_m$

$$p(q) + q \frac{dp}{dq} = \frac{dC}{dq}$$

The term on the left-hand side of the equation represents marginal revenue and that on the right, marginal cost. The monopoly equilibrium is illustrated in Figure 3.4. In this diagram the profit-maximizing output q_m is defined by the intersection of the marginal revenue and marginal cost functions and the monopoly price $p_m = D(q_m)$ is given by the demand function. Notice in particular that the shaded area represents the "welfare cost" of monopoly, because every unit of output between q_m and q_c is valued by consumers more than the cost of producing it. Fixed costs are not relevant in determining the monopolist's price and output, but as with a competitive firm, if maximum total profits are negative, then the monopoly firm will leave the market in the long run.

3.2   General competitive equilibrium

For a number of reasons, partial equilibrium analysis is incomplete, although it remains an effective tool when used with care. The more firmly founded approach is the theory of general equilibrium, which is essentially to recognize that everything depends on everything else. Although the demand for a good depends on its own price, it depends on many other prices in the economy as well. The basic tools of general equilibrium are the preferences of consumers from which demand is derived, rather than the demand function. Often preferences are represented by an ordinal utility function that expresses a utility measure for every conceivable bundle of consumption goods. Similarly, supply conditions are given by production possibility sets, which represent the set of outputs that can feasibly be produced from various combinations of inputs.

Most results in general equilibrium theory rely on the properties of convex sets and convex functions.[3] Utility functions are typically assumed to be quasiconcave,[4] which means that consumer indifference curves are convex to the origin. Convex indifference curves in turn mean that consumers face diminishing marginal rates of substitution if one good is traded for another and utility is held constant. Given convex indifference curves, an appropriately defined demand function (quantity demanded as a function of price) can be shown to be downward sloping.

Similarly, the production possibility sets, which describe feasible input-output combinations (i.e., outputs that can be technically produced from the given inputs) are assumed to be convex. This assumption, however, is a severe restriction on the technology because it precludes any form of fixed costs or more general conditions of increasing returns.

---

[3] A set T is convex if for any elements x and y in T and any number λ between 0 and 1, the "convex" combination of x and y, $\lambda x + (1 - \lambda)y$, is in T. A function f is convex if for any x, y, and λ as stated, it is true that $f[\lambda x + (1 - \lambda)y] \leq \lambda f(x) + (1 - \lambda)f(y)$.

[4] Quasiconcave and quasiconvex functions are defined more precisely in Chapter 4.

Given the basic convexity assumptions, the fundamental result of general equilibrium theory follows. There exists a price vector — one price for each good in the economy — and an output vector distributed among all producers and consumers in the economy such that every agent is at a most preferred point. That is, consumers maximize utility given prices and income, whereas producers maximize profits at the given prices.

As in the partial equilibrium analysis, a competitive equilibrium has certain optimality properties. In particular, every competitive equilibrium has the property, known as Pareto optimality, that no other feasible distribution of outputs within the economy can improve the welfare of one person without reducing the welfare of someone else.

A more extensive discussion of general equilibrium theory may be found in Debreu (1959) or Arrow and Hahn (1971). An intuitive and readable exposition is presented in Koopmans (1957).

3.3   The theory of joint production

This section will be concerned with a basic but important extension of the theory of competitive pricing. The theory of joint production is a part of the classical equilibrium analysis that is credited primarily to Alfred Marshall. It is important in the present context as a concrete example of subadditivity, which will be defined and described more completely in the following chapter.

That joint production does not conform completely to the theory of competitive pricing has a great deal to do with the definition of an economic good. For example, consider the supply and demand for sheep. The supply conditions for sheep conform to the usual conditions as discussed in Section 3.1. That is, there are many producers with upward-sloping marginal cost functions that define an upward-sloping industry supply schedule as in Figure 3.5. On the demand side, however, sheep are not relevant economic goods. Instead, they are demanded for their useful components — wool and mutton. The individual demand relationships for wool and mutton are then defined in the standard manner as in Figure 3.5.

In order to obtain a concept of market equilibrium, an additional construction is needed. For this purpose it must be noted that a supply of sheep is intrinsically a joint supply of wool and of mutton and that the relative quantities of wool and mutton that can be obtained from a single sheep are rigidly fixed. Suppose that the units of measurement for wool and mutton are chosen such that one unit of each can be produced from one sheep. Then market demand for sheep can be constructed by the vertical addition of the

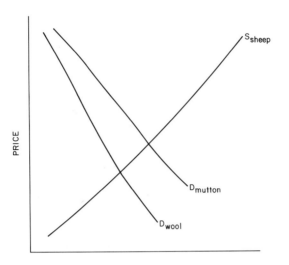

PRICE

S_sheep

D_mutton

D_wool

OUTPUT

FIGURE 3.5

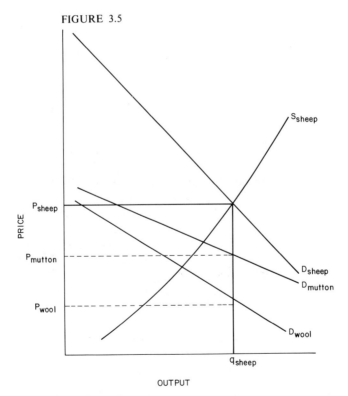

PRICE

S_sheep

P_sheep

P_mutton

P_wool

D_sheep

D_mutton

D_wool

q_sheep

OUTPUT

FIGURE 3.6

component demands as shown in Figure 3.6. The required addition is fundamentally different from the horizontal summation that is required to construct the ordinary market demand schedule. The proper interpretation is that for any given quantity q (which measures units of wool, mutton, and sheep) there is a marginal price of wool and a marginal price of mutton that consumers are willing to pay. The correct demand price for sheep, at the same quantity q is then the sum of the two component prices.

Market equilibrium is determined by the supply and demand for sheep which in the usual way generate a competitive price for sheep. The competitive prices for wool and mutton are determined from the respective demand curves at the quantities corresponding to equilibrium in the market for sheep.

Some of the characteristics of jointly produced goods are revealed by a comparative statics analysis. For example, an increase in the demand for mutton will lead to a decrease in the price of wool. The most important property of joint supply for the present discussion is, however, more obvious: There are technological conditions under which joint production is necessary and under which the standard model of market competition must be modified. Additional discussion of joint production may be found in Friedman (1962).

3.4   Fixed costs and the theory of cross-subsidization

Fixed costs have already been introduced in Section 3.1 in the discussion of the equilibrium number of firms in a competitive industry. A "fixed cost" is a cost that is insensitive to variations in output. Fixed costs arise from indivisibilities in the production process. Many of the costs associated with a railroad are fixed costs, and in fact there are several different levels in which costs are fixed. (1) In the very short run all costs are fixed, because an additional passenger or unit of freight can be carried at no increase in cost. (2) In the somewhat longer run there are fixed costs associated with adding or subtracting railroad cars in discrete units to accommodate fluctuations in demand. (3) In the very long run there are fixed costs associated with the construction of right-of-way.

Sunk costs are closely related to fixed costs. The essential characteristic of a sunk cost is that some productive activities require specialized forms of capital that are not easily converted into other productive uses. More precisely, a "sunk cost" is the difference between the ex ante opportunity cost and the value that could be recovered ex post after a commitment to a given project has been made. For example, the capital embodied in an airplane is sunk, because it cannot easily be used for a purpose other than transportation. However, the capital embodied in an airplane serving a particular market is not a sunk cost, because it is easily transferred to other markets.

Several implications of the existence of fixed costs are important. First, a competitive equilibrium cannot exist so long as any producer is operating in a region of falling average costs. This result follows because a competitive equilibrium requires that producers are price takers. But if there is a constant market price equal to average cost, while average cost is falling, then profits are necessarily increased when a larger output is produced. Therefore, as demonstrated in Section 3.1, the industry equilibrium, when there are fixed costs, requires that price is equal to marginal cost and greater than or equal to average cost. Thus the output of every firm in a competitive industry must be greater than or equal to the output at which average cost is a minimum.

Another relevant property of fixed cost concerns the production of multiple outputs. If a cost function for two outputs contains a fixed element common to both, then there are said to be common costs. Common costs are merely a more general form of joint supply (discussed in Section 3.3) in which the proportions of output are not fixed. Several additional results are possible, however.

First, consider the case of a competitive industry that supplies two different outputs for which there is a common cost. For simplicity, assume that costs for the two outputs are unrelated except through the common cost term. Then for a typical firm in the industry the cost function may be written as $C(x_1, x_2) = c_0 + c_1(x_1) + c_2(x_2)$. In Figure 3.7 the marginal cost functions for x_1 and x_2 are shown. Because the industry is competitive, each firm takes the market prices p_1 and p_2 as given. In Figure 3.7 the shaded areas represent a return to the firm in excess of variable costs. If the common cost is less than this return, then the firm is viable. Otherwise, the firm will leave the industry.

If the marginal cost curves are sufficiently flat and the common cost is sufficiently large, it is likely that a competitive industry will not be viable. An extreme case is the situation of multiproduct monopoly. As in the case of the single-product monopoly (discussed in Section 3.1), the multiproduct monopolist maximizes profits by equating marginal cost and marginal revenue in each market. Under the assumption that demands are independent, the profit maximum is illustrated in Figure 3.8. The shaded areas in this diagram represent a return in excess of variable cost. If this joint return exceeds the common cost c_0, then the monopoly is viable. Otherwise, the monopolist will choose not to produce.

It will be useful to express the profit maximum algebraically for use in a later section. Marginal revenue may be expressed as

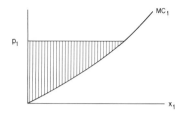

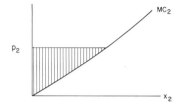

FIGURE 3.7

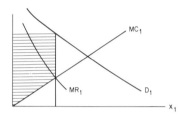

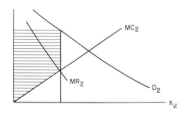

FIGURE 3.8

$$MR = p\left(1 - \frac{1}{\eta}\right) \qquad (3.1)$$

where p is price and $\eta = -(p/q)(dq/dp)$ is the elasticity of demand.[5] Then monopoly equilibrium requires that in each market separately $MR_i = MC_i$, which with use of equation (3.1) and some

---

[5] Since (dq/dp) is negative, the elasticity, as defined here, is a positive number.

rearrangement gives

$$\frac{p_i - MC_i}{p_i} = -\frac{1}{\eta_i} \tag{3.2}$$

Equation (3.2) is related to a more general result on optimal pricing in decreasing-cost industries. A survey of the latter topic will be presented in Section 3.7.

Often a multiple output monopoly firm is regulated so that its overall profits, in excess of a fair return to the stockholder owners, are set equal to zero. In this situation there is a potentially large degree of indeterminacy in the relative prices of the outputs that are produced by the firm. Naturally, consumers who purchase relatively large amounts of any one of the monopolist's outputs would like to face the lowest possible price for that output. At the same time, there may be other firms that produce outputs that are closely related to one of the monopolist's outputs. These firms prefer to see the highest possible price for that output. Each of these constituencies may on occasion complain that the prices of the regulated monopolist are such that one output is cross-subsidizing another. In order to address these issues Faulhaber (1975) and others have recently suggested a theory of cross-subsidization.[6]

The basic elements of this theory may be conveyed by means of an example, which is due to Faulhaber. Consider a water utility that is required to supply water in four distinct neighborhoods from a common well. Neighborhoods 1 and 2 are located east of the well and neighborhoods 3 and 4 are located west of the well. Suppose that the annual cost of maintaining the well and an above ground storage tank is $100. Furthermore, suppose that there is an eastbound pipeline to serve neighborhoods 1 and 2, with an annual cost of $100, and a westbound pipeline, also with an annual cost of $100. Finally, there is a cost of $100 directly attributable to each neighborhood for supplying a given quantity of water.

Total costs of the utility sum to $700. In order to break even, the utility must collect revenue from each of the neighborhoods, which is exactly equal to $700 in the aggregate. That is, if $r_1, \ldots, r_4$ represent the revenues collected from neighborhoods $1, \ldots, 4$, respectively, then $r_1 + r_2 + r_3 + r_4 = 700$ is the basic break-even constraint.

The theory of cross-subsidization seeks to determine what additional constraints need to be placed on $r_1, \ldots, r_4$ in order to ensure that the prices of the utility are subsidy-free. The concept of

[6] See, also, Zajac (1972; 1978), Sharkey (1982), and Sandberg (1975).

"subsidy-free" chosen by Faulhaber and many other economists is based on the "stand alone cost." It is conceptually possible to design a water utility that is able to serve a single neighborhood by itself or a pair of neighborhoods or a collection of any three neighborhoods. In this example the cost of serving (1) any one neighborhood is $300; (2) neighborhoods 1 and 2 together or 3 and 4 together, $400; (3) neighborhoods 1 and 3 or 2 and 4 together, $500; and (4) any three neighborhoods together, $600.

One can reasonably suppose that any neighborhood or group of neighborhoods would insist (if it had all of the appropriate information) that its contribution to the revenues of the utility not exceed the cost of constructing a separate utility exclusively for its own needs. In other words, the cost share of any group of customers in a common project should not exceed the "stand alone cost" of serving only their needs. In this example the revenues that satisfy the stand alone test are given by $r_1, \ldots, r_4$ such that

$$r_1 + r_2 + r_3 + r_4 = 700$$
$$r_i \leq 300 \qquad i = 1, \ldots, 4$$
$$r_1 + r_2 \leq 400$$
$$r_3 + r_4 \leq 400$$
$$r_1 + r_3 \leq 500$$
$$r_2 + r_4 \leq 500$$
$$r_i + r_j + r_k \leq 600$$

Manipulation of these inequalities shows that:

$$r_1 + r_2 + r_3 + r_4 = 700 \qquad\qquad\qquad (3.3)$$
$$r_i \geq 100 \qquad i = 1, \ldots, 4 \qquad\qquad (3.4)$$
$$r_1 + r_2 \geq 300 \qquad\qquad\qquad\qquad (3.5)$$
$$r_3 + r_4 \geq 300 \qquad\qquad\qquad\qquad (3.6)$$

Equation (3.3) is just the break-even constraint. Inequality (3.4) states that revenues from each neighborhood must cover at least the incremental cost of serving that neighborhood. Inequalities (3.5) and (3.6) similarly state that the revenue from certain pairs of services must be at least as great as the incremental cost or serving that pair. Thus the stand alone test for cross-subsidization is equivalent to an incremental cost test when the latter is applied to groups of services as well as to individual services.

The preceding test is significant in that it implies a set of inequality constraints that can be used to judge whether any group of customers is being treated unfairly. If the revenues from a group of customers are less than the stand alone cost of serving them, then they are better off being served by the common utility rather than by a specialty firm that supplies only their needs. If revenues are being collected from only two distinct groups, then the test for cross-subsidization reduces to the constraint that revenues must cover incremental costs of production. If more than two groups are involved, then the incremental costs of groups of customers must be considered as well.

Note also that the test for cross-subsidization simulates the operation of a competitive market with free entry. If there were truly free entry, then the constraints implied by the stand alone test would be automatically satisfied, because, if they were not, then customers would eventually learn that they could get lower prices by contracting with an alternative supplier.

Finally, observe that it is theoretically possible that no subsidy-free prices exist. In this case the break-even constraint such as equation (3.3) and the inequality constraints such as expressions (3.4) — (3.6) have no solution. This observation led to a related theory, known as the theory of sustainable natural monopoly, which will be dealt with more formally in Chapter 5.

3.5   The theory of the firm and increasing returns

The presence of a fixed cost is one example of the more general phenomenon of increasing returns. Much of the theory of natural monopoly is concerned with assigning a precise meaning to the term "increasing returns." However, for the remainder of this chapter it will be helpful to use the term loosely when considering the various ways in which economic theory has addressed this important problem. As noted in Section 3.4 a falling average cost curve is inconsistent with a competitive equilibrium. For this reason the study of increasing returns is closely related to the economic theory of the firm, in that a firm may be said to fulfill those functions in which competitive markets fail. The purpose of this section is to review those areas of economic theory that specifically treat increasing returns behavior and the theory of the firm. First, the approach of Marshall (1927) and his contemporaries will be mentioned. Second, the important contribution of Coase (1937) will be reviewed in more detail. Finally, a sample of other recent work in this area will be considered.

The basic approach of Marshall (1927) was to classify increasing returns behavior into a number of categories. Increasing returns could be either internal to the firm or external to the firm and, similarly, internal or external to the industry. The exact definitions of firm and industry were not, however, considered by Marshall. In addition, the economies of scale could be either technological — relating to the production process, or pecuniary — relating to prices paid for inputs. Of the many possibilities, only technological increasing returns that are internal to the firm will be of concern here.

One possible explanation for technological increasing returns is the unavoidable presence of fixed costs, which have already been considered. The other principal source is the economy resulting from specialized use of resources — for example, the division of labor. No adequate theory has been offered, however, to explain the circumstances under which these economies can best be realized in the context of a single firm. A final source of increasing returns is found in the statistical regularities that accompany large volumes of transactions. For instance, inventories do not need to rise so rapidly as sales in order to provide the same probability of supply in stock. Also, a large and diversified firm is less risky than a small one and can accordingly secure capital at a lower rate of interest, if investors are risk averse.

The presence of uncertainty is one of the most fundamental reasons for the existence of firms. One of the first formal presentations of this observation is contained in Knight (1921a), in which the role of the entrepreneur is defined by the need for some individuals to accept the uncertainty inherent in productive activity and to receive in return the residual element as profit.[7] Knight's theory was later criticized by Coase, but parts of it are still accepted by many economists. Numerous issues treated by Knight are now viewed from a somewhat different perspective as problems in the transfer of information.

Coase (1937) may be credited as the founder of the modern theory of the firm. His theory is based on a simple observation. In a free competitive economy a firm can exist only if it performs some function that market prices and the process of competition cannot. In other words, Coase recognized explicitly that there are costs as well as benefits involved in the use of the price system. The benefits gained through the competitive price system include the flow of information among agents and sectors of the economy, but there are other ways of achieving the same benefits. When the cost of using the price system exceeds the cost of one of its alternatives, then one would expect the alternative to be adopted.

In order to identify the activities that a firm is most likely to

---

[7] Uncertainty in this sense is defined as uncertainty that cannot be insured against. Risk, which is uncertainty with the possibility of insurance coverage, can be handled without the special role of the entrepreneur.

perform, one should examine the costs involved in using the price system. One cost is that of discovering what the relevant prices are. Another consists of the costs of bargaining and negotiating contracts for each different transaction. Finally, uncertainty enters if long-term contracts are required.

A sensible theory requires bounds on the possible economies due to the firm. The basic diseconomies of large-size firms that were identified by Coase are decreasing returns to scale in the entrepreneureal inputs. In other words, if management is regarded as a separate input into production, then it is asserted that the benefits of managing relative to the price system diminish and finally vanish as the scale and complexity of the enterprise increase. For example, the spatial dispersion of agents with which a firm is required to deal increases as its size increases.

Although the theory of Coase is largely tautological, it nevertheless offers a persuasive conceptual foundation for most of the more recent work. In fact the theory of natural monopoly may be usefully viewed as an aspect of the general theory of the firm.

Much work has been done on the theory of the firm since Coase. That of Williamson (1975) is notable in this area, and it will be surveyed in Chapter 4. In the remainder of this section I will mention some alternative approaches that are based on the role of information as an economic good.

One potential advantage of a firm over a market is due to asymmetry of information.[8] For example, a worker may have information, not directly observable in the marketplace, about his or her ability to perform certain tasks. An employer, however, may be able to use various screening devices to identify the able workers and therefore achieve a better outcome than would result from a simple competitive wage. In addition, workers may be able to monitor each other successfully, whereas a manager may only be able to measure group performance. Under these conditions, it has been shown that a firm can achieve greater efficiency in worker performance than a market solution.

A related advantage of the firm over the marketplace concerns the use of "nonlinear" prices. A "nonlinear price schedule" is one in which the average price per unit depends on the number of units purchased. A two-part tariff consisting of an entry fee in addition to a uniform price schedule is a simple example. Ordinary market

---

[8] See, for example, Spence (1974).

prices are necessarily linear, because any attempt by sellers to impose a nonlinear schedule on the buyers of their products could be frustrated by resale agreements among the buyers. Under conditions of increasing returns, a nonlinear schedule can generally achieve a more efficient outcome than a linear price schedule. For this reason a firm may be at an advantage because the transfer of resources within a firm can be determined without the constraint of demand and supply by linear prices.

A final example of information in the theory of the firm concerns the public good aspects of knowledge. Obviously, knowledge of production techniques, once gained, may be used for production at any scale of operation. Thus production that is characterized by constant returns to scale in the absence of information gathering may exhibit increasing returns when the benefits of gathering information are accounted for.[9] Essentially, larger scale makes the acquisition of more information desirable and more information makes possible a larger scale.

3.6   Public goods and collective choice

The theory of the firm is the study of a particular form of nonmarket institution. A different nonmarket institution — namely, the government or collective choice process — is studied in the theory of public goods. A public good, as conceived by economists, has some combination of the following three attributes: (1) collectivity in consumption, the most basic attribute. One person's consumption of a public good does not reduce the amount available for others to consume. All pure public goods have this property. (2) potential excludability. A private good is always excludable because one need only consume it to exclude others. For a public good, however, it is important whether or not certain individuals (e.g., those who do not contribute toward production) may be prevented at reasonable cost from consuming the good. (3) voluntary nonconsumption (or free disposability), which public goods may or may not have. Some examples of public goods are ordinary television programs that are nonexcludable but do not require consumption by all and national defense that is nonexcludable and requires common consumption.

Public goods are related to goods that are jointly supplied. In this section a simple discussion of some of the properties of a public

---

[9]   See Wilson (1975) for a discussion of this point.

good will be given in the context of general equilibrium theory. Recall from Section 3.2 the definition of a competitive equilibrium, which requires the existence of a price vector and an allocation of goods among consumers and producers such that each agent is maximizing the appropriate quantity (utility or profit). Implicit in this definition is the assumption that the total production must be allocated among consumers and producers such that the summation of individual consumption equals the total production. This concept of equilibrium will not suffice for public goods, because the total production is available in its entirety for consumption by every agent. However, there is a related theory of Lindahl pricing which generates outcomes that are in many ways similar to competitive equilibria.[10]

In a Lindahl equilibrium the role of price and quantity for a public good is exactly the reverse of the role for a private good. Instead of a common price among all consumers, there is a common quantity of consumption. Rather than an allocation of goods among consumers, there is an allocation of the total cost of the public good among all buyers such that the price facing a buyer corresponds to his or her marginal valuation of the total quantity and the sum of prices facing consumers is equal to the production cost.

It is easy to visualize the essential difference of Lindahl prices from ordinary competitive prices in a partial equilibrium context. Figure 3.9a represents the demand and supply for an ordinary private good, whereas Figure 3.9b illustrates the corresponding concept of demand and supply for a public good.

When a Lindahl equilibrium exists it has the same Pareto optimality property that a competitive equilibrium has. As with the competitive equilibrium, certain nonconvexities, such as those associated with increasing returns, may preclude existence of a Lindahl equilibrium.

There is a serious problem with Lindahl pricing, however, even when existence is assured. In a Lindahl equilibrium each consumer is required to pay a different price and an individual's price depends only on his or her personal valuation of the good. Thus there is an incentive problem, because in the absence of exclusionary devices, an individual may understate his or her value of the good and enjoy consumption without paying the proper price, or in extreme cases, without paying anything at all. This phenomenon, known as the "free-rider" problem, has received considerable attention in the public goods literature.

---

[10] See Lindahl (1958).

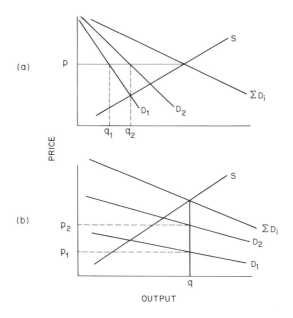

FIGURE 3.9

Recently it has been shown that the free rider problem can be avoided with a certain carefully designed incentive compatible pricing formula. The basic property of an incentive compatible pricing rule is that an individual's contribution depends on the reports or signals of everyone else, rather than on his or her reported valuation. Similarly, a buyer's own message has an impact on both the total production of the public good and the contributions of everyone else. Vickrey (1961) and Groves and Ledyard (1977) have shown that a pricing rule exists such that each individual can be given the correct incentive for truthfully revealing his or her preferences and that a Pareto optimal quantity of output will result.

Incredible Claim

A final comment concerning the relationship of the theory of public goods to natural monopoly: The outputs of a natural monopoly do not generally have the attributes of a public good. Pure public goods are usually provided by governments. However, increasing returns to scale in the production of a private good are closely related to the concept of public goods. For example, a fixed cost has the property of collectiveness, because it must be paid by the buyers in the aggregate. This observation suggests that optimal pricing in the presence of fixed costs might consist of a two-part tariff, with a Lindahl or Vickrey scheme used to cover the fixed cost and an ordinary market price to cover the variable costs. The following section treats a different and more traditional approach to the problem of pricing in the presence of increasing returns.

3.7   Public enterprise pricing and the theory of the second best

As the theory of public goods is related to the theory of joint cost from Section 3.3, the present section is closely connected to the discussion of fixed costs from Section 3.4. Recall from Sections 3.1 and 3.2 that a competitive equilibrium requires that the price of every good equals its marginal cost. The statement most appropriate to general equilibrium is that there must exist a price vector such that the ratio of any two prices is equal to every consumer's marginal rate of substitution (the ratio at which a consumer is willing to trade one good for another while holding utility constant) and every producer's marginal rate of transformation. This section will address two related questions about this concept: (1) If a competitive equilibrium does not exist, what is the appropriate pricing strategy (from the point of view of social welfare) for an individual firm, and particularly, a firm facing increasing returns to scale in production? It has been argued[11] under these conditions that the appropriate prices should be related to but not equal or even proportional to the set of marginal costs. (2) If some prices are to be unequal to marginal costs, should other prices still conform to the competitive model? This question concerns the boundary between the competitive (price = marginal cost) and the noncompetitive sector.

The first question is much easier to address. Consider the production of a single product such that average cost is declining at all levels of output. Such a cost curve would result from a fixed cost and a constant marginal cost, which is the form assumed in Figure 3.10. A usual downward-sloping demand curve is shown in the same diagram. A necessary condition for productive efficiency is that price equals marginal cost. However, marginal cost pricing in this industry would result in a budget deficit by an amount $[AC(q_1) - MC] \cdot q_1$, where q_1 is the output such that the price given by the inverse demand function is equal to marginal cost. The deficit must clearly come from some source. An earlier generation of economists, led by Hotelling (1938), argued that the deficit should be recovered from general taxation, with the government subsidizing decreasing cost industries. However, it was soon

---

[11] See Baumol and Bradford (1970).

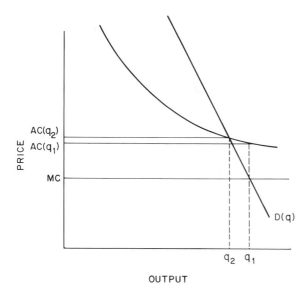

FIGURE 3.10

recognized that taxation, or any other method of raising the required subsidy, involves a welfare cost exactly analogous to the cost of having the original price greater than marginal cost.[12]

A second line of argument for pricing in decreasing cost industries is due primarily to Coase (1970). He argued that the existence of a subsidy introduces a distortion of its own because nonusers of a product are required to pay part of the cost for the users. But then there can be no market test of the overall value of a good in relation to its cost. Essentially a political process would replace an economic one in determining which goods should be produced.

The theory of pricing in public enterprises, subject to a budget constraint, is a synthesis of the views of both Hotelling and Coase, although the basic contribution by Ramsey (1927) occurred much earlier. This theory takes the position that a public utility or public enterprise must operate with its budget in balance. However, if there are multiple outputs, then the relative prices of the outputs are decision variables of the firm. The assumption of the theory is that prices should be chosen so as to maximize the aggregate net benefit to consumers from the consumption of the outputs of the firm.

[12] See Little (1951).

Like the theory of subsidy-free pricing described in Section 3.4, the theory of Ramsey pricing applies to the case of a regulated public utility that produces two or more distinct outputs. However, the results apply equally well if the utility sells essentially the same output in two or more distinct markets.

Assume for purposes of exposition that the costs to the firm take a particularly simple form. Suppose that there are two outputs and that the cost function $C(q_1, q_2)$ may be written as

$$C(q_1, q_2) = c_0 + c_1 q_1 + c_2 q_2$$

where c_0, c_1, and c_2 are positive constants. The constants c_1 and c_2 are just the marginal costs of producing additional units of outputs q_1 and q_2 respectively. The constant c_0 represents the fixed or overhead cost to the firm and is independent of either output.

Next suppose that demand functions for outputs q_1 and q_2 are independent and are given by the functions

$$q_1 = D_1(p_1)$$

$$q_2 = D_2(p_2)$$

which describe the total market demands for q_1 and q_2 respectively, as a function of p_1 and p_2.

As is generally known, the best possible outcome (which maximizes aggregate consumer welfare) occurs when both prices are equal to marginal cost. However, with prices equal to marginal costs, revenues fall short of total costs by an amount equal to the fixed costs c_0. Therefore if the public utility is required to be self-supporting, it is necessary to choose a different set of higher prices. The Ramsey prices are the "second best" prices that succeed in raising enough revenue to cover total cost with the smallest possible sacrifice in consumer welfare.

There are several ways to derive formulas for the Ramsey prices. One of the most general results states that prices should be set so as to curtail all outputs in the same proportion from the hypothetical levels at which they would have been if prices were equal to marginal costs. That is, p_1 and p_2 are Ramsey prices if

$$\frac{D_1(p_1)}{D_1(c_1)} = \frac{D_2(p_2)}{D_2(c_2)} \tag{3.7}$$

From equation (3.7) it can be seen that if the demand for good one is relatively less elastic than the demand for good two at prices close to the respective marginal costs, then the optimal price p_1 will have to be raised above marginal cost c_1 by an amount that is proportionately greater than for good two. This observation may help to motivate intuitively an alternative formula for the optimal Ramsey prices. According to this second result, p_1 and p_2 are Ramsey optimal if

$$\frac{p_i - c_i}{p_i} = - \frac{k}{\eta_i} \qquad i = 1, 2 \tag{3.8}$$

where η_i is the elasticity of demand for output i.[13] Equation (3.8) is identical to earlier equation (3.2) from Section 3.4, except for the presence of the proportionality constant k. In equation (3.8) k is assumed chosen in order to achieve overall budget balance. At $k = 1$ revenue minus variable cost is maximized, as in an unconstrained monopoly. At $k = 0$ all prices are equal to marginal costs, and so the competitive solution prevails. Further discussion of many issues associated with public utility pricing may be found in Zajac (1978). Additional results on Ramsey pricing may be found in Baumol and Bradford (1970) and Boiteux (1971).

Consider now the second problem concerning the public utility or public enterprise. Having a set of optimal prices as given by the Ramsey rule (perhaps in a more general form), one may naturally ask how the prices in the remainder of the economy should be determined. One possible answer is that other prices should be determined by the appropriate marginal costs, because it may be

---

[13] The second version of the Ramsey rule is easily derived in the case of independent demands. Let $p_i(q_i)$ represent the inverse demand function in market i and let $R(q_1, \ldots, q_n) = \sum_{i=1}^{n} p_i(q_i) \cdot q_i$ represent the revenue from sales in all markets. Let $C(q_1, \ldots, q_n)$ be the cost of producing outputs $q_1, \ldots, q_n$. Then choose outputs $q_1, \ldots, q_n$ so as to maximize the consumer surplus

$$\sum_{i=1}^{n} \left[\int_0^{q_i} p_i(t)dt - C(q) \right]$$

subject to the constraint that revenues are exactly equal to costs. First-order necessary conditions for this maximization imply that at an optimum,

$$p_i - \frac{\partial C}{\partial q_i} = -\lambda \left[\frac{\partial R}{\partial q_i} - \frac{\partial C}{\partial q_i} \right]$$

Further algebraic manipulation leads to equation (3.3) in the text, where $c_i = \partial C / \partial q_i$ and $k = \lambda/1 + \lambda$.

assumed that all decreasing cost enterprises are already accounted for. This response would be incorrect if one is interested in attaining a Pareto optimal outcome. It has been shown[14] that if prices deviate from marginal cost in one sector of an economy, then it will, in general, not be optimal to set prices equal to marginal cost in any other sector.

Of more practical, but related, interest, is the question of deciding what set of outputs to include in the computation of optimal Ramsey prices, under the assumption that all other outputs will be priced competitively. Maximization of consumer surplus, or use of any other welfare concept, is inappropriate. Consumer welfare will by definition improve (or at least not be any worse) when a new product is added to the Ramsey optimization formula. The only conclusion possible from this line of reasoning is that the entire economy should become a part of the public sector. There is no satisfactory answer to this paradox in the current literature, and thus it may be necessary to turn to a more basic theory of the firm to help assess the relative advantage of centralized optimization versus decentralized markets.

3.8   Concluding comments

I have described in this chapter a large number of results in economic theory that are necessary for understanding the material in the following chapters. Section 3.1 describes the basic tools of partial equilibrium analysis. Familiarity with these results is essential for an understanding of virtually all results in the remainder of the book. Section 3.2 on general equilibrium is less essential to the theory of natural monopoly. These results, however, are used briefly in Section 4.2 and extensively in Chapter 6. Each of the remaining more specialized sections is developed and extended in Chapters 4 through 8. Chapter 4 requires a thorough understanding of Section 3.3, 3.4, and 3.5. Chapter 5 is based upon some of the results in Sections 3.4, 3.6, and 3.7. Chapter 6 extends some of the results in Sections 3.4 and 3.6. Finally, Chapters 7 and 8 are based primarily on Sections 3.1 and 3.7.

Most of the discussion in the remaining chapters is directed only to the most basic technological and economic issues associated with natural monopoly. Therefore some of the results which are described in this chapter are not fully exploited in the remainder of the book. For example, the discussion of incentive compatible

---

[14] See Lipsey and Lancaster (1956).

pricing and nonlinear pricing could, and ultimately should, be incorporated into the analysis of market entry that is contained in Chapter 5, 7, and 8. The interested reader should feel free to use the results of this chapter and the references within it to extend when possible the results of the following chapters.

CHAPTER 4

Natural monopoly and subadditivity of costs

The most important result to be developed in this chapter can easily be stated: In a world in which competition is ideal, in a way to be described later, there is natural monopoly in a particular market if and only if a single firm can produce the desired output at lower cost than any combination of two or more firms. Natural monopoly is defined in terms of a single firm's efficiency relative to the efficiency of other combinations of firms in the industry. It is possible to test the proposition that a given firm is a natural monopoly.

Not all monopolies are natural. For example, monopoly may result from the control by a single firm of essential inputs into production, through trademarks or patents, or from the exclusive right to sell in a certain market. The essential characteristic of this form is that monopoly power is based on the inability of other firms to compete on an equal basis. Monopolies of this sort are generally transitory in nature and may also serve a useful social function, for example, when the granting of a patent gives an incentive for technological innovation. This form of monopoly, however, is not a natural monopoly.

Monopoly power may also result from unfair practices, such as predatory pricing, by one firm against its competitors, or from the formation of a cartel of several firms in a market. A monopoly of this type is based on behavioral abuses of the process of competition and is also not a natural monopoly.

The cost to society of either of these forms is shown in Figure 4.1. Monopoly power allows a firm to set a price above the marginal cost of production by setting an output q_m less than the competitive and, socially optimal output q_c. Every unit of output greater than q_m and up to the competitive output q_c is valued by consumers by an amount greater than its cost of production. Therefore a measure of the cost of monopoly is found by summing the foregone benefits, as in the shaded portion of Figure 4.1.

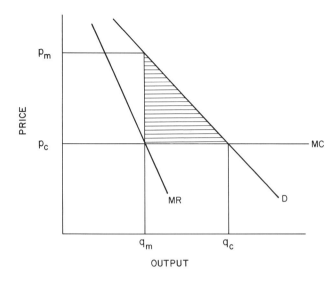

FIGURE 4.1

Suppose, however, that other firms are able to compete on an equal basis — that is, in the absence of behavioral abuses or physical and legal restrictions. Competition of this form may be referred to as ideal competition.[1] Natural monopoly is then a monopoly that results when a single firm can produce at lower cost than any collection of two or more firms in a market with ideal competition. Of course, natural monopoly may also occur in a market in which competition is less than ideal. For example, many natural monopolies are themselves regulated, and entry by rival firms is restricted. However, for the monopoly to be natural, it is necessary that a single firm remain as the most efficient producer, if the restrictions on competition are removed.

This introductory discussion may be summarized as follows. It is not monopoly but the absence of competition that imposes a cost on society. Under ideal competition, natural monopoly is consistent with maximum social welfare, as long as a single firm is as efficient as a multiple firm alternative. With other forms of monopoly, the process of competition is deficient. Social welfare could be

[1] Ideal competition will be discussed at greater length in Chapter 7. There, a market in which competition is ideal will be referred to as a contestable market.

improved by policies that encourage competition. With natural monopoly, increased competition could not improve social welfare. The entry of firms in a natural monopoly market could only reduce welfare by raising total costs of production.[2] Natural monopoly is itself the natural outcome of the competitive process under ideal competition.[3]

The present chapter is devoted to the study of conditions under which a single firm is more efficient than two or more firms. When technology is expressed in terms of a cost function, showing the monetary value of the inputs used to produce a given set of outputs, then a single firm is more efficient than two or more firms if and only if the cost function is subadditive.

Section 4.1 considers subadditivity of single output cost functions and, in particular, the relationship of subadditivity and economies of scale. The major result is that economies of scale, or equivalently average costs that fall as output increases, are sufficient for subadditivity. However, a cost function may also be subadditive if there are diseconomies of scale.

If firms in a market produce more than one output, then the conditions for subadditivity are more complex. Section 4.2 describes the basic nature of subadditivity in a multiple output market, but without the mathematical complexity of the following section. In a multiple output market, economies of scale are no longer sufficient for subadditivity. Some measure of the economies of jointly producing two or more outputs together is also needed.

The sufficient conditions for subadditivity in a multiple output market are considered more precisely in Section 4.3. The most important concepts that are introduced here are economies of scope, cost complementarity, and trans-ray convexity. Each of these expresses in some way an economy of joint production. An economy of scope exists if it is possible to produce any vector of outputs more efficiently in a single firm than in two or more specialty firms, holding constant the level of production of each output. Economy of scope is a useful intuitive property but it is not useful in deriving sufficient conditions for more general subadditivity.

Cost complementarity is said to exist if an increase in the production of any one output lowers the incremental cost of

---

[2] The entry of firms in a natural monopoly market is, however, a subtle issue. It will be examined more fully in Chapters 5 and 7.

[3] It is possible that there is no stable outcome under ideal competition. This possibility will be discussed later in Chapters 5 and 6.

producing other outputs. It will be shown that cost complementarity is by itself a sufficient condition for subadditivity.

Finally, trans-ray convexity is a measure of the behavior of the cost function on certain constrained sets, which approximately hold the overall scale of production constant. It can be shown that trans-ray convexity, together with economies of scale, or declining average costs along rays through the origin, are sufficient for subadditivity.

Section 4.4 is concerned with underlying sources of subadditivity rather than with the mathematical properties of subadditivity itself. The term "plant subadditivity" is used to describe subadditivity that ensues from the purely technical aspects of production. It can be measured through engineering cost analysis. On the other hand, firm subadditivity results from the unique role that the firm plays in organizing the set of inputs into production and in directing the transformation of inputs into outputs. Because the role of the firm is not easily quantified, firm subadditivity cannot in general be measured, except through its combined effects with plant subadditivity in econometric estimates of cost functions. Several examples are given that suggest that even in econometric studies, firm subadditivity can easily be overlooked.

The final section is devoted to a brief overview of an approach in which firm subadditivity may ultimately be quantified. Occasionally known as the transactions cost theory of the firm, this approach attempts to relate the hierarchical structure of the firm to the specific tasks that the firm must perform. We can then compare the performance of a firm with that of a market in certain stylized situations.

4.1   Natural monopoly in a single output market

This and the remaining sections of this chapter will attempt to define and characterize natural monopoly in terms of measurable attributes of the technology of a given firm. It will be convenient at this point to make the simplifying assumption that there are a large number of firms that are potentially willing to produce in the industry and that every firm has exactly the same technology. The technology of a firm will be expressed by means of a cost function that represents a dollar measure of the resources that are required to produce any conceivable level of output q.[4] Let C represent the cost function, so that $C(q)$ represents both the private and the social cost of producing q units of output when there is one firm.

---

[4]   Further discussions of the cost function and its derivation from the underlying technology will be presented in Section 4.2.

Given the preceding simplifying assumption, C represents the cost function for other firms as well. If the output q is produced by k firms with each firm i producing the output x^i then the total cost is given by $C(x^1) + \ldots + C(x^k)$. It is now a simple matter to state the necessary and sufficient condition for natural monopoly. A single firm market will be more efficient than a market in which there are k firms if and only if

$$C(q) < \sum_{i=1}^{k} C(x^i) \qquad (4.1)$$

whenever $\sum_{i=1}^{k} x^i = q$. Cost functions for which inequality (4.1) holds for all $k \geq 2$ are said to be strictly subadditive at q. If expression (4.1) holds with a weak inequality, then C is considered subadditive. An industry in which competition is ideal and the cost function is strictly subadditive at output q is then considered a natural monopoly at q.

Subadditivity depends in general on the form of the cost function and the total output that is desired. For example, the cost function in Figure 4.2 is strictly subadditive only for outputs $q \leq q^*$. I will return to a discussion of this form of cost function later in this section.

If C is strictly subadditive for all $q \leq q^*$, then the condition for subadditivity may be written more compactly as

$$C(y) < C(x) + C(y - x) \text{ for } 0 \leq y \leq q \text{ and } 0 < x < y \qquad (4.2)$$

In other words, if inequality (4.2) can be verified for all $y \leq q$, then inequality (4.1) also follows for q.[5] If q is the largest possible demand in the industry and inequality (4.2) holds, then C is strictly subadditive and the industry is a natural monopoly (unconditional on q). In general, it is more convenient to deal with unconditional subadditivity than with output specific subadditivity.

Subadditivity is a mathematically primitive concept and cannot be easily related to more familiar properties of functions. It is therefore worthwhile to contrast subadditivity with some of the better known properties of cost functions.

[5]   If inequality (4.2) holds, then

$$C\left(\sum_{1}^{k} x^i\right) < C(x^1) + C\left(\sum_{2}^{k} x^i\right)$$

$$\vdots$$

$$< \sum_{i=1}^{k} C(x^i)$$

A cost function (for one output) is said to have global economies of scale if[6]

$$C(\lambda q) < \lambda C(q) \text{ for } \lambda > 1, q \geq 0 \qquad (4.3)$$

If both sides of inequality (4.3) are divided by λq, it follows that

$$\frac{C(\lambda q)}{\lambda q} < \frac{C(q)}{q} \text{ for } \lambda > 1 \text{ and } q > 0 \qquad (4.4)$$

which implies that average cost is a decreasing function of output. Two other properties of C are of interest. C is strictly concave if

$$C[\delta x + (1 - \delta)y] > \delta C(x) + (1 - \delta)C(y) \text{ for } 0 < \delta < 1 \quad (4.5)$$

and strictly convex if

$$C[\delta x + (1 - \delta)y] < \delta C(x) + (1 - \delta)C(y) \text{ for } 0 < \delta < 1 \quad (4.6)$$

If C is a differentiable function, then strict concavity of C is equivalent to $d^2C/dq^2 < 0$ and strict convexity is equivalent to $d^2C/dq^2 > 0$. Because dC/dq is the marginal cost of output, concavity is equivalent to declining marginal cost, whereas convexity is equivalent to increasing marginal cost.

Marginal cost and average cost are related. In particular, average cost is falling if and only if marginal cost is less than average cost. It is important to note that falling average cost is consistent with either rising or falling marginal cost.

Essentially, subadditivity is more general than either falling average cost (economies of scale) or falling marginal cost (concavity). The following three propositions define the relationship more precisely.

Proposition 4.1:
      The cost function C is strictly subadditive if either of the following hold:

(i) C has economies of scale (falling average cost) for all outputs q.

(ii) C is strictly concave (falling marginal cost) for all q and $C(0) \geq 0$.

---

[6]   Economies of scale may be defined as either a global or a local concept. Local economies of scale exist when inequality (4.3) holds at a particular q and for λ in a neighborhood of 1. Because subadditivity is necessarily a global concept, the global form of scale economies has been used as the most natural form. Clearly, global economies of scale imply local economies of scale. A somewhat different definition of (local) economies of scale is given in footnote 11.

Proof:

To prove (i) note that if $q > x$

$$\frac{C(x)}{x} > \frac{C(q)}{q} \text{ and } \frac{C(q-x)}{q-x} > \frac{C(q)}{q}$$

Then $C(x) + C(q-x) > C(q)\left[\frac{x}{q} + \frac{q-x}{q}\right] = C(q)$.

To prove (ii) it is sufficient to prove that concavity and $C(0) \geq 0$ imply economies of scale. If $\lambda > 1$, then by concavity

$$C(q) > \frac{1}{\lambda} C(\lambda q) + \frac{\lambda - 1}{\lambda} C(0) \geq \frac{1}{\lambda} C(\lambda q)$$

and therefore C has economies of scale.

Proposition 4.2:

If the cost function C is strictly subadditive, then the following results hold:

$$C(kq) < kC(q) \qquad \text{for } k = 1, 2, \ldots \tag{4.7}$$

$$C(q + \delta) - C(q) < C(\delta) \qquad \text{for } \delta > 0 \tag{4.8}$$

$$\frac{dC(q)}{dq} \leq \lim_{\delta \to 0} \frac{C(\delta)}{\delta} \qquad \text{for all } q > 0 \tag{4.9}$$

Proof:

Inequality (4.7) follows directly from inequality (4.1). Inequality (4.8) follows directly from the definition of subadditivity and inequality (4.9) follows from inequality (4.8) after dividing by δ and taking the limit.

Proposition 4.3:

Neither scale economies nor concavity are necessary for subadditivity of a cost function. Subadditivity is consistent with increasing marginal cost (convexity) at all levels of output and with increasing average cost at some (but not all) levels of output.

Proof:

Counterexamples are provided in Figure 4.2 and Figure 4.3d.

Propositions 4.1 and 4.3 together are equivalent to the assertion that both scale economies and concavity of a cost function are sufficient but not necessary for subadditivity. This result is important because falling average cost and occasionally even falling marginal cost have been identified with the concept of natural

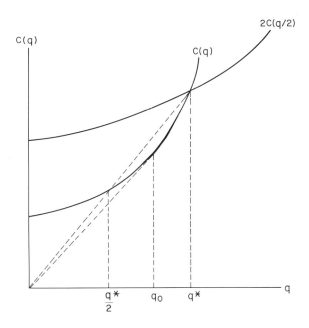

FIGURE 4.2

monopoly. Figure 4.2 provides an example of a subadditive cost function with increasing average costs (for outputs between q_o and q^*). It is clear from inequality (4.7) that the region of rising average costs is severely limited for a subadditive cost function. Inequality (4.7) requires that for any output q the average cost of integral multiples of q must be less than the average cost of q. This property is weaker than economies of scale, inequality (4.3), but is related to it.

Inequality (4.7) is a necessary condition for subadditivity. Other results contained in Proposition 4.2 are the constraints on incremental cost and marginal cost that are implied by inequalities (4.8) and (4.9). In particular, a subadditive cost function without any fixed cost (and therefore continuous at the origin) must be continuous everywhere.

Figure 4.3 presents a number of examples of subadditive cost functions. Functions (a), (d), (e), and (f) have fixed costs; (a) and (b) are concave; (a), (b), (c), and (d) show economies of scale; (d) is convex, except at the origin; and (d), (e), and (f) are discontinuous at one or more points. As these functions illustrate, subadditivity is consistent with a wide variety of possible functional forms for a cost function.

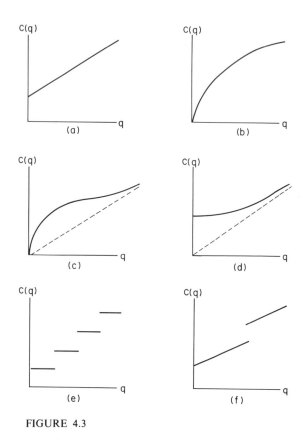

FIGURE 4.3

4.2   Multiple output natural monopoly: basic results

The basic theory of single product natural monopoly has now been stated and one may wonder what more could be said on the subject. Indeed, most of partial equilibrium theory in economics deals with the case of single output producers. General equilibrium theory allows for the existence of multiple output firms but derives few results that depend on multi-output production. Yet the fact remains that virtually all large firms in an advanced economy are multiproduct firms. Of course, it is possible, and is often the accepted practice in empirical studies, to aggregate the outputs of a firm into a single output measure. Essentially, the message of this chapter is that it would often be a mistake to perform such an aggregation. Subadditivity in a multiproduct firm is much more complex than single output subadditivity.

The basic difference can be seen in the simple, hypothetical cost function for two outputs given by

$$C(q_1, q_2) = q_1^{\frac{1}{2}} + q_2^{\frac{1}{2}} + (q_1 q_2)^{\frac{1}{2}} \tag{4.10}$$

This function is concave and exhibits economies of scale, and given Proposition 4.1 it might be expected that it would also be subadditive. Simple computation, however, reveals that it is not. For example, $C(1, 0) + C(0, 1) = 2$, whereas $C(1, 1) = 3$. This function fails to be subadditive for although there are economies of scale in each output separately (and also along any expansion path involving constant proportions), no economies of joint production exist. Instead, there is a diseconomy of joint production, and thus natural monopoly does not exist in the production of the joint output.

In Section 4.1 the technology of a firm was described by means of a cost function. Now it will be useful to introduce a more basic description of technology — the production possibility set — in order to secure a better understanding of the cost function and, secondarily, to place the theory of natural monopoly easily within the framework of both partial and general equilibrium theory.

Assume that there are n outputs in the industry that can be represented by a vector $y = (y_1, \ldots, y_n)$. Production of output involves the transformation of inputs into outputs, where inputs consist of labor, capital, raw materials, managerial ability, and so on. A typical set of inputs will then be represented by a vector $x = (x_1, \ldots, x_m)$. The production possibility set is a set in $(n + m)$-dimensional space consisting of feasible production plans. That is,

$$Y = \{(y, x): y \text{ can be produced from } x\}$$

The derivation of a cost function depends on the existence of fixed input prices.[7] That is, although a natural monopolist is necessarily the sole producer in the output market, if a cost function is to be defined, he or she must be a price taker (and therefore one among many) in the markets for inputs. If input prices are represented by the vector $w = (w_1, \ldots, w_m)$, then the cost function may be defined as the least costly method of producing y. For any (y, x) in Y the cost of producing y is just the summation of $w_i x_i$ over all inputs $1, \ldots, m$, which may be written in terms of the vector product $w \cdot x$. Then the cost function is formally defined by[8]

---

[7] Competitive input markets are required unless there is only one input, in which case the cost of output can be measured in units of input equivalents.

[8] Y must be a closed set in order for equation (4.11) to be well defined. Strictly technical assumptions, however, will be omitted from most definitions in the interest of clarity of presentation.

$$C(y) = Min\{w \cdot x \text{ for } x \text{ such that } (y, x) \text{ is in } Y\} \qquad (4.11)$$

It should be observed that the cost function could be, and often is, written as $C(y; w)$. The present discussion will assume that the firm is a price taker in input markets and that input prices do not change. It is possible, however, that a firm is a natural monopoly under one set of input prices but is not under a different set.

Natural monopoly in Section 4.1 was defined in terms of the subadditivity of the cost function. Multiproduct subadditivity may be expressed in exactly the same form as single output subadditivity.[9]

Definition:

C is subadditive if

$$C(y) + C(y') \geq C(y + y') \qquad (4.12)$$

for any output vectors y and y'.

Also, one can describe a condition on the production possibility set Y that is related to cost subadditivity and which would be appropriate in a general equilibrium analysis.

Definition:

A production possibility set Y is superadditive if for every pair of input-output bundles (y, x) and (y', x'), which are contained in Y, it is true that $(y + y', x + x')$ is contained in Y.

One can directly verify that superadditivity of the production possibility set implies subadditivity of the derived cost function,[10] but that superadditivity of Y is not necessary for subadditivity of C. Because most results in the remainder of this book are partial equilibrium in nature, cost subadditivity will be used as the defining condition for multiproduct natural monopoly. However, if input markets are not competitive, so that a cost function cannot be defined as in equation (4.11), then the appropriate definition of natural monopoly is the superadditivity of Y.

Next consider the definition of economies of scale. In terms of the production possibility set Y, the standard definition of scale economies is the following.[11]

---

[9] It will, however, be more convenient to deal with subadditivity rather than with strict subadditivity in the remaining results of this chapter.

[10] Assume Y is superadditive and let $C(y) = w \cdot x$ and $C(y') = w \cdot x'$. Then $(y + y', x + x')$ is in Y and $C(y + y')$ must be less than $w \cdot (x + x') = C(y) + C(y')$.

[11] There would be local economies of scale at a particular point $(y; x)$ if λ were confined to a neighborhood of 1. A different definition of local

Definition:

There are (global) economies of scale associated with Y if for every input-output combination (y, x) in Y and every $\lambda \geq 1$, the pair $(\lambda y, \lambda x)$ is in Y.

With single output production, economies of scale were shown to be equivalent to decreasing average cost by simple algebraic manipulation. Under multiple output production this equivalence no longer holds because a firm may not wish to operate on a linear expansion path. (In order to produce λy there may be a more efficient set of inputs than λx, even though x is efficient for y.) However, economies of scale are sufficient for the existence of declining-ray average cost which are defined as follows:[12]

Definition:

A cost function has declining ray average cost if $C(\lambda y)/\lambda y \leq C(y)/y$ for every $\lambda \geq 1$ and $y > 0$.

The first result of this section is related to Proposition 4.3 — economies of scale and the related property of declining-ray average cost are neither necessary nor sufficient for subadditivity of the cost function. The fact that they are not necessary was already demonstrated in Proposition 4.3 for the case of single output production. By Proposition 4.1, however, scale economies are sufficient for subadditivity in the single output case. Nonsufficiency in the multiproduct case has been demonstrated in the cost function given by equation (4.10).

The most important task remaining in this and the following section is the discovery of conditions that are sufficient for subadditivity. Because the conditions that prove to be sufficient are somewhat more technical in nature than the preceding work, a formal presentation will be deferred until the next section. An intuitive summary will be provided in this section.

As already noted in connection with the cost function given by equation (4.10), subadditivity in a multiproduct context requires that there be economies of joint production, as well as the more usual economies of scale. The most direct and intuitive measure of the economies of joint production is provided in the definition of economies of scope, which is only subadditivity applied to a

economies of scale is provided by Panzar and Willig (1977a). In this definition there are economies of scale at (y, x) if there exists $r > 1$ and $\delta > 1$ such that $(\lambda^r y, \lambda x)$ is contained in Y for all λ such that $1 \leq \lambda \leq \delta$. One result of this paper is that strict economies of scale under the preceding definition are equivalent, under certain regularity conditions, to the unprofitability of marginal cost pricing.

[12] The proof of this assertion is similar to that in footnote 10 and is omitted.

restricted set of output vectors.[13] A cost function C has economies of scope if

$$C(y) + C(y') \geq C(y + y') \tag{4.13}$$

whenever y and y' consist of disjoint outputs; (i.e., if for any i, $y_i > 0$, then $y_i' = 0$; and if $y_j' > 0$, then $y_j = 0$.)

A somewhat surprising result is the fact that economies of scale and economies of scope together are not sufficient for general subadditivity. What is needed is a different measure of the economies of joint production. One condition, known as cost complementarity, holds if the basic subadditivity inequality (4.12) is true for incremental costs as well as for total costs. That is, suppose that

$$C(x + y) + C(x + z) \geq C(x + y + z) + C(x) \tag{4.14}$$

holds for all nonnegative values of x, y and z. Then after some rearrangement, inequality (4.14) is seen to be equivalent to the condition that

$$[C(x + y) - C(x)] + [C(x + z) - C(x)] \geq [C(x + y + z) - C(x)] \tag{4.15}$$

Condition (4.14) is sufficient for subadditivity although it is much stronger, offering clear advantages to single firm production because it implies that a large firm can produce any given incremental output at lower cost than a small firm.

A different form of complementarity is given in the concept of "trans-ray convexity."[14] A cost function C for two outputs satisfies the property of trans-ray convexity at a point y if there is a line through y with a negative slope such that C is convex along the segment of that line bounded by the coordinate axes. Every convex function is also trans-ray convex, but trans-ray convexity is more general than simple convexity. A function that is trans-ray convex and is also concave along all rays through the origin is shown in Figure 4.4. Trans-ray convexity is not equivalent to subadditivity but is sufficient for it, given declining-ray average cost. Closely related to trans-ray convexity is the property of "quasiconvexity" which is also sufficient for subadditivity given declining-ray average cost. These as well as other sufficient conditions for subadditivity will be more formally defined in the next section.

---

[13] Economies of scope are discussed more fully in Panzar and Willig (1981).

[14] Trans-ray convexity is discussed in Baumol (1977) and Baumol, Bailey, and Willig (1977).

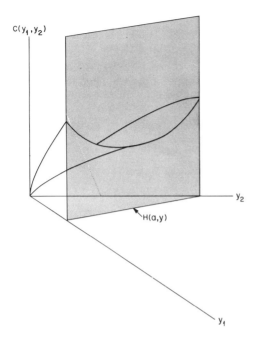

FIGURE 4.4

4.3 Sufficient conditions for subadditivity in multiple output production

For a multiple output cost function, subadditivity holds at a point y if

$$C(y) \leq \sum_{i=1}^{k} C(x_i) \qquad (4.16)$$

whenever

$$\sum_{i=1}^{k} x_i = y$$

As discussed in Section 4.1, a cost function that is subadditive for all y (i.e., all y less than or equal to the maximum possible market demand) may be more simply characterized by

$$C(y) \leq C(x) + C(y - x) \text{ for all } x \leq y \qquad (4.17)$$

Even expression (4.17), however, requires in principle that an inequality be verified for all values of $x \leq y$. This section will be devoted to finding sufficient conditions for inequality (4.17) always to hold — conditions that are stronger than subadditivity but which may be more readily verified.

The key to multiproduct subadditivity is the characterization of the economies of joint production. Although subadditivity in one dimension is implied by economies of scale or declining average costs, it will be seen that general subadditivity is closely related to certain convexity conditions.

The first step is the formal definition of two distinct components of subadditivity.

Definition:

A cost function C is ray subadditive if

$$C(\lambda_1 y) + C(\lambda_2 y) \geq C[(\lambda_1 + \lambda_2)y] \tag{4.18}$$

for any $y \geq 0$ and $\lambda_1, \lambda_2 \geq 0$.

Definition:

C is orthogonally subadditive if

$$C(y) + C(y') \geq C(y + y') \tag{4.19}$$

whenever $y \cdot y' = \sum_{i=1}^{n} y_i y_i' = 0$.

A ray is merely a half line beginning at the origin. A multiple output cost function is ray subadditive if it is subadditive when restricted to any ray. A cost function with declining-ray average costs is necessarily ray subadditive, but as shown in Section 4.1 for single output cost functions, ray subadditivity may hold in the absence of declining-ray average costs.

Orthogonal subadditivity is merely another name for economies of scope. For any given output vector $y = (y_1, \ldots, y_n)$ there are economies of scope if it is more efficient to produce y in a single multiproduct firm than to produce the same set of outputs in two or more specialty firms.

Intuitively, one might expect that orthogonal subadditivity and ray subadditivity together would imply global subadditivity. Such is not the case, as the following cost function demonstrates.

$$C(y_1, y_2) = \begin{cases} y_2 + \dfrac{y_1^2}{y_2} & \text{if } y_1 \leq y_2 \\[2ex] y_1 + \dfrac{y_2^2}{y_1} & \text{if } y_2 \leq y_1 \end{cases} \tag{4.20}$$

The reader may verify that this function has both economies of scale and economies of scope at all outputs. It is not, however, subadditive. For example, $C(3, 3) = 6$ and $C(1, 2) = C(2, 1) = 2.5$. Something more than economies of scope is needed. There are several alternative ways to define conditions on the cost function that are stronger than economies of scope. In Propositions 4.4 through 4.7 these conditions, along with others previously defined, will be shown to be sufficient for subadditivity.

Definition:

C satisfies cost complementarity if[15]

$$C(x + z) - C(x) \geq C(x + y + z) - C(x + y) \tag{4.21}$$

whenever $x, y, z \geq 0$.

If C is twice continuously differentiable, then inequality (4.21) is equivalent to the condition $\partial^2 C / \partial y_i \partial y_j \leq 0$. Also, notice that inequality (4.21) is completely equivalent to inequalities (4.14) and (4.15).

Definition:

C satisfies weak cost complementarity if inequality (4.21) is satisfied for all $x, y, z \geq 0$ such that

$$\sum_{i=1}^{n} y_i z_i = 0.$$

Weak cost complementarity expresses a pure complementarity effect.[16] As previously defined, cost complementarity requires that marginal or incremental costs of any output decline when that output or any other output increase. Weak cost complementarity requires the incremental cost of a given output to fall only when other outputs are increased. For a single output cost function, cost complementarity implies concavity, whereas weak cost complementarity places no constraints on the cost function.

Proposition 4.4:

If C satisfies cost complementarity, then C is subadditive.

Proof:

This result follows immediately from inequality (4.21) by setting $y = 0$. Then

$$C(x + z) \leq C(x) + C(z) - C(0)$$
$$\leq C(x) + C(z)$$

---

[15] Cost complementarity is discussed in Panzar and Willig (1977b).

[16] Weak cost complementarity is equivalent to a property known as submodularity in the mathematical literature. Also, note that weak cost complementarity is related to cost complementarity in the same way that orthogonal subadditivity is related to subadditivity.

Proposition 4.4 states that cost complementarity is by itself sufficient for subadditivity. Although it is a plausible condition, complementarity is also restrictive.

For example, if two or more outputs require a particular input that is not supplied in a competitive market, then an increase in production of one of the outputs might bid up the price of the required input and so increase the incremental cost of some of the other outputs. Similarly, if there is common machinery or equipment used in producing two or more outputs, then cost complementarity would fail to hold if capacity constraints on individual machines become binding. Finally, it should be noted that cost complementarity like subadditivity, is a global concept that must be verified on an infinite number of inequalities such as inequality (4.21).

The remainder of this section will be concerned with an alternative set of sufficient conditions for subadditivity. The economies of joint production will be described by restricting aggregate production to a particular set and by examining the cost function on that restricted set. There are numerous restrictions that might be made, but only two such possibilities will be considered.

The first alternative is the most straightforward. Previously the properties of a cost function along rays have been discussed. In order to describe the properties of the cost function on sets other than rays, one can define a set of outputs that are perpendicular to a given ray and which contain a particular output vector $\bar{y}$. Thus let $\bar{y} \geq O$ be any output vector. Let $a = (a_1, \ldots, a_n)$ be a vector such that $a_i > 0$ for $i = 1, \ldots, n$. Together a and $\bar{y}$ define the set

$$H(a,\bar{y}) = \{y \geq 0 : \sum_{i=1}^{n} a_i y_i = \sum_{i=1}^{n} a_i \bar{y}_i\}$$

which is a subset of an $n - 1$ dimensional hyperplane containing the vector $\bar{y}$ and perpendicular to the vector a. A cost function C is said to be "trans-ray convex" at $\bar{y}$ if there is at least one set H on which C is convex. More formally, trans-ray convexity is defined as follows:

Definition:

$\quad$ C satisfies trans-ray convexity if for every $\bar{y} \geq 0$ there is a vector $a > 0$ such that C is convex when restricted to the set $H(a,\bar{y})$.

A function that is trans-ray convex is illustrated in Figure 4.4. In a hypothetical test for trans-ray convexity one restricts aggregate output to the set H. Convexity of the cost function C on H is then roughly equivalent to a diminishing marginal rate of transformation as some outputs increase and others decrease in a movement along H.

Closely related to trans-ray convexity is the property known as quasiconvexity. Now instead of being restricted to a hyperplane, output is restricted to the set of outputs that can be produced at a cost less than or equal to a given amount. That is, given an output vector $\bar{y}$, let the set $L(\bar{y})$ be defined such that

$$L(\bar{y}) = \{y \geq 0 : C(y) \leq C(\bar{y})\}$$

Definition:
  C is quasiconvex if the sets $L(\bar{y})$ are convex for every $\bar{y} \geq 0$.
  A cost function that is quasiconvex is illustrated in Figure 4.5.
  Each of the subsequent propositions demonstrates that an appropriate convexity condition, in combination with a condition on costs along rays, is sufficient for subadditivity.

Proposition 4.5:
  If C is convex and ray subadditive, then C is subadditive.

Proof:
  For any y and y' it is necessary to show that $C(y) + C(y') \geq C(y + y')$. By convexity,

$$C\left[\frac{y + y'}{2}\right] \leq \frac{1}{2} C(y) + \frac{1}{2} C(y')$$

And by ray subadditivity,

$$C(y) + C(y') \geq 2C\left[\frac{y + y'}{2}\right] \geq C(y + y')$$

Figure 4.6 illustrates a cost function that satisfies the conditions of Proposition 4.5. Notice that this cost function does not pass through the origin, indicating the presence of a fixed or start-up cost. In fact if there is either strict ray subadditivity, that is, a strict inequality in expression (4.18), or strict convexity, then a fixed cost is necessary in order for the hypotheses of the proposition to be internally consistent.

The next two results are similar to Proposition 4.5, but use weaker forms of convexity and stronger assumptions on cost restricted to rays.

Proposition 4.6:
  If C is trans-ray convex and has declining-ray average costs, then C is subadditive.

Proof:
  Suppose that y, y' and $H(a, y + y')$ are given as in Figure 4.7, where C is convex on $H(a, y + y')$. Let

$$\lambda = \frac{a \cdot y}{a \cdot (y + y')} \quad \text{and} \quad (1 - \lambda) = \frac{a \cdot y'}{a \cdot (y + y')}$$

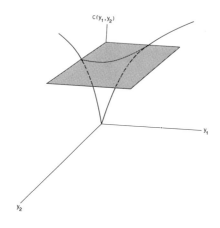

FIGURE 4.5

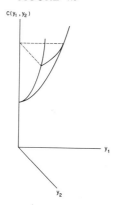

FIGURE 4.6

Then it is seen that both y/λ and $y'/(1 - \lambda)$ are contained in $H(a, y + y')$. Given that $0 \leq \lambda \leq 1$, trans-ray convexity implies that

$$\lambda C(y/\lambda) + (1 - \lambda)C[y'/(1 - \lambda)] \geq C(y + y')$$

Then by declining-ray average costs,

$$C(y + y') \leq C(y) + C(y')$$

Proposition 4.7:

If C is quasiconvex and has declining-ray average costs, then C is subadditive.

Proof:

The proof of this proposition is the same as that of Proposition 4.6. One needs only to interpret $H(a, y + y')$ as the "tangent plane" to $L(y + y')$ at $y + y'$.

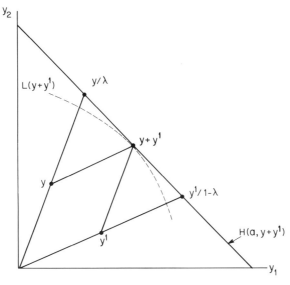

FIGURE 4.7

This concludes the discussion of the properties of multiple output cost functions and subadditivity. The results previously described were originally derived in a number of papers. Some basic references on cost subadditivity and related issues are Baumol (1975; 1977), Baumol and Braunstein (1977), Baumol, Panzar, and Willig (1982), Panzar and Willig (1977a; 1981), Sharkey and Telser (1978), Teece (in press), and Willig (1979b). A discussion of the general mathematical properties of subadditive functions may be found in Rosenbaum (1950).

4.4   Plant subadditivity and firm subadditivity

Natural monopoly has been defined to exist when a single firm can produce the total market demand at lower cost than two or more firms can. This simple definition belies considerable complexity. A single firm may be more efficient than two for many reasons. It will be useful, however, to consider two generic forms of subadditivity. The strictly technological aspects of subadditivity will be called "plant subadditivity." "Firm subadditivity," on the other hand, will refer to the organizational advantages of a single firm. Whereas plant subadditivity is based on the technology of production, firm subadditivity is based on the technology of transactions in the marketplace. Firm subadditivity exists when the organization of productive activities within a firm is more efficient than organization through the competitive market.

Clearly, of the two forms of subadditivity, firm subadditivity is the more fundamental. An industry is a monopoly (whether natural or not) only if there is a single firm that makes decisions regarding price and output. Given technical, or plant subadditivity, it is conceivable that more than one firm could operate in a workable competitive market. For example, despite the fixed costs associated with the roadbed, tracks, and so forth, it is possible that several railroad firms might share the same right-of-way if an agreement could be reached on the proper share of fixed cost for each firm to bear. Similarly, given an economy of scope, such as is thought to exist in the production of iron and steel, independent firms could potentially share in the various stages of the production process.

On the other hand, firm subadditivity may exist in the absence of plant subadditivity. Indeed, many firms, including those in competitive industries, operate more than one physical plant. Thus the cost advantages of single firm production transcend the purely technical economies of plant subadditivity and contain organizational economies as well. It is the purpose of this and the following section to shed some light on the nature of these organizational economies.

By now it should be apparent that the concept of firm subadditivity is only an application of modern theories of the firm to the case of natural monopoly. At present, there is not a single coherent theory of what a firm is and why it exists. Rather, there are many theories and models that are concerned with such apparently diverse topics as the failure of competitive markets, the reasons for vertical integration, the relative advantages of centralized versus decentralized economies, and the nature of hierarchical organizations. This is the context in which it is appropriate to question whether a single firm can produce the industry output at lower cost than two or more firms can. The remainder of this section will consider briefly some examples of both plant and firm subadditivity. Then the following section will summarize some of the results of a different approach to the theory of the firm, in which the costs of carrying out a transaction within a firm, or in a market, are described explicitly.

Consider now the sources of plant subadditivity, which one may loosely think of as economies of scale and economies of scope. A number of conditions have been suggested by economists as to why there may be significant economies of scale. The first, and perhaps the most widely known, is derived from Adam Smith's remarks on the economies due to specialization. As an activity is conducted on an ever larger scale it becomes possible to devote more specialized resources to production and the presumption is that specialized production is more efficient. In Smith's time, specialization was primarily a matter of allocating labor resources. An economy of specialization may result if a simple task can be learned more rapidly. In a modern economy, specialization allows the application of automated equipment to replace human craftsmanship. The classic example is the automobile assembly line, although more recent times have seen the rapid growth of electronic automation. Both forms of automation represent a virtually inexhaustible source of economies of scale.

A second source of large economies of scale is the existence of unavoidable indivisibilities in the production process. Consider again the example of a railroad. If the cost function of a typical firm is approximated by $C(x) = a + bx$, then the fixed cost a results from an indivisibility. No traffic can be carried until right-of-way is secured and track laid. These costs, however, are relatively insensitive to the volume of traffic actually carried. It is important to point out that the economy of scale occurs only to the extent that the indivisibility is unavoidable. A smaller gauge of railroad is conceivable and might be less costly for small volumes of traffic. Ultimately, the indivisibilities in production reside in the indivisibility of the human agent. Beyond a certain point, a small-scale railroad or assembly line could not be operated by human agents.

Finally, there is an economy of scale that follows from a mathematical result of probability theory. The size of a firm's inventory is a productive input, and the firm must balance the costs of carrying an inventory against the sales that would be lost if stocks on hand fall short of demand at any given time. It is a well-documented observation[17] that the size of the inventory, as a proportion of total sales, falls as sales expand because the behavior of a large group of customers is more easily predicted than the behavior of a small group.

Each of the preceding factors contributes to the existence of economy of scale. The other component of subadditivity is economy of scope, which is essentially an unavoidable externality in the production of two or more goods. For example, production of bees and apple orchards is more profitable when the two activities are coordinated than when they are not. The bee orchard example is commonly used as an example of an economic externality.

---

[17] See Baumol (1952). For a related result concerning the risk of failure of machines, see Feller (1957, pp. 416-419).

However, if a simple contractual agreement could induce separate producers of bees and honey to cooperate optimally, then the economy of scope could not be said to exist.[18] An externality in production that is clearly unavoidable is the example of the joint production of wool and mutton.

Other than externalities, the conditions likely to lead to economies of scope are identical to those that promote economies of scale. Specialized use of labor and machinery can result in an economy in the production of related products, as well as in larger outputs of a homogeneous product. For example, automobile producers may also produce household appliances. Indivisibilities may be reflected in common costs in addition to fixed costs as the possibility of joint production readily demonstrates. Finally, an economy of scope is reflected in the laws of probability as firms decrease risks through diversification. For instance, a farmer may plant two crops — one suitable for wet weather and another suitable for dry weather — even though in a world of certainty it would be most efficient to specialize.

Now consider firm subadditivity. Firm subadditivity may be said to exist if and only if there is a market failure. Economists have for a long time been interested in market failure outside the natural monopoly context and have accumulated a substantial body of results and examples. The present discussion will focus on two distinct types. The first form of "market failure" occurs if a market fails to exist because of either an insufficient number of traders in the marketplace or an inherent instability that prevents an equilibrium from being obtained. These possibilities will be described in Section 4.5 and Chapter 6, respectively. A different form of "market failure" occurs when a market equilibrium involving two or more firms exists but is suboptimal. In the remainder of this section I will describe three examples of firm subadditivity due to suboptimal competition.

The first example, which is due to Hotelling (1929), concerns the competition between two stores for location along a segment of road. Suppose that buyers for a product are uniformly distributed on a finite segment of a road, which will be represented by the line segment [0,1] in Figure 4.8. Assume that only two stores are competing for business along the road and that the items that the stores wish to sell can be produced at zero cost. Suppose, however, that there is a positive transportation cost for each customer, which is directly proportional to the distance from the nearest store. Also, assume that the two stores compete for the most desirable location but do not compete in price.

[18] See Cheung (1973) for further discussion of this example.

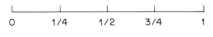

FIGURE 4.8

The optimal locations for the stores are the points 1/4 and 3/4. With these locations the total transportation costs of the buyers are minimized. Competition, however, results in a different outcome. If one store locates at any point in the interval [0,1/2], for example, at the optimal location 1/4, then the best competitive response of the other store is to locate as closely as possible to the right of the first (in Figure 4.8). The unique competitive equilibrium in this simple game occurs when both stores locate at the midpoint of the road. Consequently, both stores have exactly the same set of customers as they would have at the optimal locations 1/4 and 3/4, but buyers pay higher transportation costs in the aggregate.

The second example is based on the well-known prisoners' dilemma from the theory of noncooperative games. Suppose that the fish in a lake, or region of the ocean, are a common property resource, which two competing firms are able to exploit. The population of fish grows according to exogenous biological laws, and so if more fish are caught in any one period, there are fewer fish available in the future. Suppose that each firm must choose to take either a large catch or a small catch in every period, where the small catch is set at a level that maximizes the joint discounted profits over all future intervals.

In any one period there are four possible payoff combinations as shown in Figure 4.9. Here the first number in each box represents the payoff to firm 1 and the second number, the payoff to firm 2 under the indicated sizes of catch. The upper left-hand box represents the joint profit-maximizing payoffs. However, if each firm takes the other's size of catch as given, then the only equilibrium in a one-period game is the lower right-hand box, in which each firm takes the largest possible catch.

The same outcome can easily be shown to be the only equilibrium in any finite number of plays.[19] However, with an infinite number of repetitions there are a large number of equilibrium outcomes, including the one in which each firm pursues the joint profit-maximizing strategy in every period. Similarly, if there are a

---

[19] In the last period each firm is in the same position as in a one period game. Thus there is a unique final period outcome in every equilibrium. But once the final period is determined, the next to last period offers the same strategic prospects as the final one to each firm. Thus, by backward iteration, it follows that a unique outcome in any finite number of plays exists.

Size of Firm 2
Catch

		Small	Large
Size of Firm 1 Catch	Small	3,3	1,4
	Large	4,1	2,2

FIGURE 4.9

potentially infinite number of periods but a probability that the game will terminate at the end of any particular one, then it can be shown that the cooperative solution may or may not be an equilibrium, depending on the probability that the game will extend into the future.[20] The essential conclusion to be drawn, in any repeated game of the preceding form, is that competition will result in a suboptimal outcome whenever firms in the industry are sufficiently short sighted or the prospects for the industry itself are sufficiently uncertain.

The final example of firm subadditivity is based on the dynamic capacity expansion problem. Suppose that demand is growing over time and that there are fixed costs associated with the installation of new capacity. Capacity must then be installed in discrete units. If large units are installed at infrequent intervals, then a firm can economize on the fixed costs of installation. However, a large unit of capacity takes longer to become fully utilized, and the average level of excess capacity over time is therefore large. An optimal capacity expansion sequence, as derived, for example, in Manne (1961), Chenery (1952), or Skoog (in press) requires a balance of these two opposing forces.

[20] One model of this type is described in Telser (1972). One can also think of the equilibrium strategies that sustain cooperative behavior as implicit contracts among players in the game. Radner (1980a) has shown that a cooperative outcome may result, under certain conditions, even if each player is uncertain about, or can only monitor imperfectly, the past behavior of other players. It has also been shown by Radner (1980b) that an outcome arbitrarily close to any cooperative outcome can be sustained in a finite game if the number of periods is large enough.

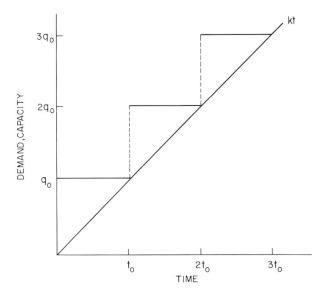

FIGURE 4.10

Figure 4.10 illustrates an optimal expansion sequence in the case of linearly growing demand. Given a linear growth rate of demand and an infinite time horizon, then it is easy to see that the optimal expansion sequence must involve the addition of a given size of plant at equally spaced time intervals. Suppose, for example, starting at $t = 0$ in Figure 4.10, that a firm decides to install a capacity of q_0 units of capacity. This plant will be exhausted at $t_0 = q_0/k$, where k is the growth rate of demand. At $t = t_0$, the future looks exactly the same as at $t = 0$, and so it must be optimal again to install a plant of size q_0 at time $2t_0$.

In this type of problem there is clearly a short run economy of scale, or economy of fill. But, in the long run there would appear to be constant returns to scale, because the same size of plant is installed at regular intervals. Constant returns to scale, however, applies only to plant costs. The cost function to a firm may exhibit substantial firm subadditivity.

Firm subadditivity arises from the basic nature of an optimal capacity expansion sequence. An optimal sequence requires the installation of a particular piece of equipment at a particular time. If two or more firms are jointly responsible for determining additions to the industry capacity, then an optimal sequence could be sustained only by a detailed agreement among the firms, which in effect would constrain many firms to act as one.

A more likely alternative, however, is that each firm would choose its own expansion sequence independently of the others.[21] Then if there are two firms in the industry and total demand at any time is equal to kt, each firm would perceive demand equal to $(k/2)t$ at each unit of time. If capacity costs are exponential in form, so that $C(q) = q^\alpha$, for $0 < \alpha < 1$, then it can be demonstrated[22] that the optimal expansion sequences of two independent firms would involve each firm adding a plant of size $q_0/2$ at intervals of t_0, where q_0 and t_0 represent the optimal solution for a single firm. (In other words, given exponential capacity costs, the optimal fill time is independent of the growth rate of demand.) Since $2(q_0/2)^\alpha > (q_0)^\alpha$ for $0 < \alpha < 1$, it follows that the long run total cost in the industry is necessarily higher when there are two firms than when there is one.

This concludes the discussion of plant subadditivity and firm subadditivity. A related discussion is contained in Gold (1981). The reader may also wish to refer to several recent studies of scale economics in the multiplant firm such as Beckenstein (1975), Ginsberg (1974), and Scherer et al. (1975).

4.5   Transactions costs and firm subadditivity

This section reviews some results of Williamson and others that relate firm subadditivity to the transactions costs that may exist in a competitive market. Before determining when a single firm can produce a given output at lower cost than two or more firms can, one must describe more precisely what is meant by a firm and what a firm actually contributes to the production process. Indeed, the most basic question in an investigation of firm subadditivity concerns the existence of the firm, whether there be one or many in a given market. Coase (1937) was one of the first to recognize that firms exist for purely economic reasons. That is, a firm must perform some essential functions in the process of production more economically than a market. According to Coase, the distinguishing characteristic of a firm is the supersession of the price mechanism.

A firm may supersede the price mechanism because the price system is itself costly. Individuals must expend resources to learn

---

[21] It is also possible that the dynamic nature of the problem will lead to an inherently unstable competitive market. See Section 6.3 for further analysis of this possibility.

[22] For details, see Skoog (in press, Chapter 4). Choosing an optimal size q_0 for additions to capacity is equivalent to choosing an optimal fill time $t_0 = (q_0/k)$. But the optimal fill time is found by minimizing $f(t) = k^\alpha \left[t^\alpha / (1 - e^{-rt}) \right]$, where r is the rate of interest. It is easily seen that the optimal t_0 does not depend on k.

about the relevant prices. When competitive prices do not exist, parties must negotiate in order to reach an agreement. Uncertainty about future events and states of the world poses a particularly severe problem. Long-term contracts may be essential so as to economize on the costs of search or negotiation. In a long-term relationship a loosely defined hierarchical organization within a firm can be more adaptable to changing circumstances than a more structured set of contingency contracts.

The essence of Coase's analysis is that marginal analysis applies to the creation of firms just as it does in other aspects of economic organization. The firm will expand until the marginal value of making an additional transaction internal to the firm equals the cost at the margin of increasing the size of the firm. These costs, or diseconomies of scale to firm size, are in turn related to the fixed supply of entrepreneurial input. Thus in Coase's theory, firms of optimum size would tend to arise in a freely functioning market economy. Virtually all later reviewers have accepted Coase's view of the firm and have sought to identify more carefully the specific costs and benefits of the firm relative to the price mechanism.

The work of those who have built up on Coase's theory may be grouped into two categories: (1) contributions of authors who focused on the costs inherent in the price system, deriving basic insights about the failure of competitive markets — for example, Arrow (1971) and Koopmans and Beckmann (1957) and (2) recent contributions of those who directed their analysis to the specific benefits and functions of the firm — including Alchian and Demsetz (1972), Goldberg (1976), Klein, Crawford, and Alchian (1978), and Williamson (1975; 1979). Although different writers generally choose to emphasize different aspects of the role of a firm, or internal organization, the work of Williamson is broadly representative of this group and is by far the most comprehensive.

Williamson's analysis builds directly on the insights of Coase. In his own words Williamson briefly sketches his approach as follows:

(1) Markets and firms are alternative instruments for completing a related set of transactions; (2) whether a set of transactions ought to be executed across markets or within a firm depends on the relative efficiency of each mode; (3) the costs of writing and executing complex contracts across a market *vary with the characteristics of the human decision makers who are involved with the transaction on the one hand, and the objective properties of the market on the other*; and (4) although the human and environmental factors that impede exchanges between firms (across a market) manifest themselves somewhat differently within the firm, the same set of factors apply to both. (1975, p. 8; emphasis as in original.)

Thus in Williamson's theory, market failure, and the consequent supersession of a market by a firm, results from the particular combination of certain human and environmental factors in a given market setting. Among the environmental factors, the most important are uncertainty or complexity and the small numbers of decision makers, or thinness of markets. Uncertainty is, of course, a central factor in all theories of market failure, and as elsewhere, it refers to the difficulties of writing and specifying contingent claims contracts for all possible future events. Williamson, however, emphasizes that uncertainty itself is a problem only to the extent the human decision makers are constrained by bounded rationality. That is, human beings are limited in their ability to calculate or enumerate contingent future events and are likewise limited in their ability to communicate either verbally or in writing what information they do possess.

Similarly, complexity of a given task may impede the efficient operation of market forces, given the preceding sources of bounded rationality. The central point is that uncertainty and complexity impede transactions among firms in a market only as long as human decision makers within firms are constrained by bounded rationality. On the other hand, bounded rationality is itself a constraining factor only so far as events are highly uncertain or unusually complex. In a static and simple world, competitive markets could be expected to operate smoothly and flawlessly.

A second and related environmental factor is the existence of small numbers of participants. The small number condition may result from an underlying subadditivity condition in the technology of production, or from the uncertainty or complexity of the object to be negotiated. (A common example is a pollution externality in which a separate contract might be required between every resident of a community and a factory that emits a harmful pollutant.) Small numbers will lead to a market failure, however, primarily because it is inevitably associated with opportunistic behavior on the part of human agents. In this context Williamson defines opportunism as self-interest combined with guile. That is, individuals can reasonably be expected to pursue maximizing behavior within the context of a set of rules, as well as to attempt to change or perhaps to cheat on the rules themselves.

In order to translate these observations into a viable theory of the firm, Williamson observes that the same factors that make transactions difficult or costly in a market also tend to operate in an internal organization. Thus by far the largest part of his study consists of an investigation of the characteristics of hierarchical organizations that tend to ameliorate the consequences of bounded rationality and opportunism in the presence of uncertainty or complexity and small numbers.

4.6   Concluding comments

This chapter has considered the study of cost subadditivity. Costs are said to be subadditive if a single firm can produce a given output or set of outputs at lower cost than two or more firms can. Although subadditivity is a straightforward and easily understood concept in itself, it is more difficult to verify directly whether or not a given cost function is subadditive. A direct test for subadditivity requires a comparison of the cost of producing a given output in a single firm with every conceivable alternative involving two or more firms. Therefore this chapter has attempted to relate subadditivity to other specific properties of the cost function, which can more readily be verified empirically. The most important conclusions are:

1. For a single output cost function, economies of scale are sufficient for subadditivity. However, costs may also be subadditive if there are diseconomies of scale.

2. For a multiple output cost function, economies of scale are not sufficient for subadditivity. In a multiple output market subadditivity holds only if there are economies of joint production.

3. One measure of the economies of joint production is the concept of cost complementarity. Cost complementarity holds if an increase in the output of one output tends to reduce the incremental cost of producing other outputs. Cost complementarity is by itself sufficient for subadditivity.

4. Another measure of the economies of joint production is the concept of trans-ray convexity, which is closely related to the more familiar property of quasiconvexity. Either trans-ray convexity or quasiconvexity in combination with economies of scale is sufficient for subadditivity.

Going beyond the purely mathematical properties of cost subadditivity, this chapter has also discussed some of the reasons that costs may be subadditive. The terms plant subadditivity and firm subadditivity were used to describe two different aspects of a subadditive cost function. Plant costs are the costs of physical units of production and firm costs are the costs of acquiring and disseminating information about the production process. Firm subadditivity is difficult to quantify but is just as important as the more easily measured plant subadditivity.

Readers who are interested primarily in subadditivity may wish to proceed directly to Chapter 9, where the technological characteristics of the telecommunications industry will be discussed in detail. The following four chapters will be concerned with the economic structure and performance of natural monopoly markets.

CHAPTER 5

Sustainability of natural monopoly

Chapter 4 was concerned with the technological conditions for the existence of natural monopoly. This and the following three chapters will deal with some of the economic issues associated with natural monopoly. Perhaps the most important one to be addressed is the role that competition by rival firms should play in an industry that is considered a natural monopoly. That is, should there be open and unrestricted entry into some or all of the natural monopolist's markets?

Given the discussion in Chapter 4, it may seem strange to pose the preceding question, for a natural monopolist is by definition more efficient than any collection of firms that could result from effective entry by rival firms. However, it should be remembered that the condition of cost subadditivity, although easy to state, is by no means simple to verify in practice. By the very nature of subadditivity, which requires comparison of a single firm's costs with an infinity of alternatives, no regulator can be entirely certain that the firm that it regulates is a natural monopoly. Potential rivals will not generally accept the monopolist's claims of subadditivity if they perceive that there is profit to be made upon entry into the industry. Even monopolists cannot be entirely sure that their position is a natural monopoly.

The purpose of this chapter will be to point out some surprising and potentially serious consequences of a policy of free entry into natural monopoly markets. It will be shown that although entry may occur because the industry cost function is not, in fact, subadditive, it may also occur when costs are unquestionably subadditive. In other words, the incentives that rival firms perceive as they decide whether to enter a market do not in general correspond to the conditions for socially desirable entry.

The results in this chapter, and the next two, differ in a fundamental way from those in Chapter 4. Whereas subadditivity of costs is due to technological or organizational economies, which can, in principle, be measured empirically, the question of entry involves a model of the strategy of potential entrants, their perceptions of the monopolist's response, and similarly, the strategy of the monopolist. There is an unavoidable game theoretic context to any model that considers entry behavior. Here two approaches will be considered: the highly intuitive concept of sustainability and a concept of stability based on the theory of cooperative games. Neither approach captures all the aspects of the behavior that one would like, but it is a fortunate result that two dissimilar approaches lead to essentially the same conclusions.

In Section 5.1 the basic concept of sustainability is defined for a single output natural monopoly market. A natural monopoly is said to be sustainable if there exists a price and an output such that entry by rival firms is unattractive, while all demand is satisfied and revenues cover total costs of production. A sufficient condition for sustainability is that average costs of production fall as output expands. In this case, by producing the total market demand, the monopolist can achieve an average cost that is at least as low as any potential rival. However, if average costs first fall and then rise with output, a possibility that was shown in Chapter 4 to be consistent with overall subadditivity, then natural monopoly is not sustainable.

The definition of sustainability is extended to markets in which two or more outputs are produced in Section 5.2. Here the concept of sustainability must account for fundamentally different ways in which entry may occur. In a single output market, entry can take place only at outputs less than or equal to the monopolist's, assuming the monopolist chooses to produce the entire market demand and does not earn positive profits (in excess of the normal return on investment). However, in a multiproduct market there may be entry by firms that specialize in one, or a small subset, of the monopolist's outputs. Furthermore, if there are nonzero cross-elasticities of demand, and particularly if goods are substitutes, then a rival firm may enter by producing a larger output than the monopolist in one or more sectors of the market.

The study of multiple output sustainability therefore begins with a special case in which demand is assumed to be totally inelastic with respect to price. A monopolist is assumed to choose an output vector satisfying total consumer demand in all markets, and entry is assumed possible in any output or vector of outputs less than or equal to the choice of the monopolist. If entry in these circumstances is unattractive to rival firms, the cost function of the natural monopolist is said to be supportable. Thus supportability is a natural extension of the property of declining average costs to the case of multiple output production, where average costs cannot be defined.

Supportability of the cost function is a necessary condition for sustainability. The remainder of Section 5.2 is devoted to finding sufficient conditions for the sustainability of multiproduct natural monopoly. There are two major results: (1) If demands are independent, so that the cross-price elasticities are equal to zero, then sustainability is shown to follow from the weak cost complementarity of the cost function and a set of subsidiary inequalities. (2) If trans-ray convexity and declining-ray average costs hold in combination with some plausible technical conditions on demand, then they are also sufficient for sustainability.

Section 5.3 is devoted to a parallel approach to the question of entry in a natural monopoly market and the related question of cross-subsidization. This approach is based on the theory of cooperative games and will be extended in the following chapter. In the game theoretic context it is shown that cost complementarity and independence of demand are sufficient for stability for one special class of cost functions. However, if demands are not independent, it is demonstrated by means of an example that stability is more elusive. Even with a well-behaved linear cost function, a market may be unstable due to conflicts of interest on the demand side.

5.1   Sustainability of single output natural monopoly

The most straightforward and intuitive approach to modeling entry in natural monopoly markets is the theory of sustainability that was developed by Baumol, Bailey, and Willig (1977) and Panzar and Willig (1977b). [Also see Baumol, Panzar, and Willig (1982), Baumol and Willig (1981), and Panzar (1980).] In this approach a natural monopoly is viewed as a dominant firm in the industry, which must choose prices and outputs subject to a number of constraints. Entry into the industry is assumed to be possible for rival firms that are unconstrained but are allowed to enter if it is profitable for them to do so.

The relevant constraints on the behavior of the natural monopolist are as follows. The monopolist must choose a price and an output level such that

1. The chosen output is equal to total market demand at the chosen price;

2. Revenues collected are equal to the total cost of producing the chosen output;

3. If entry should occur, the monopolist is not allowed to deviate from the chosen price and is implicitly required to satisfy the residual demand at that price.[1]

Then a natural monopoly is sustainable if, under these conditions,

4. No other firm would wish to enter the industry at any level of output.

From these conditions it follows that in the theory of sustainability a natural monopolist is assumed not to respond in any way when entry occurs in a market. This is, of course, an unrealistic assumption but is a useful first approximation for a number of reasons. To begin with, a natural monopoly is likely to be regulated, so that any price changes that it would prefer to implement are apt to be slow in coming, due to lags in the regulatory process. Furthermore, even if a price response is allowed in principle, it is not easy to define a set of rules that would guarantee fair but effective competition between a natural monopoly firm and its rivals. If a natural monopoly is sustainable under the severe restrictions imposed by the theory, then a strong statement about market entry can be made. That is, in a market without restrictions or barriers to entry, there can be no entry by a rival unless that firm possesses a technology superior to the natural monopolist, or unless the monopolist happens to choose, by mistake or by regulatory decree, a price outside the set of sustainable prices.

In order to determine the conditions under which a natural monopoly is sustainable, one must formulate a more precise definition of sustainability. Let $D(p)$ represent the industry demand function — that is, the number of units of output desired by all consumers in the market when the price is equal to p. Let q represent a potential output and $C(q)$ the cost of producing q. The industry is a natural monopoly if and only if C is subadditive.

Definition:

A natural monopoly with cost function C and market demand D is sustainable if there is a price p and an output q such that

(i) $q = D(p)$,

(ii) $p \cdot q = C(q)$,   (5.1)

(iii) $p' \cdot q' < C(q')$ for all $p' < p$ and all $q' \le D(p')$.

---

[1] The assumption that the monopolist continues to supply residual demand is important in the case of a multiproduct natural monopoly and nonzero cross-elasticities of demand.

The major result of this section is contained in the following proposition.

Proposition 5.1:

A natural monopoly need not be sustainable.

For a proof of this result, consider the cost and demand functions in Figure 5.1. Here q_o represents the minimum average cost and q^* represents the largest output that is consistent with natural monopoly. Suppose that market demand is given by $D(p)$ in Figure 5.1. If the monopolist chooses any price other than $\bar{p}$, given by the intersection of demand and average cost, the resulting price and output will be nonsustainable. If $p < \bar{p}$ were chosen, then the monopolist could not produce the entire market demand except at a loss. If $p > \bar{p}$ were chosen, the potential entrant could enter with the choice of $\bar{p}$ and $\bar{q}$. However, if the monopolist chooses $\bar{p}$, entry is still possible at a price between $\bar{p}$ and p_o, the minimum average cost. For example p' slightly less than $\bar{p}$ and $q' = q_0$ would guarantee a positive profit. The essential feature of this result is that the entrant is not assumed to be under obligation to serve the entire market demand.

The proof of Proposition 5.1 strongly suggests that sustainability is related to economies of scale or declining average cost. For single output firms this intuition is indeed correct. The result is contained in the following:

Proposition 5.2:

(i) A natural monopoly is sustainable at an output q [assuming (i) and (ii) in the definition] if and only if $AC(q) \leq AC(x)$ for every $x \leq q$, where $AC(x) = C(x)/x$.

(ii) A natural monopoly is sustainable for every output q if and only if there are economies of scale at all outputs.[2]

Propositions 5.1 and 5.2 together suggest an obvious question. Is natural monopoly more likely to be sustainable or nonsustainable? Unfortunately, there is no way to answer this question precisely. Cost functions may take a bewildering variety of forms and yet satisfy the basic subadditivity condition for natural monopoly. However, assuming a certain amount of regularity to the cost function, one can make the following observations. In almost any industry there are economies of scale at low levels of output due to

[2] The proof of Proposition 5.2 is essentially the same as that of Proposition 5.1. The natural monopolist must choose a price-output pair (p,q) where market demand intersects the average cost curve. As before, profitable entry cannot occur at any output greater than q. But if $AC(q) \leq AC(q')$ for every $q' \leq q$, entry will be unattractive in all cases because it is required that $p' < p = AC(q) \leq AC(q')$.

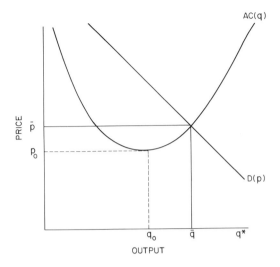

FIGURE 5.1

unavoidable fixed costs of production. And at very high levels of output there are apt to be diseconomies of scale in the cost function of a single firm. The industry is a natural monopoly if the fixed costs are large relative to the market demand. A growing industry is therefore likely to pass through stages as suggested by the long-run average cost curve in Figure 5.2.

Initially, when the industry is new and demands are low as in D_1 production is subject to rapidly falling average costs. New opportunities for exploiting economies of scale are learned in this stage. At the output q_1, the minimum average cost is reached, and average costs are likely to be flat as output grows further. The industry is, of course, a sustainable natural monopoly in both the region of falling average cost and the initial portion of constant average costs. At some output q_2, however, average costs will probably rise again. At the output $q_3 = 2q_1$ the industry is no longer a natural monopoly, because two firms can produce at the same average cost as one firm can. The region of unsustainable natural monopoly is bounded by the outputs q_2 and q_3. In some sense the probability that natural monopoly is unsustainable is given by $(q_3 - q_2)/q_3$. Notice, however, that the size of $(q_3 - q_2)$ depends on both q_1 and q_2. For example, if $q_2 \geq 2q_1$, then $q_3 \leq q_2$ and natural monopoly in this case is always sustainable. It should also be apparent that if $q_3 > q_2$, then even after the transition from natural monopoly to natural oligopoly, the minimum feasible price will exceed minimum average cost. Thus there is reason to suspect an

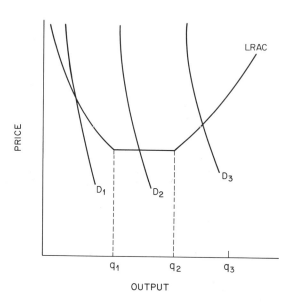

FIGURE 5.2

instability similar to that which is suggested by the theory of sustainability. This question will be pursued further in Chapters 6 and 8.

5.2   Sustainability of multiple output natural monopoly

Under multiproduct natural monopoly the options for competitive entry are much greater than for single product monopoly. Competitors may produce the entire product line if they choose, or they may also concentrate on one or a small set of goods. In addition, competitors can produce even more output than natural monopolists may have chosen in some of the markets.

The task of determining sustainable prices is greatly complicated by the possibility of cross-elasticities of demand. When demands are interrelated it is likely that total market demand will depend on the prices of both the monopolist and the competitor whenever entry is attempted. Behavioral responses of a monopolist are therefore crucial in determining the attractiveness of entry. For example, a competitor may perceive a profitable price-output combination, but the output may be contingent on the monopolist's original price structure. Successful entry, however, might make the monopolist's prevailing prices unprofitable at his or her reduced output. Clearly, entry could be unstable for both the monopolist and the competitor and it is not clear what would happen.

Therefore before the general case of multiproduct sustainability is considered, a related special case will be discussed. In Proposition 5.2 it was possible to obtain a complete characterization of sustainability, based entirely on the properties of the cost function. A natural monopoly with price p and output $q = D(p)$ is sustainable if

$$p = \frac{C(q)}{q} \leq \frac{C(q')}{q'} \text{ for all } q' \leq q \tag{5.2}$$

or equivalently

$$p \cdot q' \leq C(q') \text{ for all } q' \leq q \tag{5.3}$$

In Figure 5.3 the average cost $C(q)/q$ is given by the slope of a ray through the origin, which coincides with the cost function at q. The price p equal to average cost is then sustainable if this ray lies below the cost function for all outputs less than or equal to q.

One can generalize this aspect of sustainability to the case of multiple output cost functions. Thus let $C(q)$ represent a multiple output cost function, and suppose that a natural monopolist is interested in producing at a particular output vector q. The cost function C is said to be supportable at q if there exists a price vector p such that the hyperplane[3] through the origin defined by $p \cdot q = C(q)$, which coincides with the cost function at q, lies below the cost function at all outputs $q' \leq q$. More formally, a supportable cost function is defined as follows:

Definition:
A cost function is supportable at output q if there exists a price p such that

$$p \cdot q = \sum_{i=1}^{n} p_i q_i = C(q) \tag{5.4}$$

and

$$p \cdot q' \leq C(q') \text{ for all } q' \leq q \tag{5.5}$$

In Figure 5.4 a cost function in a market with two outputs is illustrated. The two-dimensional rectangle in this figure represents the set of outputs q' such that $0 \leq q' \leq q$. This cost function is

[3] More precisely, the hyperplane is given by (x, α) such that $p \cdot x - \alpha = 0$, where p is such that $p \cdot q = C(q)$.

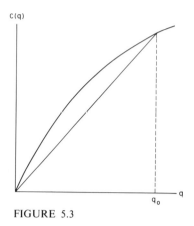

FIGURE 5.3

therefore supportable if there is a plane (not shown in the figure) that passes through the origin, intersects the cost function at q, and lies below the cost function on the indicated rectangle.

The type of entry that is envisioned in the definition of supportability is entry on a small scale with respect to each of the natural monopolist's outputs. If potential entry is known to be on a small scale, and if the natural monopolist is required to follow a nonresponsive pricing policy in which prices do not change if entry occurs, then the concept of supportability accurately describes the prospects for entry in a multiple output market. If the cost function is supportable, then entry should not take place so long as a price vector satisfying equation (5.4) and inequality (5.5) is chosen. If the cost function is not supportable, then no matter what price vector is chosen, small-scale entry can be expected.

The relative simplicity of the concept of supportability is due to the fact that prices are required only to allocate total costs among the consumers and not to determine the total market demand in any of the markets. A sustainable price is one that both allocates costs and determines total demand through nonzero own price and cross-price elasticities. Therefore, as will be seen later in this section, the conditions that are sufficient for sustainability are substantially more complex than those for supportability.

In order for a cost function to be supportable, it must have decreasing-ray average cost. It is also necessary that the cost function be subadditive. If $C(q) > C(x) + C(y)$ for some outputs x and y such that $x + y = q$ and

$$p \cdot x \leq C(x)$$
$$p \cdot y \leq C(y)$$

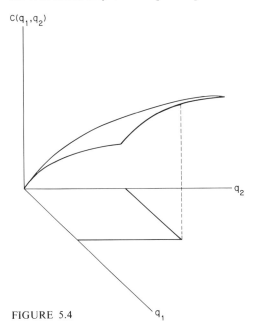

FIGURE 5.4

as required by inequality (5.5) then it necessarily follows that

$$p \cdot (x + y) = p \cdot q \leq C(x) + C(y) < C(q)$$

Thus equation (5.4) could not hold.

Therefore supportability is a property of a cost function that is stronger than subadditivity. Supportability is a potentially useful concept primarily because of the large number of conditions that are related to it. The most important results are listed without proof in the following proposition. Proofs and additional discussion may be found in Sharkey and Telser (1977). An interesting extension of the concept of supportability is contained in Faulhaber and Levinson (1981) and ten Raa (1981).

Proposition 5.3:
    A cost function C is supportable at q if and only if

$$\sum_{i=1}^{n} \delta_i C(q^i) \geq C(q)$$

whenever

$$\sum_{i=1}^{n} \delta_i q^i = q$$

and for each $i = 1, \ldots, n$

$$\delta_i \geq 0 \text{ and } q^i \leq q$$

Furthermore, any one of the following properties is a sufficient condition for C to be supportable at any output q.

(i) $C(q)/a \cdot q$ is nonincreasing for some vector $a > 0$.

(ii) C satisfies cost complementarity.

(iii) C is convex and subadditive.

(iv) C is linearly homogeneous and subadditive.

(v) C is quasiconvex and has declining-ray average costs.

(vi) C is twice differentiable, $\partial^2 C/\partial q_i \partial q_j \geq 0$ and

$$C(q) \geq \sum_{i=1}^{n} (\partial C/\partial q_i) q_i$$

Supportability is also potentially useful as a necessary condition for the more general concept of sustainability. That is, a natural monopoly is sustainable at an output q only if it is supportable at q. The remainder of this section will characterize a number of sufficient conditions for sustainability. First, sustainable natural monopoly will be explicitly defined in the context of a multiple output market.

Definition:

   A natural monopoly with cost function C and demand function D is sustainable if there is a price vector $p = (p_1, \ldots, p_n)$ and an output vector $q = (q_1, \ldots, q_n)$ such that

$$q_i = D_i(p) \quad i=1, \ldots, n \tag{5.6}$$

$$p \cdot q = \sum_{i=1}^{n} p_i q_i = C(q) \tag{5.7}$$

$$p' \cdot q' < C(q') \text{ for all } p' \leq p \tag{5.8}$$

and all $q' \leq D(q')$ such that

$$q_i' = 0 \text{ if } p_i' = p_i$$

The definition of sustainability is illustrated by a simple but instructive special case.[4] Consider a natural monopolist producing two outputs that are substitutes in demand. Assume that the market demand functions are linear and the cost function is linear and subadditive. Then it is possible to represent the price vectors that satisfy the budget constraint, as required by (5.7), by an ellipse as shown in Figure 5.5. In fact the only prices of interest are the

---

[4] The following graphical analysis is due originally to Zajac (1972). The application of Zajac's analysis to the theory of sustainability is due to Panzar and Willig (1977b).

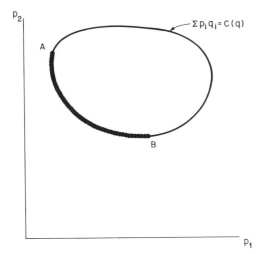

FIGURE 5.5

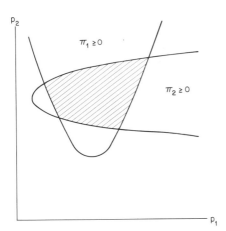

FIGURE 5.6

undominated portion of the ellipse, between points A and B in Figure 5.5.[5]

Now consider the prospects of a single product firm entering only one of the markets. Because the goods are assumed to be substitutes, the prices at which entry is profitable are those that were contained in the parabolic sets as shown in Figure 5.6. The shaded region in Figure 5.6 represents the set of prices at which two single

5   A price vector p is undominated if there does not exist a different price $p' \leq p$, which also lies in the zero profit set available to the natural monopolist.

product firms could simultaneously operate and earn nonnegative profits. Given the assumption of subadditivity, this region must lie above and to the right of the undominated portion of the monopolist's zero profit ellipse.

To apply this analysis to the theory of sustainability, consider two possible cases. The first is portrayed in Figure 5.7. As in Figure 5.5 the curve AB represents the set of undominated zero profit price vectors available to the monopolist. Not all such price vectors are sustainable, however. Consider, for example, the price vector represented by E in Figure 5.7. E is contained in the set of profitable price vectors for a rival firm specializing in the production of good 1. If the monopolist maintains the price p_2^E for good 2 then a rival firm could make a profit by setting a price $p_1^e < p_1^E$ and satisfying all the market demand at that price. Therefore condition (5.8) in the definition of sustainability is violated.

A similar result obtains if the monopolist chooses prices represented by the points F, G, or H in Figure 5.7. For example, at point F a rival firm producing good 1 could again earn a positive profit at the price $p_1^e < p_1^F$, assuming the monopolist maintains the price p_2^F for good 2.

If the monopolist chooses a price pair between points C and D on his or her zero profit set, however, the resulting prices are sustainable. For instance, if the monopolist maintains p_2^I in Figure 5.5, there is no price $p_1 < p_1^I$ at which entry can occur in market 1 nor is there a price $p_2 < p_2^I$ at which entry is attractive to market 2, assuming p_1^I is maintained by the monopolist.

Figure 5.8 portrays a situation in which there are no sustainable prices available to the monopolist. At any price vector on the zero profit set AB there is a price p_2^e at which entry is attractive in market 2.

It should be noted that the kind of entry that occurs in Figure 5.8 is fundamentally different from the entry that can occur when a single product natural monopoly is unsustainable. Panzar and Willig (1977b) refer to the two possibilities as cooperative (or segmented market) entry and market entry. Under cooperative entry a rival firm enters one or more of the natural monopolist's markets but does not serve the entire market demand. This form of entry, as illustrated in Figure 5.1, results essentially from the nonmonotonicity of ray average costs. Market entry, on the other hand, occurs when the entrant serves all demand in those markets that he or she chooses to enter. Nonsustainability resulting from market entry is possible only in multiproduct natural monopoly and the conditions under which it may take place depend in a complex

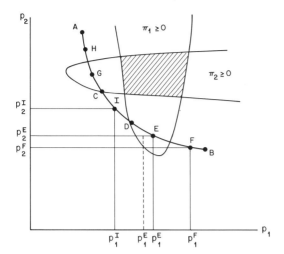

FIGURE 5.7

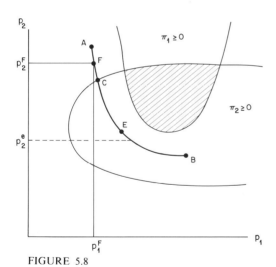

FIGURE 5.8

way on the "trans-ray" properties of the cost function, as well as on demand.

With respect to cooperative entry, Panzar and Willig (1977b) derive conditions under which cooperative entry cannot succeed unless market entry can also succeed. The relevant conditions are that goods are weak gross substitutes in demand and that costs satisfy a condition that is known as declining average incremental cost, which is somewhat stronger than declining-ray average cost. The reader is referred to Panzar and Willig (1977b) for further details.

The remainder of this section will discuss the conditions under which multiproduct natural monopoly is sustainable against market entry, although most results will apply equally well to both cooperative and market entry. First consider the case of independent demands. Figure 5.9 is relevant if there are only two outputs. The sets of prices at which entering single product firms earn nonnegative profits are rectangular, given the independence of demands. The shaded rectangle contains the prices at which two single product firms could simultaneously operate. By subadditivity, the monopolist's zero profit price set must lie below and to the left of the shaded rectangle. Points between C and D in this set are necessarily sustainable. That is, in a natural monopoly industry that produces two outputs with independent demands, sustainable prices always exist.

Unfortunately this result does not generalize to the case of three or more outputs. It was previously shown that supportability of the cost function is a necessary condition for sustainability, and with three or more outputs, supportability is not implied by subadditivity. Furthermore, it follows from the results of Sharkey (1981) that even with a supportable cost function and independent demands, sustainable prices may not exist.

However, two related results that apply in the case of independent demands. The first, due to Panzar and Willig (1977b), is that under certain conditions, it is possible to guarantee sustainability against market entry by testing for sustainability at only a finite number of points, although if there are many outputs the number of points to test could be quite large. More specifically, if $D_i(p_i)$ is market demand for output i, and q^S is a vector of outputs defined by $q_i^S = D_i(p_i)$ if $i \in S$ and $q_i^S = 0$ otherwise, then the test for sustainability of a price vector p is given by

$$\sum_{i \in S} p_i q_i < C(q^S) \text{ for all proper subsets } S \subset N \tag{5.9}$$

The formal result is the following:

Proposition 5.4:

If the cost function of a natural monopolist satisfies weak cost complementarity and the demands for all outputs are independent, then a price vector p, chosen from the undominated zero profit set, is sustainable if conditions (5.9) hold.

In its original form, Proposition 5.4 applied only to the case of sustainability against market entry. However, because the condition

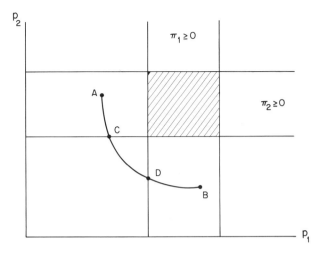

FIGURE 5.9

of weak cost complementarity also implies decreasing average incremental cost, this result implies general sustainability, given the previously cited additional conclusion of Panzar and Willig. For the proof of Proposition 5.4 the reader is referred to Panzar and Willig (1977b).

In a result that is closely related to Proposition 5.4, Sharkey (1981) derived a sufficient condition for the existence of sustainable prices that does not require explicit verification of conditions (5.9). Suppose that the cost function can be written in the form

$$C(q) = F(S) + \sum_{i=1}^{n} c_i q_i \qquad (5.10)$$

where S is the set of outputs for which $q_i > 0$, F(S) is the fixed cost associated with the set S, and c_i is the constant marginal cost of producing the output i. Then if costs satisfy weak cost complementarity and demands are independent, it can be shown that a sustainable price vector always exists. In fact, under these conditions, it is possible to define an algorithm that can explicitly calculate a sustainable price vector.

Given the above results, one can reasonably conjecture that weak cost complementarity and independent demands are together sufficient for sustainable prices to exist with cost functions more general than those given in equation (5.10). In addition, it is possible that a similar result holds for the case in which demands are complementary rather than independent.

An alternative approach to sustainability is taken in a paper by Baumol, Bailey, and Willig (1977). This work describes a set of

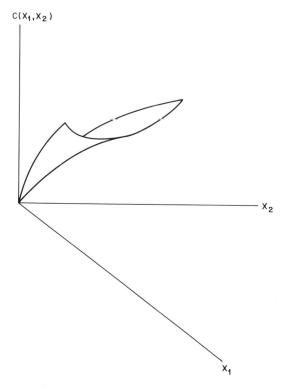

FIGURE 5.10

conditions that are sufficient for the existence of sustainable prices. Furthermore, if the assumed conditions prevail, the authors' conclusion is operationally useful, because the prices that are shown to be sustainable are exactly the same as those that satisfy the Ramsey first-order conditions for optimal pricing in the presence of a budget constraint.

Before proceeding let us recall from Section 3.7 the Ramsey conditions for welfare optimality. If p, MR, and MC represent vectors of price, marginal revenue, and marginal cost for the n different outputs that are produced by a natural monopolist, then the Ramsey prices are given by the solution to[6]

$$p_i - MC_i = -\lambda(MR_i - MC_i) \quad i = 1, \ldots, n \quad (5.11)$$

[6] In Section 3.7 the definition of Ramsey prices was based on the simplifying assumption of independent demands, which allows the substitution $MR_i = p_i(1 - 1/\eta_i)$ to be made, where η_i is the price elasticity of demand.

On the demand side, it is assumed that outputs produced by the natural monopolist are weak gross substitutes. That is, the demand for any one good cannot decline when the prices of any other good or set of goods rise. In addition, the set of outputs for which nonnegative profits are possible for either the natural monopolist or a competitor is assumed to be bounded and convex and to have no flat sections in its undominated portion.[7]

On the cost side, the required conditions have been defined and used in Chapter 4. They require that ray average costs are declining and that costs are trans-ray convex. A cost function that has these properties is shown in Figure 5.10. Then given some additional technical conditions, the Baumol, Bailey, Willig (1977) result is as follows:

Proposition 5.5:

If the cost function of a natural monopolist is trans-ray convex and has declining-ray average costs, outputs are weak gross substitutes, and the region of feasible entry is suitably convex, the Ramsey prices defined in equation (5.11) are sustainable.

The principal virtue of this result is the demonstration of the surprising conclusion that optimal prices can be contained in the set of sustainable prices. In addition, although there may be other sustainable prices, only the Ramsey prices are certain to be sustainable if local information about the cost function is all that is available.

One should not be tempted to conclude, however, that there is a truly general "invisible hand" theorem that is capable of guaranteeing the optimality of natural monopoly prices with free entry. As Faulhaber (1975) observes, the optimal Ramsey prices are in general not sustainable if the conditions of Baumol, Bailey, and Willig do not hold. For example, if fixed costs are associated with individual outputs (instead of a fixed cost common to all outputs), the Ramsey rule will allocate these fixed costs so as to achieve the highest aggregate welfare, regardless of the possibility of entry in some of the markets. An output for which demand is highly inelastic will bear a disproportionate share of the total fixed costs under the Ramsey rule, perhaps inviting entry by a rival producer who is not constrained to serve the aggregate welfare. In addition, the Ramsey rule is not well suited to determine which goods should fall within the boundaries of a natural monopoly industry. Even without a cost advantage in assigning a given good to a natural

---

[7] There are alternative assumptions that do not require the assumption of weak gross substitutability. In addition, specific costs associated with entry may also be included in the analysis, with only minor modification of the assumptions and statement of the theorem.

monopolist, welfare will generally improve if that good is produced by a natural monopolist and prices are set according to the Ramsey rule. In short, the Ramsey rule is primarily a tool that is useful in the context of centralized planning in a well-defined industry, where competitive entry is not a serious policy question. Some further discussion of the application of Ramsey pricing in the case of markets with free entry is contained in the papers of Braeutigam (1979) and Sharkey (1981).

A final comment on the usefulness of the results on sustainable prices concerns the implicit restriction in the existing literature to the case of linear price schedules. Because nonlinear or multipart tariff schedules may result in superior performance and higher welfare to consumers, this restriction is a serious one. However, one should not assume that the possibility that natural monopoly firms may use nonlinear prices in any way eliminates the possibility that a price schedule may be nonsustainable. Tentative results indicate that even with the ability to use a completely general nonlinear tariff schedule, a natural monopolist may still be unable to find a sustainable tariff schedule. In fact the results of the following section support this finding. Although the game theoretic models to be developed do not explicitly consider nonlinear pricing, neither do they assume that firms are constrained to use linear price schedules. Instead, they assume that a firm and its customers are free to enter into coalitions in which outputs may be internally allocated optimally without any explicit use of a pricing schedule. It will be seen that in these models the stability of a natural monopoly producer is no more secure than it is when a simple linear price schedule is assumed.

5.3   A game theoretic approach to cross-subsidization and the stability of natural monopoly

The concept of sustainability of natural monopoly, discussed in the previous two sections, is an attempt to describe what might happen in a market in which a monopolist competes with one or more rival suppliers. Because the number of potentially active firms is likely to be small, competition in such a market is necessarily imperfect. That is, individual firms recognize that their own decisions regarding price and output will have an effect on the market price and may induce a response from other firms in the industry. The theory of games is a tool that has been developed in recent years to deal with such situations.

In fact the theory of sustainability may be viewed as a noncooperative game in which one firm, the natural monopolist, is required to make the first move by announcing a price. A single rival is then allowed to respond by staying out of the market, or by entering at some price lower than the monopolist's. Thus in the sustainability "game" firms are active players while consumers are treated as passive agents whose behavior is specified, via their demand functions, in the rules of the game.

This section will examine a different game in which the active players will be consumers while firms will be assumed to pursue passive behavior, which will be built into the structure of the game. More precisely, a cooperative game will be defined, where each player in the game represents a single consumer, or group of similar consumers. The objective of consumers in this game will be to convert their own resources or endowments into a vector of outputs. To do this, they will generally find it advantageous to form coalitions because of the assumed subadditivity of the underlying production process. Firms in this approach may therefore be identified with the set of possible coalitions of buyers. Active firms will correspond to the coalitions that actually form at the conclusion of the game, whereas the inactive, but potentially competitive, firms will correspond to the unsuccessful coalitions. In this approach a stable natural monopoly results if the coalition of all buyers is a stable outcome of the game.[8]

First consider a game known as the "cost-sharing game," which was introduced in Section 3.4.[9] Suppose that a public utility is engaged in the production of n distinct goods. For example, the utility might produce a homogeneous output such as electricity or water, which is then sold in n different neighborhoods or communities. More generally, the utility might produce a different good in each of its markets. Assume however, that each market can be represented by a single buyer. The set of all buyers will then become the players in the game.

Let $N = \{1, \ldots, n\}$ represent the set of all buyers or markets and let S represent a subset of N. Assume that the utility incurs a fixed

---

[8]   The reader who is familiar with the theory of cooperative games will notice that the concept of stability that will be developed in the remainder of this section is based on a solution concept known as the core. Chapter 6 will formally analyze the core of a market in a more general context. Also, it should be noted that there are game theoretic solutions other than the core, that could be used to describe a type of stability. However, they will not be pursued in this or the following chapter.

[9]   This game was analyzed by Faulhaber (1975) and Littlechild (1975) in the context of public utility pricing. There were, however, earlier applications of game theory to similar problems. See, for example, Borch (1962), for an analysis of subsidization in the insurance industry. Also, for a nongame theoretic approach to cross-subsidization and related issues see Sandberg (1975; 1979).

cost in providing service to each possible collection of buyers that may be represented by a set function $C(S)$, and that $C(\emptyset) = 0$, where $\emptyset$ represents the empty set. If the utility is a natural monopoly, then C is subadditive. That is,

$$C(S) + C(T) \geq C(S \cup T) \quad \text{whenever} \quad S \cup T = \emptyset \tag{5.12}$$

Suppose that there is free entry in the industry, so that competing firms are allowed to serve some or all of the utility's buyers. Furthermore, assume that all firms in the industry have access to the same technology and therefore produce according to the same cost function C.

Given this scenario, the natural monopoly utility must determine prices to charge each of its buyers that satisfy a number of constraints. The prices must be high enough so that revenues are equal to total costs. Thus if $p = (p_1, \ldots, p_n)$ is a price vector, then

$$\sum_{i=1}^{n} p_i = C(N) \tag{5.13}$$

In addition, to prevent coalitions of buyers from seeking service from an alternative supplier, one must set prices that also satisfy the constraints

$$\sum_{i \in S} p_i \leq C(S) \quad \text{for all} \quad S \subseteq N \tag{5.14}$$

Prices that satisfy expressions (5.13) and (5.14) together are said to be in the core of the cost-sharing game.[10]

This analysis highlights a number of issues that are associated with the stability of natural monopoly pricing and the formally identical problem of cross-subsidization. First, in order to determine whether subsidization is occurring (or whether entry is attractive), one must examine all possible groups of services instead of individual services by themselves. Second, and more important, it becomes obvious that for strictly technological reasons there may be no prices that simultaneously generate revenues equal to total cost and deter entry by rival firms. In other words, subadditivity of the cost function C is not a sufficient condition for the existence of a core to the cost-sharing game.

To illustrate the possibility of an empty core, consider the example of a water utility that was discussed by Faulhaber (1975). The utility wishes to provide service to three neighborhoods in a

---

[10] In usual game theoretic terminology a cooperative game with side payments is represented by a set of players N and a real-valued characteristic function v, which is defined in all subsets $S \subseteq N$. The core of the game (N, v) is then the set of vectors x such that $\sum_{i \in N} x_i = v(N)$ and $\sum_{i \in S} x_i \geq v(S)$.

new community that does not have access to any existing facilities. Each neighborhood has a projected demand of 10,000 gallons/day. In order to satisfy this demand, the company can dig shallow wells at several locations, each of which can provide a maximum of 20,000 gallons/day, or it can dig a single deep well, which can provide 30,000 gallons/day. The cost of a shallow well is $200, whereas a deep well costs $350. In addition, there are local distribution costs of $100 per neighborhood.

Thus letting $N = \{1, 2, 3\}$ it can be seen that total costs, including drilling and distribution, are given by

$$C(\{1\}) = C(\{2\}) = C(\{3\}) = 300$$

$$C(\{1, 2\}) = C(\{1, 2\}) = C(\{2, 3\}) = 400$$

$$C(\{1, 2, 3\} = 650$$

This cost function is subadditive so that only one well is needed in the community. However, to prevent entry by rival firms, the price vector $p = (p_1, p_2, p_3)$ must satisfy

$$p_1 + p_2 \leq 400$$

$$p_1 + p_3 \leq 400$$

$$p_2 + p_3 \leq 400$$

which implies that

$$p_1 + p_2 + p_3 \leq 600$$

Thus there is no way that prices can cover the total costs of $650 and deter entry simultaneously.

Although the preceding analysis is useful, it fails to consider consumer demand. It is possible, however, to integrate demand into the analysis by means of relatively simple addition to the model. Assume that each buyer has a maximum price that he or she is willing to pay, which will be represented by a vector $y = (y_1, \ldots, y_n)$.[11] No buyer can be asked to pay more than the maximum which he is willing to pay. Therefore in addition to the constraints in expressions (5.13) and (5.14), prices must also satisfy

$$p_i \leq y_i \quad i = 1, \ldots, n \qquad (5.15)$$

[11] The vector y could also have been defined to represent the total consumer surplus that each buyer i receives from the consumption of good i. In addition, because the present discussion has considered only the fixed costs of production, y_i is actually the maximum amount that consumer i is willing to contribute in excess of his or her marginal costs. It is, of course, a simple matter to incorporate marginal costs into the analysis, which has been done in Sharkey (1981). Also, it should be observed that the present model is closely related to the discussion of sustainability with independent demands in the previous section.

Even though this addition of a simple demand constraint to the model is a seemingly minor change, the results of the new model are actually quite different. One must now determine whether production of a given good or collection of goods is desirable, by examining both the consumers' willingness to pay and the costs of production. (Before, it was implicitly assumed that all goods were worth producing and the only relevant test was for subadditivity, to see if production should be carried out by one firm or several.)

The appropriate cost test to determine if production is desirable is an incremental cost test. The incremental cost of producing a collection of goods S, out of a total collection N, is given by $C(N) - C(\bar{S})$, where $\bar{S}$ represents the set of goods contained in N but not in S. Therefore the production of S is desirable if

$$\sum_{i \in S} y_i \geq C(N) - C(\bar{S}) \tag{5.16}$$

The collection N is a feasible product set if inequality (5.16) holds for all $S \subseteq N$. Furthermore, N is said to be the optimal product set if it is feasible and there is no larger collection N' from among the set of potentially producible goods, such that inequality (5.16) holds for all $S \subseteq N'$.

Given that an optimal product set N, has been determined, it is necessary to determine if there exists a vector p satisfying expressions (5.13), (5.14), and (5.15). Such a price will be called a "stable price vector." It is readily apparent that a necessary condition for a stable price vector to exist is that the core of the cost-sharing game be nonempty. If this core is empty, then expressions (5.13) and (5.14) are by themselves inconsistent.

The existence of a core to the cost-sharing game is not, however, sufficient for the existence of a stable price vector. Consider, for example, an industry with an optimal product set $N = \{1, 2, 3, 4\}$ and a cost function given by

$$C(S) = \begin{cases} 200 & \text{if } S \text{ contains 1 good} \\ 300 & \text{if } S \text{ contains 2 goods} \\ 500 & \text{if } S \text{ contains 3 goods} \\ 600 & \text{if } S \text{ contains 4 goods} \end{cases}$$

and a willingness to pay vector given by

$$y_1 = 100$$

$$y_2 = y_3 = y_4 = 200$$

One can easily verify that this cost function is subadditive and that the product set N is optimal, assuming that no other goods are potentially producible. Furthermore, the core of the cost-sharing game is nonempty and is given by the unique price vector

$$p = (150, 150, 150, 150)$$

However, this price vector is not a stable price vector, for buyer 1 has been required to pay more than the maximum that he or she is willing to pay. Because the price vector in the core of the cost-sharing game is unique, it is clear that any price vector that satisfies the demand constraints, inequalities (5.15), must fail to satisfy the core constraints, expressions (5.13) and (5.14). In other words, no stable price vector can exist in this game.

Games that have a stable price vector for every optimal product set are discussed in Sharkey (1981). The most important result of that paper is the following:

Proposition 5.6:

If a cost function C on a set of goods N satisfies weak cost complementarity, then a stable price vector always exists for any willingness to pay vector as long as N is an optimal product set.

In the present context it should be pointed out that weak cost complementarity is equivalent to the following condition on C.

$$C(S) + C(T) \geq C(S \cup T) + C(S \cap T) \tag{5.17}$$

for all subsets $S, T \subseteq N$

The results of these models are applicable to industries in which the demands for various goods are independent. However, when there is a possibility that individual consumers may consume more than one type of output or substitute one output for another as relative prices change, a different type of model is called for. Some of the issues that arise from the possibility of substitution in demand may be illustrated in the following example. Further discussion of this example and related issues is contained in Sharkey (1982).

Suppose that three neighborhoods or communities are located, as shown in Figure 5.11, at the vertices of an equilateral triangle. Each community is interested in constructing a public good, such as a swimming pool, for the use of its residents. The only suitable locations for such facilities lie on the perimeter of the triangle connecting the three communities. The communities are willing to cooperate in the construction of a pool that residents of all three communities may use, and serious discussion of sites is restricted to the locations 1, 2, and 3 in Figure 5.11.

Suppose that the cost of constructing a pool at each location is $100. If two pools are built, the cost is $200 and if all three sites are used the cost is $300. Thus there are no economies or diseconomies of scope. On the demand side, however, each community has definite preferences, which are summarized in terms of each community's willingness-to-pay function:

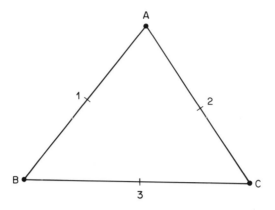

FIGURE 5.11

$$U_A(S) = \begin{cases} 120 & \text{if } S \text{ contains location 1 or 2} \\ 40 & \text{if } S = \{3\} \\ 0 & \text{if } S = \varnothing \end{cases}$$

$$U_B(S) = \begin{cases} 120 & \text{if } S \text{ contains location 1 or 3} \\ 40 & \text{if } S = \{2\} \\ 0 & \text{if } S = \varnothing \end{cases}$$

$$U_C(S) = \begin{cases} 120 & \text{if } S \text{ contains location 2 or 3} \\ 40 & \text{if } S = \{1\} \\ 0 & \text{if } S = \varnothing \end{cases}$$

Thus each community is willing to pay $120 for a nearby location, but only $40 for a more distant location.

As bargaining over locations proceeds, each pair of communities observes that it can achieve a joint surplus of $140 = [2 \times 120] - 100$ by constructing a pool at the location between them. Thus if u_a, u_b, and u_c represent the payoffs resulting from any final decision regarding pool location, then

$$u_a + u_b \geq 140$$

$$u_a + u_c \geq 140 \tag{5.18}$$

$$u_b + u_c \geq 140$$

Together inequalities (5.18) imply that $u_a + u_b + u_c \geq 210$. But the highest level of surplus attainable by all three communities together is $180 = [120 + 120 + 40] - 100$. (If two pools were constructed, the total surplus would be $360 - 200 = 160$ and the communities would be even worse off.) That is, payoffs in the game must collectively satisfy

$$u_a + u_b + u_c \leq 180 \qquad (5.19)$$

Because inequalities (5.18) and (5.19) are inconsistent, it appears that the coalition of all three communities will not form. Suppose then that two communities, say, A and B agree to form a coalition and to share the costs of a pool at location 1. A and B will then each receive a surplus of $70, while C will receive a surplus of $20 if it builds a pool for its own use. Notice, however, that C has a strong incentive to disrupt the coalition of A and B. For example, C could approach A with an offer to pay 75 percent of the costs of a pool at location 2 if only A would withdraw from the agreement with B. The surplus of C would then increase from $20 to 45, and of A from $70 to 95. Of course, any provisional agreement between A and C would be threatened with disruption by a counteroffer from B.

From the preceding example, it is apparent that the instability of the underlying game results entirely from the special demand conditions present. Thus in any model that allows similar possibilities for substitution in demand, sufficient conditions for stability are likely to depend on restrictions on demand as well as on costs. This issue will be pursued further in the more general game theoretic framework of the following chapter.

5.4   Concluding comments

This chapter has considered two models that attempt to characterize the nature of market equilibrium if there is free entry in a natural monopoly industry. Of the two, the theory of sustainability is more intuitive. However, the theory of sustainability should be regarded as only a first stage in a more complete model of entry and exit in natural monopoly markets. It is not by itself a theory of market equilibrium. In Chapter 8 an attempt will be made to construct an equilibrium model of market entry, which in some respects parallels the theory of sustainability.

Models based on cooperative game theory offer an alternative theory of entry in natural monopoly markets. However, at present the game theoretic models suffer from many of the same deficiencies as the sustainability models. For example, models based on the core solution concept fail to predict what would happen when a core fails to exist. A fruitful avenue for future research may be the application of other game theoretic solution concepts to the problem of market entry.

Despite their differences, the fundamental results of both the sustainability and the game theoretic approaches are the same. In a natural monopoly market there may be an incentive for entry to occur even though minimum cost production requires only one firm in the market.

CHAPTER 6

A game theoretic analysis of destructive competition

The term "destructive competition" has been widely used, and much abused, in the nontechnical and popular literature on natural monopoly and regulated industries. This chapter will investigate the possible merits of the proposition that competition is at times destructive by setting out a formal economic model based on the theory of cooperative games.

In many respects this chapter is a continuation of the work that was begun in Chapter 5. For example, the game theoretic approach to market stability is the same as that used in Section 5.3, although now it will be developed on a more formal and rigorous level. In addition, a nonsustainable natural monopoly may be correctly viewed as a particular example of a market in which competition is destructive. In Chapter 5 it was argued that although the theory of sustainability of natural monopoly is highly intuitive and useful, it is by no means a total theory of entry or competitive behavior in a natural monopoly industry. The results of this chapter may be seen as an attempt, from the point of view of cooperative game theory, to construct a model of competitive behavior in a market that is a natural monopoly or natural oligopoly. As will be seen later, it is convenient to build a cooperative theory of market stability on the demand side of the model. That is, the players in the game will represent buyers who wish to form coalitions with other buyers in order to gain access to their desired consumption bundles at favorable terms. Firms do not enter explicitly as players in this formulation. Instead, the technology of supply is incorporated into the opportunity sets that are available to coalitions of buyers.

An alternative and equally promising approach to the study of entry behavior and competition could be based on the supply side of the market. This alternative will be pursued in Chapter 8 in the construction of a noncooperative game theoretic model in which firms use price as a strategic variable. The noncooperative model will offer a different but complementary perspective on the issues raised in this chapter.

A word of warning to the nontechnical reader is in order. This chapter is considerably more demanding than any of the other chapters in this book. There is more mathematical structure, and unavoidably, a considerable amount of notation that must be used to describe it. In Section 6.1 the basic theory of cooperative games will be discussed and the structure of the economic model will be defined. Some positive results will be presented in Section 6.2 on conditions that are sufficient for markets to be stable. Although presented in a more formal and rigorous manner, these results bear a close resemblance to those of Chapter 5. In this chapter a market will be called stable if a core, which is defined in Section 6.1, exists in the game that is derived from the underlying market. Proposition 6.1 states that if the cost function is quasiconvex and has declining-ray average costs, and if consumer preferences obey some mild regularity conditions, then the market is stable. Proposition 6.2 gives conditions that are sufficient for a stable market if the cost function satisfies cost complementarity. However, in Proposition 6.2, it is necessary to make an additional strong condition on the preferences of consumers. All outputs must be complementary in a sense to be defined later. Besides these two basic findings on ordinary markets for private goods, Section 6.2 contains two other results for markets in which outputs have the qualities of a public good. Proposition 6.3 demonstrates that if there is only one public good that is desired by all consumers, then the market is necessarily stable. This result is extended to the case of many public goods in Proposition 6.4 by showing that if there is a concensus among consumers on the desired bundle of public goods, and if the cost function is supportable, as defined in Chapter 5, then the market is again stable.

Just as a stable market is defined in terms of the existence of a core in a certain cooperative game, destructive competition is said to occur when the core of the underlying game is empty. Section 6.3 contains three examples of destructive competition. In the first one the core is empty due to a persistent imbalance of demand and available capacity in the market. This imbalance may take place if demand fluctuates periodically or is uncertain and if capacity cannot adjust in a sufficiently flexible manner.

The remaining two examples are static in character. One is based on the location of stores, or indivisible production units, when there is a continuum of buyers. Here the core is empty unless the size of the total market is an exact integer multiple of the optimal market size for a single store. The final example is based on the costs of transmitting information or physical output through a network. A specific network is constructed in which the core is empty despite the fact that the costs of constructing capacity on each link are concave and exhibit economies of scale.

6.1 Game theoretic preliminaries

In order that this chapter may be as nearly self-contained as possible, the next few pages will define a large number of game theoretic tools that will be used later in the chapter. The reader who has had no previous exposure to the theory of cooperative games may find some of the concepts or notation confusing, but in general, this theory does not require knowledge of advanced mathematics.

In general terms a game may be defined whenever a group of individuals find themselves in a situation in which each may choose from a set of alternatives, and in which each player recognizes that his or her own payoff depends on the choices of other players and that his or her choice affects the payoff of other players. In the theory of cooperative games, however, few of the strategic aspects of game playing are analyzed explicitly. In a cooperative game, players are assumed to have the ability to enter into binding agreements, called coalitions, with other players.[1]

Thus the basic ingredient in a cooperative game is a specification of the set of players. If there are n players in the game, the set of all players is given by $N = \{1, \ldots, n\}$.[2] Coalitions of players then consist of subsets $S \subseteq N$, including the empty set $\varnothing$ and N itself.

In order to complete the description of a cooperative game, one must specify the opportunities that are available to each coalition. A possible outcome of the game can be represented by a vector $u = (u_1, \ldots, u_n)$ of payoffs representing the utility of every player in the game. Players in the game are interested in achieving the

[1] In fact, the only choice available to a player in a cooperative game is the decision of which coalition to join. Because in a noncooperative game the players presumably have the option of forming binding agreements in coalitions, it would appear that the noncooperative theory is much more general. This is indeed the case. However, noncooperative models of cooperative behavior are quite complex and at the same time are not sufficiently general to be of interest in most economic models of cooperative behavior.

[2] In some contexts it is more convenient to assume a continuum of players — for example, the set of points in the real interval $[0, n]$, or the set of vectors $x = (x_1, \ldots, x_n)$ such that $0 \leq x \leq x^0$. Most results in this and the following section, however, will use a finite set of players.

highest possible utility and are assumed in this theory to enter the coalition that offers the most favorable prospects. The prospects of a coalition S may be completely described by the set of utilities that the members of S can guarantee themselves if they choose to cooperate. Thus let $V(S)$ denote the set of utility outcomes u such that each member $i \in S$ can be guaranteed to receive at least u_i.

Certain mild technical conditions are generally imposed on the sets $V(S)$.[3] For the present discussion the essential property of V is the following. If $u \in V(S)$ and u' is such that $u_i' \leq u_i$ for all $i \in S$, then $u' \in V(S)$. Thus if the players in S can be guaranteed a vector u, they can be guaranteed of a vector u', which is less favorable to the members of S. In addition, if $u \in V(S)$ and $i \notin S$, then the component u_i is arbitrary, in the sense that $u \pm me^i$ is contained in $V(S)$ for any value of m. (Here e^i is the vector with $e_i^i = 1$ and $e_j^i = 0$ for $j \neq i$.)

Definition:

A cooperative game without side payments is a pair (N, V) where N is the set of players and $V(S)$ is a nonempty set of attainable utility vectors for every $S \subseteq N$.

Among the coalitions, the "grand coalition" N deserves particular attention, because the set $V(N)$ describes the largest possible set of utility vectors available to players in the game. A subset of $V(N)$ that is of particular interest is the Pareto optimal set

$$\overline{V}(N) = \{u \mid u \in V(N) \text{ and if } u_i' > u_i$$
$$\text{for all } i \in N, \text{ then } u' \notin V(N)\}$$

The Pareto optimal set contains all likely candidates for solutions to the game (N, V). However, some outcomes $u \in \overline{V}(N)$ are more reasonable than others. For example, if $u \in \overline{V}(N)$, there may exist a coalition S and a vector $u' \in V(S)$ such that $u_i' > u_i$ for all $i \in S$. (In other words, u is contained in the interior of $V(S)$.) In such a case the vector u can be improved on by the coalition S. A particular stable set of Pareto optimal vectors, known as the core, consists of all vectors $u \in \overline{V}(N)$, which cannot be improved on by any coalition $S \subseteq N$. The core of a two-person game is shown in Figure 6.1.

Definition:

The core of (N, V) consists of the set of utility vectors $u \in \overline{V}(N)$ such that there does not exist $S \subseteq N$ and $u' \in V(S)$ for which $u_i' > u_i$, $i \in S$. More concisely,

$$\text{core } (N, V) = V(N) - \underset{S \subseteq N}{U} \text{ interior } V(S)$$

The game (N, V) as previously defined does not require side

---

[3] See Aumann (1967) and Scarf (1967).

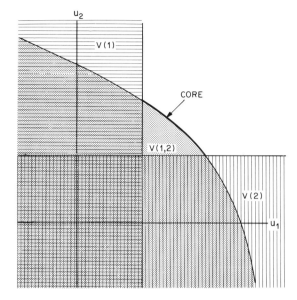

FIGURE 6.1

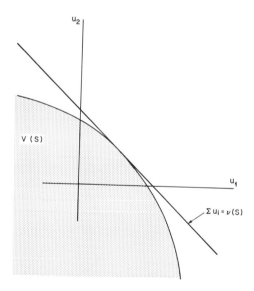

FIGURE 6.2

payments among players. If side payments are allowed in all coalitions, and in addition, if utility is freely transferable among players, as might happen if payoffs to the game are made in money, then the sets $V(S)$ take on the simplified form

$$V(S) = \{u : \sum_{i \in S} u_i \leq v(S)\}$$

The effect of allowing side payments is to enlarge the set of attainable utility vectors, as shown in Figure 6.2. A game with side payments and transferable utility is denoted by the pair (N, v) where v is a real-valued function (called the characteristic function) on the coalitions $S \subseteq N$. It is required that $v(\varnothing) = 0$, where $\varnothing$ represents the empty set.

The core of a side payment game then consists of all vectors u such that

$$\sum_{i \in N} u_i = v(N)$$

$$\sum_{i \in S} u_i \geq v(S) \text{ for } S \subseteq N$$

It is possible to characterize the core of a side payment game as follows. Consider the linear program

$$\min_u \sum_{i \in N} u_i$$

$$\text{subject to } \sum_{i \in S} u_i \geq v(S), S \subseteq N \tag{6.1}$$

The core is nonempty if and only if every optimal solution u^0 to inequality (6.1) satisfies

$$\sum_{i \in N} u_i^0 = v(N)$$

Now consider the dual linear program

$$\max_\delta \sum_{S \subseteq N} \delta_s v(S)$$

$$\text{subject to } \sum_{i \in S} \delta_s = 1, i=1, \ldots, n \tag{6.2}$$

$$\delta_s \geq 0, S \subseteq N$$

From the duality theorem for linear programming, it follows that the core of the side payment game is nonempty if and only if

$$\sum_{S \subseteq N} \delta_s v(S) \leq v(N)$$

for every vector δ that satisfies the constraints in expression (6.2).

Let δ be any feasible solution in expression (6.2) and let $S = \{S \subseteq N \text{ such that } \delta_s > 0\}$. Every such collection S of coalitions is known as a balanced collection. For example, $\{N\}$ is a balanced collection as is every partition $\{P_1, \ldots, P_k\}$ of N. In general, balanced collections contain coalitions with overlapping membership.

In the language of balanced collections it follows that the core of a game (N, ν) is nonempty if and only if

$$\sum_{S \in \mathbf{S}} \delta_s \nu(S) \le \nu(N) \tag{6.3}$$

for every balanced collection $\mathbf{S}$ of coalitions in N.[4] This basic result was first derived independently by Shapley (1967) and Bondareva (1962), and the reader should consult these sources for further details.

A particular form of continuous transferable utility game will be useful in Section 6.3. Let $T = [0, t]$ be the set of players. Suppose that only the number of players in a coalition, rather than the identities of individual players, matter. Then all coalitions may be represented by intervals $[0, s]$ for $0 \le s \le t$. Let $\nu(s)$ be the characteristic function.

Then it follows that the core of (T, ν) is nonempty if and only if $\nu(t)/t \ge \nu(s)/s$ for $0 \le s \le t$.

It is also possible to consider continuous games in which there are finitely many types of players and a continuum of players of each type. Telser (1978) presents a formal analysis of such games. In addition, many of the results on supportable cost functions, which were introduced in Chapter 5, apply to continuous games with several types of players.

Balance conditions also prove useful in the theory of nonside payment games. As before, a balanced collection $\mathbf{S} = \{S_1, \ldots, S_k\}$ is a collection such that

$$\sum_{j \in S_i} \delta_i = 1 \quad \text{for } j = 1, \ldots, n$$

for some set of positive weights $\delta_1, \ldots, \delta_k$. Now suppose that a vector u is attainable by every coalition S_i in the balanced collection $\mathbf{S}$. Then the game (N, V) is said to be balanced if u is also attainable by the grand coalition.

Definition:

A game (N, V) is balanced if for any balanced collection $\mathbf{S}$ and any vector $u \in V(S_i)$, for all $S_i \in \mathbf{S}$, it follows that $u \in V(N)$.

In a game without side payments, balancedness is not equivalent to having a nonempty core, as was the case in side payment games. However, Scarf (1967) proved the following important result.

---

[4] Side payment games in which inequality (6.3) is satisfied for every balanced collection are known as balanced games. Therefore a side payment game has a nonempty core if and only if it is a balanced game.

Theorem:

A balanced game without side payments has a nonempty core.

Thus balancedness is a stronger condition on the class of nonside payment games than the property of having a nonempty core, and it is often easier to verify that a game is balanced than directly to construct a vector in the core.

A final preliminary result from game theory concerns games with transferable utility. Suppose that the characteristic function v satisfies the following property

$$v(S) + v(S') \leq v(S \cup S') + v(S \cap S') \text{ for all } S, S' \subseteq N \qquad (6.4)$$

Then the characteristic function is a "convex" set function[5] and the game (N,v) is said to be a convex game. Convexity of v is equivalent to the following more intuitive property. If $S \subseteq S'$ and a particular player $k \in N - S'$, then v is convex if and only if

$$v(S \cup k) - v(S) \leq v(S' \cup k) - v(S')$$

for all such S, S', and k. Thus convexity implies that a game has a particular form of increasing returns to scale in coalition size.

Shapley (1971) proved the following theorem.

Theorem:

A convex game with side payments has a nonempty core.

The theory of games that has been described thus far is very general and can be used in a number of contexts. A simple economic model will now be described in which the theory of cooperative games, and in particular, the core, can give some useful insights into the stability of a market and the possibility of destructive competition. In the remainder of this chapter the term "market" will be used to refer to a collection of agents, to be called buyers, and a set of outputs. The model that will be developed is sufficiently general to allow the set of buyers and the set of outputs to comprise an entire economy. However, the model does not address all the issues that are typically of concern in general

---

[5] The term "convex" should not be confused with the more usual convexity of a real-valued function, as the two concepts are unrelated. For this reason the term "supermodular" is often used in the mathematical literature. See, for example, Topkis (1981). An advantage of this terminology is that supermodularity easily generalizes to functions defined on real variables, and so considerable confusion can be avoided. The generalization of inequality (6.4) to real-valued functions is closely related to the concept of cost complementarity, which was defined in Chapter 4.

equilibrium theory. A more convenient, partial equilibrium interpretation of the model is that it represents a particular industry in which the boundaries of that industry are determined by the largest group of buyers who are able to form a "coalition" and the largest set of outputs that are desired by at least one buyer in the grand coalition.[6]

Let $N = \{1, \ldots, n\}$ be the set of buyers in the market, and suppose that there are m goods available. Let $q = (q_1, \ldots, q_m)$ represent a vector of outputs and let q^i represent a particular vector that is consumed by buyer $i \in N$. If each of the outputs is a private good, then each buyer may consume whatever output q^i that he chooses. Then the total consumption bundle of a coalition S is the summation of q_i over all $i \in S$. On the other hand, if each of the outputs is a public good, then each member of a coalition must consume the same bundle of q, and the total consumption of a coalition S is also equal to q.

The following section contains results for both markets with private goods and markets with public goods.[7] The reason for considering a market for public goods, as well as for private goods, is twofold. (1) Some industries in the private sector produce outputs that have many attributes of public goods. (2) Fixed costs of production constitute a pure public good, even in a market for purely private goods. Therefore industries in which fixed costs are a large component of total costs may be better approximated by the public good than the private good version of the model.

Preferences of each buyer will be described by means of a real valued utility function $U_i(q^i)$, which will be defined over the set of all nonnegative consumption bundles q^i. Various combinations of the following properties of utility functions will be used in the following section.

---

[6] Buyers in this model form coalitions because of their commonality of interests and not because they necessarily meet together in order to coordinate their behavior jointly. In fact, firms in this model exist primarily to bring coalitions of buyers into existence. Thus the most important "output" of a firm, although it is not explicitly modeled, is the information flow that allows widely separated groups of buyers to act as one unified coalition.

[7] Markets for mixed collections of public and private goods will not, however, be considered, although many results could be generalized in this context.

Conditions on preferences

1. The function U_i is monotonic if $U_i(q) \leq U_i(q')$ whenever $q \leq q'$.

2. The function U_i is quasiconcave if $U_i[\lambda q + (1 - \lambda)q'] \geq \min\{U_i(q)\ U_i(q')\}$ for any q, q' and $0 \leq \lambda \leq 1$.[8]

3. The outputs q are strict complements to buyer i if $U_i(q \wedge q') - \min\ \{U_i(q), U_i(q')\}$, where $q_j \wedge q_j' - \min\ \{q_j, q_j'\}$ and $q \wedge q' = (q_1 \wedge q_1', \ldots, q_m \wedge q_m')$.

Condition 1 is largely self-explanatory and requires only that buyers continue to place a nonnegative value on increments to output at each level of output. Monotonicity is also satisfied if output can be disposed of costlessly. Condition 2 is equivalent to the convexity of indifference curves as shown in Figure 6.3. This is the usual assumption in consumer demand theory, and it is roughly equivalent to the assumption of downward-sloping demand curves.

Condition 3 is much stronger, as it requires that consumer indifference curves have a right angle shape, as shown in Figure 6.4. This is the usual interpretation of product complementarity. However, condition 3 is also satisfied under a particular form of demand independence in which each buyer's utility depends only on a single component of vector q.

It will be assumed that each buyer is endowed with a resource, ω_i, which may be used as an input in production but that inputs do not enter into the utility function of any buyer.

Technology will be described by the cost function C, which measures in units of consumer input ω, the cost of producing any nonnegative output q. Various combinations of the following properties of C will be required.

Conditions on the cost function

1. C is nondecreasing if $C(q') \geq C(q)$ whenever $q' \geq q$.

2. C is unbounded if

$$\lim_{q_j \to \infty} C(q_1, \ldots, q_j, \ldots, q_n) = \infty$$

for each j and all outputs $\{q_i\}$, $i \neq j$

---

[8] It follows by repeated application of this definition that $U_i[\sum_{i=1}^{k} \lambda_i q^i] \geq \min_{i=1,\ldots,k} \{U_i(q^i)\}$ whenever $\sum_{i=1}^{k} \lambda_i = 1$.

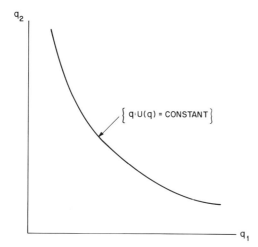

FIGURE 6.3

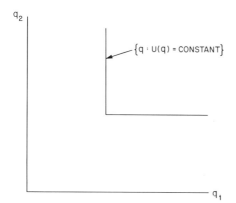

FIGURE 6.4

3. C has declining-ray average cost if $C(\lambda q) \leq \lambda C(q)$ for any $q \geq 0$ and any $\lambda \geq 1$.

4. C is quasiconvex if $C[\lambda q + (1 - \lambda)q'] \leq \max\{C(q), C(q')\}$ for any $q, q' \geq 0$ and $0 \leq \lambda \leq 1$.[9]

---

[9] As with quasiconcavity, it follows that $C(\sum_{i=1}^{k} \lambda_i q^i) \leq \max_{i=1,...,k} \{C(q^i)\}$ whenever $\sum_{i=1}^{k} \lambda_i = 1$.

5. C satisfies cost complementarity if $C(x + z) - C(x) \geq C(x + y + z) - C(x + y)$ for any outputs $x, y, z \geq 0$.

6. C is supportable if

$$\sum_{i=1}^{k} \delta_i C(q^i) \geq C(\sum_{i=1}^{k} \delta_i q^i)$$

whenever $\delta_i \geq o$ and

$$q^i \leq \sum_{i=1}^{k} \delta_i q^i$$

for each $i = 1, \ldots, k$.

Each of these conditions is discussed in greater detail in Chapters 4 and 5.

It is now possible to associate with each market a game without side payments. Players in the game will be the set N of buyers. The set of attainable utility vectors for each coalition S will consist of the utilities that can be obtained from outputs that are produced using the combined inputs of members of the coalition and distributed among the members. More precisely, the game is defined as follows:

Definition:

Given a market for a set of private goods, there is an associated game (N, V) where N is the set of buyers in the market and V is defined for every $S \subseteq N$ by

$$V(S) = \{u \,|\, U_i(q^i) \geq u_i \text{ for all } i \in S \text{ and } C(\sum_{i \in S} q^i) \leq \sum_{i \in S} \omega_i\}$$

In a market for public goods, the game is defined in a similar fashion.

Definition:

Given a market for a set of public goods, there is an associated game (N, V) where N is the set of buyers in the market and V is defined for every $S \subseteq N$ by

$$V(S) = \{u \,|\, U_i(q) \geq u_i \text{ for all } i \in S \text{ and } C(q) \leq \sum_{i \in S} \omega_i\}$$

Definition:

A market is said to be a stable market if the core of the associated game is nonempty. Competition in a market is said to be destructive if the core of the associated game is empty.

The following section will consist of a collection of results that are sufficient for a market to be stable. Section 6.3 will consider several examples of markets in which there is destructive competition.

6.2 Sufficient conditions for a stable market

This section contains four propositions that establish conditions under which the core of the game associated with a market is nonempty. A brief discussion and economic interpretation will follow each result. Additional information on the existence of cores in markets with increasing returns to scale in production may be found in Scarf and Hansen (1973), Champsaur (1975), Telser (1978), Quinzii (1980), and Ichiishi (1980).

Proposition 6.1:

> If each buyer's utility function is monotonic and quasiconcave, and the cost function is unbounded, quasiconvex, and has declining ray average cost, then the core of (N, V) is nonempty.[10]

Proof:

> I will show that (N, V) is a balanced game. Let S be a balanced collection, and suppose that $u \in V(S)$ for all $S \in \mathbf{S}$. Then there must exist for each $S \in \mathbf{S}$ an output vector $q^i(S)$ for each $i \in S$ such that

$$U_i[q^i(S)] \geq u_i, i \in S$$

and

$$C[\sum_{i \in S} q^i(S)] \leq \sum_{i \in S} \omega_i \tag{6.5}$$

In this model one may assume, with no loss in generality, that expression (6.5) holds as an equality. Let

$$q(S) = \sum_{i \in S} q^i(S)$$

and define

$$x^i = \sum_{\substack{S \in \mathbf{S} \\ i \in S}} \delta_s q^i(S), i \in N$$

Then by the properties of balance weights, it follows that

$$\sum_{i \in N} x^i = \sum_{i \in N} \sum_{S \in \mathbf{S}} \delta_s q^i(S) = \sum_{S \in \mathbf{S}} \delta_s \sum_{i \in S} q^i(S) = \sum_{S \in \mathbf{S}} \delta_s q(S)$$

---

[10] This result is adapted from a previously published theorem in Sharkey (1979).

Then

$$C\left[\sum_{i \in N} x^i\right] = C\left[\sum_{S} \delta_s q(S)\right]$$

$$= C\left[\sum_{S \in \mathbf{S}} \frac{\delta_s C[q(S)]}{\sum_{T \in \mathbf{S}} \delta_T C[q(T)]} \frac{\sum_{T \in \mathbf{S}} \delta_T C[q(T)]}{C[q(S)]} q(S)\right]$$

where the last equality follows by multiplying both the numerator and the denominator of each term $\delta_s q(S)$ by $C[q(S)] \sum \delta_T C[q(T)]$.
Let

$$\alpha_s = \frac{\delta_s C[q(S)]}{\sum_{T \in \mathbf{S}} \delta_T C[q(T)]}$$

Then

$$\sum_{S \in \mathbf{S}} \alpha_s = 1$$

and so by quasiconvexity of C,

$$C\left[\sum_{i \in N} x^i\right] \leq \max_{S \in \mathbf{S}} \left\{ C\left[\frac{\sum_{T \in \mathbf{S}} \delta_T C[q(T)]}{C[q(S)]} q(S)\right] \right\}$$

By hypothesis,

$$C[q(T)] = \sum_{i \in T} \omega_i$$

for all $T \in \mathbf{S}$, and by the properties of balance weights, it can be seen that

$$\sum_{T \in \mathbf{S}} \delta_T \sum_{i \in T} \omega_i = \sum_{i \in N} \omega_i$$

Therefore

$$C\left(\sum_{i \in N} x^i\right) \leq \max_{S \in \mathbf{S}} \left\{ C\left[\frac{\sum_{i \in N} \omega_i}{\sum_{i \in S} \omega_i} q(S)\right] \right\}$$

By declining-ray average cost, for each $S \in \mathbf{S}$, we see that the following holds true

$$C\left[\frac{\sum\limits_{N}\omega_i}{\sum\limits_{S}\omega_i}\, q\,(S\,)\right] \le \frac{\sum\limits_{N}\omega_i}{\sum\limits_{S}\omega_i}\, C\,[q\,(S\,)]$$

$$= \sum\limits_{N}\omega_i$$

and therefore

$$C\,(\sum\limits_{i\in N} x^i\,) \le \sum\limits_{i\in N}\omega_i$$

To complete the proof, observe that quasiconcavity of U_i for each $i \in N$ and the fact that

$$\sum\limits_{\substack{S\in \mathbf{S}\\ i\in S}}\delta_s = 1$$

imply that

$$U_i\,(x^i\,) \ge \min\limits_{S\in \mathbf{S}}\{U_i\,[q^i\,(S\,)]\} = u_i$$

Therefore $u \in V(N)$ and so (N, V) is balanced. By Scarf's theorem from the previous section, it follows that the core of (N, V) is nonempty.

Q.E.D.

Proposition 6.1 is remarkably similar to a result, demonstrated by Baumol, Bailey, and Willig (1977), on the sustainability of natural monopoly. (See Proposition 5.5 of Chapter 5.) In particular, the required conditions on the cost function C are virtually the same in the two results.

Because of the assumption of declining-ray average cost, Proposition 6.1 applies only to markets that are natural monopolies. There is, however, a straightforward generalization of Proposition 6.1, which allows for a multiple firm stable market. Consider a market for a single homogeneous output q for which the average cost does not decline everywhere, and in which $C(q)/q$ reaches a minimum at q_0, as in Figure 6.5. Such a cost function is subadditive for outputs $0 \le q \le q_1$, where $q_1 > q_0$. Beyond q_1, however, minimum cost production requires production by two independent firms. If both firms have the same cost function, then industry average cost falls from q_1 to a minimum average cost for two firms at an output $2q_0$. Beyond an output $q_2 > 2q_0$, minimum cost production requires three firms. The industry average cost function is then given in Figure 6.6.

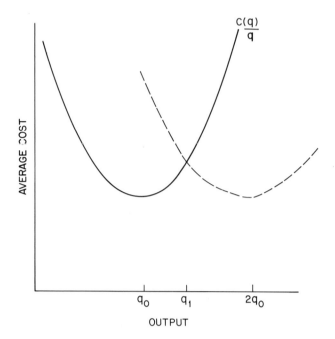

FIGURE 6.5

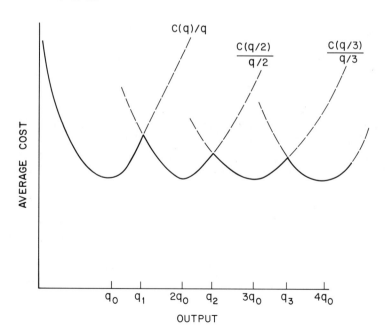

FIGURE 6.6

In order to investigate the status of the core, I will assume that all buyers are identical, and each buyer is infinitesimally small relative to the size of the market. Then the grand coalition of all buyers may be represented by the real interval $[0, t]$. Assume also that each buyer wishes to consume one infinitesimal unit of output for which he is willing to pay an amount b. Now it is possible to define a continuous game with transferable utility, where the characteristic function v is given by

$$v(s) = sb - C(s) \text{ for } 0 \leq s \leq t$$

It can be shown[11] that such a game has a core if and only if

$$\frac{v(t)}{t} \geq \frac{v(s)}{s} \text{ for all } s \in [0, t] \tag{6.6}$$

But the inequalities in expression (6.6) hold if and only if

$$\frac{C(t)}{t} \leq \frac{C(s)}{s} \text{ for all } s \in [0, t]$$

which is possible only if $t < q_0$ or $t = kq_0$ for some integer k.

In other words, a multiple firm stable market is possible, but only if the grand coalition of all buyers is able to purchase output at minimum average cost. It should be noted that if t is large relative to q_0, then $C(t)/t$ is necessarily close to $C(q_0)/q_0$ and it is reasonable to think that a market in such a situation is "almost" stable. For intermediate cases, however, in which the optimal number of firms is small, but greater than one, it follows from the model that the conditions for a market to be stable are very restrictive.

The preceding analysis can also be carried out in a multiple output setting. For example, if Figure 6.6 is taken to represent ray average cost along the particular ray s_q, where q is output that is desired by the grand coalition, then a multifirm stable market is possible under the same conditions as previously described. In addition, in a multiproduct setting there is also the possibility that two or more specialty firms may coexist in equilibrium. The details of this analysis are left to the interested reader.

The next result provides a different set of conditions for a market with private goods to be stable.

Proposition 6.2:

If each buyer's utility function is monotonic, outputs are strict complements, and the cost function satisfies cost complementarity, then the core of (N, V) is nonempty.

Proof:

Let $u = (u_1, \ldots, u_n)$ be a vector of utilities and define the

---

[11] See, for example, Telser (1978, Chapter 4).

real-valued function $\phi(u, S)$ such that $\phi(u, \varnothing) = 0$, and for each $S \subseteq N$,

$$\phi(u, S) = \min\left\{C(\sum_{i \in S} q^i) | U_i(q^i) \geq u_i \text{ for all } i \in S\right\}$$

If $u \notin V(S)$, then by convention, $\phi(u, S) = \infty$. The function ϕ is well defined for $u \in V(S)$ if the sets $Q_i = \{q^i | U_i(q^i) \geq u_i\}$ are closed for each $i \in S$ and C is unbounded. I assume that both conditions are satisfied.

$\phi(u, S)$ represents the minimum cost to coalition S of achieving the utility vector u. Using the function ϕ, one can analyze a game without side payments by employing some of the techniques and results of transferable utility games. I will first show that for every u, and every $S, S' \subseteq N$, ϕ satisfies the inequality

$$\phi(u, S) + \phi(u, S') \geq \phi(u, S \cup S') + \phi(u, S \cap S') \tag{6.7}$$

To demonstrate inequality (6.7), consider the output vectors $q^i(S)$ such that $U_i[q^i(S)] \geq u_i$ for all $i \in S$ and $q^i(S')$ such that $U_i[q^i(S')] \geq U_i$ for all $i \in S'$. Then, for all $i \in S \cap S'$, let

$$x^i = q^i(S) \wedge q^i(S')$$
$$y^i = q^i(S) \vee q^i(S')$$

where for arbitrary vectors a and b,

$$a_j \wedge b_j = \min\{a_j, b_j\}$$
$$a_j \vee b_j = \max\{a_j, b_j\}$$

and

$$a \wedge b = (a_1 \wedge b_1, \ldots, a_m \wedge b_m)$$
$$a \vee b = (a_1 \vee b_1, \ldots, a_m \vee b_m)$$

Finally, let

$$y^i = \begin{cases} q^i(S) & \text{for all } i \in S - S' \\ q^i(S') & \text{for all } i \in S' - S \end{cases}$$

Since outputs are strict complements for each buyer, it follows that

$$U_i(x^i) \geq u_i \text{ for all } i \in S \cap S' \tag{6.8}$$

Since each U_i is monotonic,

$$U_i(y^i) \geq u_i \text{ for all } i \in S \cup S' \tag{6.9}$$

Since C satisfies cost complementarity, for all output vectors a, b, and $c \geq 0$,

$$C(a + b + c) - C(a + b) \leq C(a + c) - C(a)$$

which is equivalent to

$$C(a) + C(a + b + c) \leq C(a + b) + C(a + c) \tag{6.10}$$

Let

$$a = \sum_{S \cap S'} x^i$$

$$b = \sum_{i \in S} q^i(S) - a$$

$$c = \sum_{i \in S'} q^i(S') - a$$

Then

$$a + b + c = \sum_{S-S'} q^i(S) + \sum_{S'-S} q^i(S') +$$

$$\sum_{S \cap S'} [q^i(S) + q^i(S') - x^i]$$

$$= \sum_{S \cup S'} y^i$$

since $x^i + y^i = q^i(S) + q^i(S')$ for all $i \in S \cap S'$.

Therefore inequality (6.10) implies that

$$C(\sum_{S \cap S'} x^i) + C(\sum_{S \cup S'} y^i) \le C[\sum_S q^i(S)] + C[\sum_{S'} q^i(S')] \qquad (6.11)$$

From inequalities (6.8), (6.9), (6.11) and the definition of ϕ, it follows that

$$\phi(u, S \cap S') + \phi(u, S \cup S') \le C(\sum_{i \in S \cap S'} x^i) + C(\sum_{i \in S \cup S'} y^i)$$

$$\le C[\sum_S q^i(S)] + C[\sum_{S'} q^i(S')] \qquad (6.12)$$

But inequality (6.12) holds for all vectors $q^i(S)$ and $q^i(S')$ such that $U_i[q^i(S)] \ge u_i, i \in S$ and $U_i[q^i(S')] \ge u_i, i \in S'$. Therefore

$$\phi(u, S \cap S') + \phi(u, S \cup S') \le \phi(u, S) + \phi(u, S')$$

and so inequality (6.7) is established.

To complete the proof of Proposition 6.2, I will show that (N, V) is balanced. Let S be a balanced collection and suppose $u \in V(S)$ for all $S \in S$ Then it must be true that

$$\phi(u, S) \le \sum_{i \in S} \omega_i \qquad (6.13)$$

for each $S \in S$. Since $-\phi(u, \emptyset) = 0$, $(-\phi)$ is a characteristic function in a game with transferable utility, and by inequality (6.7), it follows that the game $(N, -\phi)$ is convex. By Shapley's theorem from the previous section, $(N, -\phi)$ has a nonempty core. Let x be a vector in the core of $(N, -\phi)$. Then it follows that

$$\sum_{i \in S} x_i \geq -\phi(u, S) \quad \text{for all } S \subseteq N \tag{6.14}$$

and

$$\sum_{i \in N} x_i = -\phi(u, N) \tag{6.15}$$

By the properties of the balance weights for $S \in \mathcal{S}$ and conditions (6.13) to (6.15) it follows that

$$-\phi(u, N) = \sum_{i \in N} x_i = \sum_{S \in \mathcal{S}} \sigma_s \sum x_i$$

$$\geq \sum_{S \in \mathcal{S}} \sigma_s [-\phi(u, s)]$$

$$\geq \sum_{S \in \mathcal{S}} \sigma_s \sum_{i \in S} (-\omega_i)$$

$$= -\sum_{i \in N} \omega_i$$

Therefore

$$\phi(u, N) \leq \sum_{i \in N} \omega_i$$

and so $u \in V(N)$. Thus (N, V) is balanced and therefore has a nonempty core.

Q.E.D.

Proposition 6.2 is related to Proposition 5.4 of Chapter 5, in that both results assume complementarity of the cost function. In addition, the most likely circumstance in which outputs would be strict complements, in this result, would be if each buyer's utility function depends on only one component of the output vector q. This is a similar condition to the demand independence assumed in Chapter 5.

The general condition of strict output complementarity, however, is quite restrictive. An example of an industry in which this condition might be satisfied is a transportation network in which each user depends on several links in the system to travel from start to finish. Then it is plausible to think that the value of the service would be a function of the weakest link, and so the condition of strict complementarity would be satisfied.

Another interesting point is that the assumption of strict complementarity of demand gives a powerful incentive for large coalitions of buyers to form even in the absence of cost advantages to a large coalition. This is one aspect of the coordinating function of a firm that is entirely separate from the strictly technical condition of cost subadditivity.

Finally, note that Proposition 6.2 remains true, with only minor changes in the proof, for a market with public goods. The next two results convey further information about markets for public goods.

Proposition 6.3:

If there is only one public good, and each buyer's utility function is monotonic, then the core of (N, V) is nonempty.[12]

Proof:

As in the previous result, define the function

$$\phi(u, S) = \min\{C(q) | U_i(q) \geq u_i \text{ for all } i \in S\}$$

representing the minimum cost to coalition S of attaining the utility vector u. I will again show that $-\phi$ is a convex characteristic function.

Let $q(S)$ be such that $U_i[q(S)] \geq u_i$ for all $i \in S$; and let $q(S')$ be such that $U_i[q(S')] \geq u_i$ for all $i \in S'$. Let

$$x = \min\{q(S), q(S')\}$$
$$y = \max\{q(S), q(S')\}$$

Then

$$U_i(y) \geq u_i \text{ for all } i \in S \cup S'$$
$$U_i(x) \geq u_i \text{ for all } i \in S \cap S'$$

Therefore

$$\phi(u, S \cup S') + \phi(u, S \cap S') \leq C(x) + C(y)$$
$$= C[q(S)] + C[q(S')] \qquad (6.16)$$

Since expression (6.16) holds for all $q(S)$ such that $U_i[q(S)] \geq u_i, i \in S$ and $U_i[q(S')] \geq u_i, i \in S'$ it follows that

$$\phi(u, S) + \phi(u, S') \geq \phi(u, S \cup S') + \phi(u, S \cap S')$$

Therefore $-\phi$ is convex and it follows exactly as in Proposition 6.2, that the core of (N, V) is nonempty.

Q.E.D.

Proposition 6.3 confirms the intuitive result that for a public good there are powerful incentives for large coalitions for form.[13] The "free-rider" problem does not arise in the present context because in the definition of the game (N, V) it is assumed that coalitions S are concerned only with utility vectors that the members of S can

[12] This result was first demonstrated in Champsaur (1975).

[13] Public goods are also studied from the point of view of the core in Telser (1972; 1978; 1979).

guarantee with their own resources. If a public good is produced in a private market, one would expect exclusion of nonmembers of a coalition who do not contribute to the cost of production. In this case the assumptions underlying the definition of the sets $V(S)$ are quite reasonable.

However, one issue that is not adequately addressed in the present theory is the revelation of preferences among the members of a coalition. In the model it is assumed that buyers enter coalitions with an endowment ω_i, all of which must be used for production, because buyers are assumed to place no value on the unused portion of their endowment. In general, players do value resources that are used in the production of public goods, and for this reason each player has an incentive to misrepresent his or her true preferences for the public good.

One might expect that Proposition 6.3 could be generalized to the case of many public goods. However, the example at the end of Chapter 5 (which could easily be reformulated as a nonside payment game) shows that this expectation is not justified. The problem is that with several public goods, opinions may differ among the buyers about which goods should be produced, or at what levels they should be produced. (The proof of Proposition 6.3 depended crucially on the fact that there was only one public good that all buyers valued monotonically.) What is needed in a market with several public goods is a consensus among the buyers on the choice of an output vector by the coalition. If the public good outputs are strict complements to all buyers, then a particularly strong form of consensus exists, and a public goods version of Proposition 6.2 can be used to demonstrate a nonempty core. A different interpretation of a social consensus is contained in the following result.[14]

Definition:

Let S be balanced collection of coalitions, with weights δ_S, and suppose $u \in V(S)$ for all $S \in S$. Let

$$\phi(u, S) = \min\{C(q) | U_i(q) \geq u_i \text{ for all } i \in S\} \tag{6.17}$$

---

[14] Many issues that arise in social choice theory are also related to the existence of a core in a public goods economy. For example, if preferences are described by "ideal points" that are distributed over the real line, then it is known that a sufficient condition for a group consensus to exist is that the distribution of ideal points be single peaked.

and let $Q(u, S)$ represent the set of output vectors at which the minimum in inequality (6.17) is attained. Suppose that $q(S)$ is chosen from $Q(S)$ for each $S \in S$. Then preferences are said to be "supportable" if

$$q(S) \leq \sum_{S \in S} \delta_S q(S) \qquad (6.18)$$

for each $S \in S$.[15]

The term on the right-hand side of inequality (6.18) represents the "average" choice over all coalitions $S \in S$. Thus inequalities (6.18) require that no coalition in a balanced collection can find it advantageous to select a vector of outputs $q(S)$ that exceeds in any component the average choice of all players.

With this result it is now a simple matter to prove the following claim.

Proposition 6.4

In a market for public goods, if each buyer's utility function is monotonic, preferences are supportable, and the cost function is supportable, then the core of (N, V) is nonempty.

Proof:

Let S be balanced. Let $u \in V(S)$ and choose $q(S) \in Q(u, S)$ for each $S \in S$. Then

$$C[q(S)] \leq \sum_{i \in S} \omega_i$$

By hypothesis,

$$q(S) \leq \sum_{S \in S} \delta_S q(S) = \tilde{q}$$

for each $S \in S$ and by monotonicity of U_i,

$$U_i(\tilde{q}) \geq U_i[q(S)] \geq u_i$$

for each $i \in N$. By supportability of the cost function,

$$C(\tilde{q}) \leq \sum_{S \in S} \delta_S C[q(S)] \leq \sum_{S \in S} \delta_S \sum_{i \in S} \omega_i = \sum_{i \in N} \omega_i$$

Therefore $u \in V(N)$; (N, V) is balanced; and so the core of (N, V) is nonempty.

Q.E.D.

---

[15] The condition of supportable preferences is, of course, a condition on both preferences and costs because the vectors $q(S)$ depend on both the cost function C and the utility functions U_i.

6.3   Destructive competition: examples of unstable markets

Two general conclusions can be extracted from the previous section. In a market for private goods the core of the associated game is nonempty if there are uniformly increasing returns to scale in production. In a market for public goods the core is nonempty if the preferences of buyers are supportable or if other conditions favoring a concensus are satisfied. In this section I will present three detailed examples of markets in which the core is empty. As a general rule, in a private goods market with an empty core, there are increasing returns to scale in production that are followed by decreasing returns. This characterization applies to an unsustainable natural monopoly and in one way or another to each of the examples in this section. In each example, however, the phenomenon of decreasing returns to scale arises from somewhat subtle sources. Even when the apparent production function exhibits economies of scale throughout the range of outputs, the derived cost function, reflecting the cost of serving coalitions of buyers, may introduce decreasing returns characteristics, which may therefore lead to an empty core.

Much of the formality of the previous section can be dispensed with because only examples rather than theorems will be considered here. In order to maintain an economy of notation, I will in all cases describe games in transferable utility terms, instead of in the more general nonside payment terms. (Of course, a counterexample that assumes transferable utility is also a counterexample in a nonside payment game.)

Example 1:   A market with uncertain demand:
        The first example is a continuation of the discussion of a market for a single private good in which firms have identical U-shaped average cost functions. In the discussion following Proposition 6.1 it was shown that if there are two or more active firms, then the core is empty unless the total market demand is exactly equal to the total capacity (defined as output that minimizes average cost) of an integral number of plants. If there are no forces in the market that tend to equate aggregate demand with aggregate capacity, then it would appear that the core is nearly always empty.

There are two possible explanations for a persistent imbalance of demand and aggregate capacity. One is that there are large, unavoidable indivisibilities in the production process, so that the output at which average cost is a minimum is rigidly set by the technology. Then if demand is also inelastic, an unstable market may result.

Production processes, however, are not totally inflexible. In most industries, in the long run, plants of almost any capacity can be constructed with little loss in efficiency. (In other words, the long-run average cost function is thought to be flat over wide ranges of output.) By this logic it follows that the instability of a market that results from an imbalance of demand and supply is only a short-run, or transitional, problem.

The second possibility for an imbalance of demand and supply is that demand itself may be fluctuating or fundamentally uncertain, and as long as demand changes more rapidly than supply can adjust, there will be no long run tendency toward equilibrium. These conditions can lead to a persistently unstable market.

To describe this possibility more formally, consider the following model.[16] Suppose that there is a collection of identical buyers, each of whom is small relative to the size of the market. Also, suppose that each buyer demands one unit of a single homogeneous output and is willing to pay a price of b units if he or she receives that output. Assume that the total number of buyers is uncertain. Let t be the actual number of buyers that results from a drawing from the underlying distribution, and assume that t is distributed uniformly on the interval $[0, 1]$. The density function for this distribution is given by

$$f(t) = \begin{cases} 1 & \text{if } t \in [0, 1] \\ 0 & \text{otherwise} \end{cases}$$

Suppose that there is free entry into the industry, but that in order to enter, a firm must commit itself to a plant of capacity q. Let the cost of a plant of size q be given by $f + cq$, with the following interpretation. The constant "f" is a fixed cost of entry that must be incurred before any production can take place. The term "cq" is to be regarded as a fixed, but avoidable, cost of production. That is, if a plant of size q is used in production, then the cost of operation is given by cq and any output t, $0 < t \leq q$ can be produced. However, the firm also has the option of shutting the plant down and avoiding the cost cq.

Because average cost of production is falling, it would appear that this is a classic natural monopoly industry. However, the

[16] A more detailed analysis of this model is contained in Sharkey (1977). See also, Telser (1978).

uncertainty of demand, indicates that this is not necessarily the case. Consider the optimal choice of scale of a single plant. The firm wishes to choose q so as to maximize the total expected surplus in the market. (As a monopolist, the firm could appropriate the entire surplus for itself.) This expected surplus is shown as the shaded area in Figure 6.7. If the number of buyers is $t < cq/b$, surplus is zero, as the firm would prefer to avoid the cost cq. If $t > q$, surplus is $(b - c)q$ because the plant is operating at full capacity. Total expected surplus is given by

$$S(q) = \int_{\frac{cq}{b}}^{q} (bt - cq)dt + (1 - q)(b - c)q$$

and one may readily calculate that the optimal q is given by $q^* = b/(b + c)$.

Now suppose that the firm decides to operate two plants q_1 and q_2 such that $q_1 + q_2 = q^*$. Then it may be seen in Figure 6.8 that for fixed q^* total surplus increases by an amount equal to the heavily shaded region of the diagram. Actual surplus may increase somewhat more, with an optimal choice of q_1 and q_2 because the firm may wish to choose a total capacity other than q^*. However, it is clear that as long as the increase in surplus is greater than the increase in fixed cost f, then the firm will prefer to operate with two separate plants. A discussion of the full optimum, including the optimal number of plants, is described in Sharkey (1977).

An important result of the preceding model is the following. If one firm chooses to operate multiple plants in the industry, then there is room in the industry for multiple firms.[17] Suppose, as an extreme case, that each plant in the industry is managed by a different firm. Then one can investigate the status of the core for all possible realizations of demand.

I will assume that there are two firms in the industry that have plants with capacities q_1 and q_2. In Figure 6.9(a) the heavily shaded function $C(t)$ represents the true cost of supplying any coalition $t \in [0, 1]$, including the cost of foregone demand if some buyers in the coalition do not receive output. A characteristic function $v(t) = bt - C(t)$ may therefore be defined giving the maximum net surplus that any coalition t of buyers could obtain. As shown in Figure 6.9(b), v is a piecewise linear function, which is everywhere

---

[17] However, the end result of multiple firm competition in the market is instability. Thus one may also use this example as a justification for firm subadditivity, which is independent of plant subadditivity. See Section 4.4 for further details.

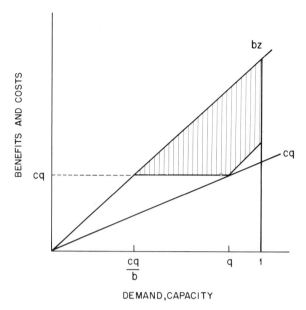

FIGURE 6.7

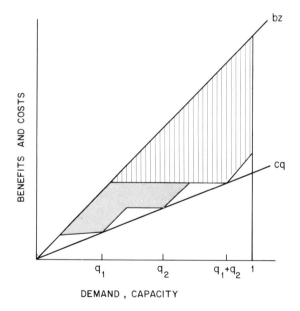

FIGURE 6.8

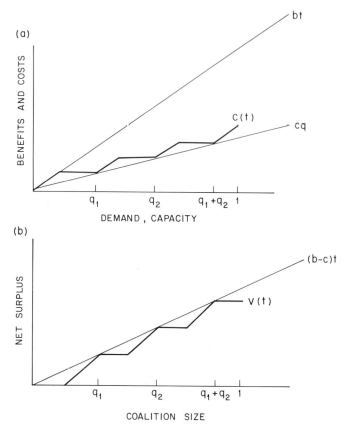

FIGURE 6.9

less than or equal to the ray $(b - c)t$, with equality at $t = q_1$, $t = q_2$, and $t = q_1 + q_2$.

Recall from Section 6.1 that in a continuous game with one type of player the core is nonempty if and only if $v(t)/t \geq v(s)/s$ for all s, such that $0 \leq s \leq t$. Thus in this example the core is nonempty only if $t \leq q_1$, $t = q_2$, or $t = q_1 + q_2$. As in a multifirm market with U-shaped average cost, the core is nearly always empty.

Needless to say, there are many important issues that are not addressed by a model like the preceding one, in which firms do not explicitly enter as participants in the market behavior. However, the simple analysis does suggest that uncertainty, or periodicity of demand, coupled with rigidity of supply, may result in market instability.

Example 2:   A model of retail sales

In this example I consider a spatial model of demand that in other variations has received considerable attention.[18] The essential feature of a spatial model is that consumers are distributed more or less continuously over a region and that stores that satisfy consumer demand can be located at only a finite number of locations due to the fixed costs of operating a store. A particularly simple version of the model assumes that buyers are located on the circumference of a circle and that all travel is restricted to the circumference. A straight line would do just as well but would require treating buyers near the end points as a special case. Even greater realism could be obtained by placing buyers on a two-dimensional surface. These variations, however, serve more to complicate the model than to add new insight.

Therefore assume that the market consists of a circle of unit circumference on which a continuum of buyers is uniformly distributed. Let S denote the grand coalition of all buyers. Suppose that each buyer desires one unit of a good for which he or she is willing to pay a price b. Assume that stores can locate at any point on the circle and that the only cost of operating a store is the fixed cost f. Suppose, however, that there are delivery costs of c per unit of distance.

Now consider the game in which coalitions of buyers form and construct stores at locations so as to maximize the net consumer surplus. It is necessary to consider only coalitions of buyers that are connected subsets of S. Therefore one can describe coalitions by their total size s, where $0 \leq s \leq 1$.

Throughout this example I will assume that $b \geq c/2$, so that all buyers will be served under all possible configurations of stores. Consider a coalition of size s. If it chooses to build one store, the total net surplus that the coalition can achieve is given by

$$\psi(s, 1) = bs - \frac{cs^2}{4} - f$$

which corresponds to the shaded area in Figures 6.10, minus the fixed cost f. More generally, with a coalition of size s and k stores the total net surplus is given by

---

[18] The original spatial model is due to Hotelling (1929). Telser (1978) also analyzes a spatial model using the theory of the core and reaches substantially the same conclusions as the present example.

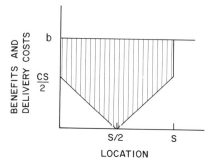

FIGURE 6.10

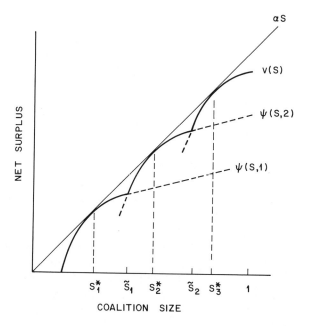

FIGURE 6.11

$$\psi(s, k) = bs - \frac{cs^2}{4k} - kf$$

Observe that for all $s \in [0, 1]$ and $k = 1, 2, \ldots,$

$$\psi(s, k) = k\psi(\frac{s}{k}, 1)$$

A coalition may choose the number of stores that gives it maximum net surplus. Therefore

$$v(s) = \max_{k=0,1,2,\ldots} \psi(s, k)$$

In other words, $v(s)$ is the upper envelope of the family of functions $\psi(s, k)$. The function v is illustrated in Figure 6.11. Observe that $v(s) = 0$ for small s due to the fixed cost f.

It is now possible to determine the status of the core in this example. Let s_k^* be the size of coalition that maximizes $\psi(s, k)/s$. It is easily seen that

$$s_k^* = \left[\frac{4k^2 f}{c}\right]^{\frac{1}{2}} = ks_1^* \text{ for } k = 1, 2, \ldots$$

Now let $\tilde{s}_k$ be the size of the coalition that is just indifferent between having k and $k + 1$ stores. Solving $\psi(s, k) = \psi(s, k + 1)$ gives the result

$$\tilde{s}_k = \left[\frac{4k(k+1)f}{c}\right]^{\frac{1}{2}} > s_k^* \text{ for } k = 1, 2, \ldots$$

Therefore, it may be seen that as in Figure 6.11, $v(s)/s$ attains a maximum of $\alpha^* = b - (cf)^{\frac{1}{2}}$ at $s = s_k^*$, $k = 1, \ldots$. At all other values of s, $v(s)/s < \alpha^*$. Therefore from the results on cores of continuous games from Section 6.1 it follows that the core of the retail trade model is empty unless $s_1^* \geq 1$ or $s_k^* = 1$ for some $k = 2, 3, \ldots$.

As in other examples of this type, the core constraints are violated by the largest amount when there are a small number of stores. The largest deviation of $\alpha^* - v(s)/s$ occurs at $s = \tilde{s}_1$. If the market can accommodate a much larger number of stores, then it is true that the core constraints are almost satisfied.

Example 3: A simple model of network flows[19]

Consider a finite set $K = \{1, \ldots, k\}$ of agents among whom there is a demand for pairwise traffic flows. For example, telephone subscribers may wish to communicate with other subscribers in the network, individual users may wish to be connected to a central supplier of gas or electricity, or a planner may be interested in designing a transportation network among cities.

K defines the set of nodes in a network. The total number of pairs of nodes, or arcs, is equal to $k(k - 1)/2$. Let A be the set of all arcs. Let $N = \{1, \ldots, n\}$ be a subset of A representing the set of players in a game, where $n \leq k(k - 1)/2$, and such that each pair

---

[19] This example is derived from Topkis (1981).

$i \in N$ has traffic flow $h_i > 0$ to be carried by the network. Thus the set of players is the subset of the set of all arcs, on which there are positive traffic flows.

It is not necessary to construct a link connecting every pair $i \in N$ in order to minimize total network costs. If there are economies of scale in the construction of capacity on individual links, traffic from several pairs can use the same links and therefore achieve lower costs. In addition, it may be desirable to use arcs that connect pairs of nodes in the network for which there is no traffic. Let $C_j(z)$ be the cost of constructing z units of capacity on the arc j. Let P_i be the collection of all paths joining the pair $i \in N$ and let Q_j be the set of all paths that include arc j.

Then each coalition S must determine a path $T_i \in P_i$ for each $i \in S$ so as to minimize

$$\sum_{j \in A} C_j \left[\sum_{\{i : i \in S, T_i \in Q_j\}} h_i \right]$$

If the minimum cost is given by $C(S)$ and each player achieves a utility of $U_i(h_i)$, then a characteristic function in a transferable utility game may be defined by

$$\nu(S) = \sum_{i \in S} U_i(h_i) - C(S)$$

Necessary and sufficient conditions for the existence of a core in the preceding game could be expressed in terms of certain balancedness conditions.[20] It is not sufficient, however, to place restrictions only on the cost function C. Even with a well-behaved cost function and strongly increasing returns to scale, the core may be empty.

Consider, for example, the network in Figure 6.12 that has seven nodes and nine arcs. Suppose that there are positive traffic flows on three nodal pairs, which are then the players in the game. Let $N = \{(a, g), (c, g), (e, g)\} = \{1, 2, 3\}$ be the set of players. Assume that $h_i = 1$ and that $U_i(1) = 2$ for $i = 1, 2, 3$. Also, assume that $C_j(z) = z^\alpha$ for every arc j and some α such that $0 < \alpha < 1$. Costs on each link are concave, so that both average and marginal cost are decreasing functions of capacity. However, increasing returns on individual links do not translate into increasing returns for the game.

One may easily determine that ν has the following values:

[20] See Kalai and Zemel (1980, 1981).

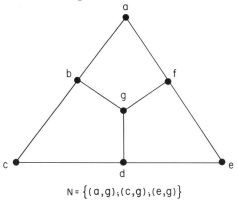

$$N = \{(a,g);(c,g);(e,g)\}$$

FIGURE 6.12

$$\nu(\varnothing) = 0$$
$$\nu(\{i\}) = 0 \qquad i = 1, 2, 3$$
$$\nu(\{i, j\}) = 2 - 2^\alpha \quad i, j = 1, 2, 3; i \neq j$$
$$\nu(\{1, 2, 3\}) = 2 - 2^\alpha$$

The three pairs of players form a balanced collection, with weight vector $(\frac{1}{2}, \frac{1}{2}, \frac{1}{2})$. Since

$$3(\frac{1}{2})(2 - 2^\alpha) > (2 - 2^\alpha)$$

it follows that the core of (N,v) is empty.

6.4   Concluding comments

In this chapter it has been demonstrated that a reasonably simple model of cooperative game may be used to describe the underlying stability of a market in which there is free entry. It was shown that there are plausible conditions under which a market with a single firm is stable. These conditions include some familiar properties of the cost function that are essentially the same as the conditions that were shown in Chapters 4 and 5 to be sufficient for subadditivity or sustainability. In addition, it was observed in the examples that a market with a large number of firms is "almost" stable in that there are outcomes in the game that violate the core constraints by only a small amount.

The examples of destructive competition are most persuasive in cases in which the optimal number of firms in a market is greater than one, but still small. Even with a small number of firms, however, it must be concluded that competition is destructive only in particular circumstances, as were, for example, described in the three examples of the previous section.

A number of caveats are in order with respect to the analysis of this chapter. First, in a cooperative game model, coalitions are generally assumed to form costlessly. In the present context it was also suggested that coalitions could be usefully identified with firms and that the mechanism of coalition formation was an essential part of a theory of the firm. One striking characteristic of real firms, however, is that they do not at all times operate with perfect efficiency. Capital market imperfections may impede the birth of new firms; and sunk costs may prevent existing firms from seizing new opportunities. Each of these effects may tend to promote stability in an oligopolistic market that would otherwise be unstable.

A second caveat concerns the use of a cooperative game model itself. Any cooperative game is derived from an underlying noncooperative game, and it is possible that important aspects of the strategic interaction of players are lost. In the present model, for example, the strategic behavior of firms in an oligopoly setting is not in any way captured.

The basic conclusion of this chapter, however, remains valid, despite these caveats. In a market in which there is free entry and the number of firms is small, but greater than one, there will be no broadly applicable theorems that guarantee stability and there will be a number of examples of markets that are unstable.

CHAPTER 7

Competition in natural monopoly and natural oligopoly markets

This chapter has two objectives: (1) to describe some basic issues associated with the regulation of natural monopoly firms and (2) to set out a theoretical framework in which to examine both the nature of competition and the need for regulation in natural monopoly or natural oligopoly markets. A "natural oligopoly" is a market in which the number of firms that minimizes total industry cost is greater than one but not so large as to make the market competitive.

Section 7.1 is concerned with the possible objectives of regulation in a natural monopoly or natural oligopoly market. These may include a desire to promote efficiency, fairness, or stability. In this section five more specific objectives are enumerated and discussed, with special attention to the interrelationships and possible conflicts among the objectives.

The need for regulation to promote efficiency in a market is considered in more detail in Section 7.2. In particular, it is argued that the need for this form of regulation may be less than commonly imagined. Although in an efficient natural monopoly market there can be only one active firm, many inactive firms may exist. That is, there may be firms producing closely related products that would be willing and able to enter into competition with, and ultimately replace, the incumbent firm if that firm does not produce at the lowest possible cost or produce the set of outputs desired by consumers. The appropriate question is therefore whether or not the potential competition of inactive firms can be more effective in promoting efficiency than direct regulation of the market. A market in which potential competition operates in an ideal form is called a "contestable market." In a contestable market both entry and exit of firms must be free and unconstrained — there can be no barriers to entry or exit of firms. Thus Section 7.2 discusses the nature of contestable markets and barriers to entry.

The most important result of Section 7.2 is that fixed costs do not by themselves constitute a barrier to entry. However, sunk costs are by nature costs that must be incurred by a new entrant but which are not recognized as costs by an incumbent firm. Therefore sunk costs are a barrier to entry.

The distinction between a fixed cost and a sunk cost is necessarily dynamic in character. At issue is the difference between the ex ante value, or cost, of the resources required for a given project and the value ex post, after the resources have been fully committed to the project. Section 7.3 contains a short discussion of dynamic markets, suggesting that markets that are growing or undergoing technological change are particularly likely to have sunk costs. Therefore these markets are less likely to be contestable.

Finally, Section 7.4 considers two of the more complex pricing strategies, namely, limit pricing and predatory pricing, which firms may use in a natural monopoly or natural oligopoly market. A limit pricing strategy by an incumbent firm in an industry involves a price that is set so as to limit entry into the industry and thereby to maximize the discounted sum of long-run profits to the incumbent. However, a limit price is one that is stationary over time unless external circumstances, other than the entry or exit of rival firms, change. Thus a "limit price" is a price set by an incumbent firm in recognition of the possibility of entry but without intending to intimidate the potential entrants.

A "predatory pricing strategy," on the other hand, is one that explicitly uses price as a threat against potential rivals. In a predatory pricing strategy the incumbent firm clearly indicates that it is willing to lower its price temporarily if entry should occur and thereby inflict short-run losses both on itself and on the entrant. After the rival has left the industry, the incumbent can then raise its price to the monopoly level and therefore recover its short-run losses.

The analysis in Section 7.4 consists of an economic (but not a legal) interpretation of limit pricing and predatory pricing in the context of U.S. antitrust laws. Two conclusions are reached: (1) Although predatory pricing is quite clearly anticompetitive, it is not easy to define precisely what a predatory pricing strategy is. (2) Although some interpretations of the law are ambiguous, it is argued that limit pricing is generally acceptable under the antitrust laws. There may also be some difficulty in practice in distinguishing a limit pricing strategy from a predatory pricing strategy.

7.1   The rationale for regulation

I will argue in this section that there are five essentially distinct objectives that justify the imposition of some regulation in a natural monopoly market. These objectives can be briefly described as follows:

1. Society may wish to protect buyers from a price that is too high and to recapture the loss in consumer surplus associated with monopoly pricing.[1]

2. Society may wish to protect a natural monopolist from opportunistic behavior on the part of customers or other firms.

3. Society may wish to promote stability in an unstable market.

4. Society may wish to delineate the market boundaries that separate a natural monopoly sector from a closely related competitive sector of a given market.

5. Society may wish to prevent collusion among incumbent firms or certain behavioral abuses, such as predatory pricing.

The argument for type 1 regulation is familiar to all economists. An unconstrained monopolist will set a price equal to marginal revenue rather than to marginal cost, and in general, the price will be set at a level greater than the average cost of production.[2] The traditional view is that regulation can improve both consumer welfare and economic efficiency in such circumstances by setting a price equal to average cost of production, as in Figure 7.1. The mechanism by which average cost pricing is usually enforced is the rate of return constraint, whereby a regulator determines a rate base (which corresponds roughly to the capital inputs used in production) and an allowed rate of return. This mechanism may introduce a distortion[3] in the firm's choice of inputs, and at best, regulation by rate of return can drive the price down only to average cost. Thus it may conceivably prevent the firm from using a multipart tariff or other nonlinear pricing schedule that could bring the price (for the marginal unit sold) closer to marginal cost.

Despite these objections the underlying rationale for type 1

---

[1] This loss in surplus is explained in Chapter 3 in the discussion of unconstrained monopoly pricing.

[2] If the profit-maximizing price for a monopolist is equal to average cost, then regulation can do nothing to improve consumer welfare or productive efficiency.

[3] See Averch and Johnson (1962) and Bailey (1973).

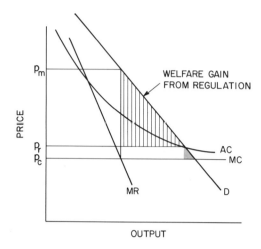

FIGURE 7.1

regulation went unquestioned for many years. Recently, however, the need for this type of regulation has been examined in more detail by Demsetz (1968) and later by Bailey and Panzar (1981) and Baumol, Panzar, and Willig (1982). These authors observed that in the long run a monopoly firm can earn a positive profit only if there is a barrier to the entry of new firms. In a market without barriers to entry, also known as a contestable market, monopoly firms, whether or not natural, cannot earn positive profits. The traditional view of type 1 regulation may therefore be reformulated as the proposition that markets are generally not perfectly contestable, which will be explained in more detail in the following section.

Also of interest in the theory of type 1 regulation are some recent attempts to design mechanisms that are to an extent self-enforcing or which require minimal intervention on the part of the regulator. For example, Vogelsang and Finsinger (1979) have proposed a procedure in which a multiproduct monopolist is given an incentive to choose a Ramsey optimal price vector. A different proposal, suggested by Loeb and Magat (1979), uses a subsidy to encourage a single-product monopolist to set a price equal to marginal cost.[4] More results of this type are likely in the future, which may

---

[4] The advantage of this proposal is that costs need not be known or verified by the regulator.

ultimately enhance the desirability of type 1 regulation.

A less familiar basis for regulation is the need to protect explicitly a natural monopolist from the forces of competition. As demonstrated at length in Chapter 5, entry may possibly occur in a natural monopoly market even if the monopolist produces efficiently and does not earn positive profits. Thus to the extent that entry results in inefficient production, it may be desirable to place restrictions on the competitive process when an unsustainable natural monopoly is known to exist.

Independently of the sustainability literature, it has also been recognized that monopoly firms may at times be vulnerable to opportunistic behavior on the part of their consumers and other firms.[5] If production requires the commitment of large amounts of nonfungible plant (i.e., if there are large sunk costs), then a monopoly firm may be forced to lower its price to the variable cost of production, under the threat that its customers could seek an alternative supplier. In a growing market in which there are economies of scale, or in an industry with continuous technological advancement, such threats may be particularly troublesome. In order to satisfy demand, a monopoly firm must commit itself to a plant of a given vintage or a given scale. Before the existing plant has worn out, however, or been allowed to depreciate fully, pressure is likely from a new set of customers who would like to secure the advantages of the current technology or scale of production. In other words, in a dynamic market a natural monopoly with sunk costs may be inherently unsustainable.[6]

Thus type 2 regulation requires constraints on the process of competition. For example, minimum prices may be set and entry may be limited by the regulatory agency. Although these forms of regulation have been used, largely in the transportation and communications industries, the results have been disappointing. It is not clear whether regulations of this type have ever been proven more efficient than the market-generated solution. An example of a market response to opportunistic behavior, or nonsustainability, is the long-term contract between a firm and its customers. Furthermore, as Klein, Crawford, and Alchian (1978) note, there is

[5] See Goldberg (1976), Klein, Crawford, and Alchian (1978); and Williamson (1975).

[6] The unsustainability, or opportunistic behavior, arises because sunk costs act as a "barrier to exit." In the next section it will be argued that sunk costs are also a barrier to entry.

also an incentive toward vertical integration if integration is expected to be more efficient than the contractual equilibrium.

The justification for type 3 regulation is substantially the same as for type 2 regulation, although the argument is perhaps more compelling for type 3, if the market is known to be unstable. An unsustainable natural monopoly can be viewed, in fact, as a special type of unstable market. There is a distinction, however, which is useful to maintain. In an unsustainable monopoly the existing competition is asymmetric between an incumbent monopolist and one or more rivals outside the industry. In a market with unstable competition the presumption is that all firms compete on an equal basis. It would seem then that the consequences of totally unregulated competition would be more severe in an unstable market, due to the possibility of total market failure — that is, the inability of any firm to survive.

The next case that can be made for regulation concerns the definition of the market boundaries for a natural monopoly. If all markets are contestable, then the boundaries of a natural monopoly market are no more a subject for regulation than are the boundaries of a perfectly competitive industry. Thus a single firm can be active in both natural monopoly and competitive markets. If some markets are not contestable, however, the regulatory mechanism in the uncontestable sector and the competitive process in the contestable sector may be difficult to coordinate, in practice, if not in theory.[7]

Finally, the need for type 5 regulation, where regulation is broadly construed so as to include antitrust laws, is similar to the need for type 1 regulation. Collusion may allow several firms to act as one and so inflict on consumers all the costs of unconstrained monopoly. Similarly, predatory behavior may be used by an incumbent monopolist to forestall entry by rival firms. In either case, social welfare could be potentially improved by policies that promote entry by new firms.

The preceding discussion highlights some of the complexity that may be present in regulatory situations. For example, it might be argued that encouraging entry and competition is desirable in the case of a sustainable natural monopoly, in order to reduce the need

---

[7] In theory, a natural monopoly firm should be allowed to participate in any market in which its incremental cost is less than the total cost of the specialty firms in that market, if the total cost of production in all markets is to be minimized. In practice, however, neither the regulatory agency, nor the specialty firms in the contestable sector, know with any accuracy the incremental costs of the natural monopolist, and so charges of anticompetitive conduct seem inevitable.

for type 1 regulation. However, if the natural monopoly is unsustainable, then easier entry and more competition increase the need for type 2 regulation. Furthermore, a market solution to the problem of unsustainable natural monopoly, which would eliminate the need for type 2 regulation, may result in a larger, vertically integrated monopoly, which would require more careful consideration of the market boundaries of the natural monopoly.

On the other hand, it might be argued that the possibility of market instability may be the prime factor that tends to make a market uncontestable, due to the resulting uncertainty on the part of incumbent firms and potential competitors about the final equilibrium if entry should occur. In this case, policies that discourage entry, where entry is clearly destabilizing, may actually encourage it more generally, and such policies would therefore enhance the contestability of the market.

Finally, it should be observed that behavior appearing to be anticompetitive may in fact serve a useful function if it increases either the stability of an otherwise unstable market or the efficiency with which outputs are produced. A long-term contract, or an exclusive right to sell in a particular market, may allow a firm to serve an unsustainable market at lower cost than would be achieved in a regulated market.

To resolve these issues, or even to begin to formulate a blueprint for regulatory policy will not be possible in the remainder of this chapter. Instead, the analysis will focus on two of the more manageable questions. Sections 7.2 and 7.3 will be concerned with the entry and exit of firms in a market, and Section 7.4 will deal with the behavior of an incumbent natural monopolist.

7.2   Contestable markets and barriers to entry

The theory of a contestable market has been developed by Baumol, Panzar, and Willig (1982) in order to describe a market with perfect freedom of entry and exit. [See also Bailey and Panzar (1981), Bailey (1981), Baumol and Willig (1981), and Willig (1980).] Much of the material in Chapters 4, 5, and 6 was presented under the implicit assumption that markets are contestable. For example, a natural monopoly was said to be sustainable if a price-output pair exists such that the monopolist satisfies all demand at the quoted price, earns nonnegative profits, and no rival firm would wish to enter any portion of the monopolist's market. Because entry into a natural monopoly market necessarily results in higher costs of production, a possible goal of regulation would be to prevent such entry as suggested in the previous section. However, if there are barriers to entry, such regulation would be unwarranted.

On the other hand, the traditional view of regulation has held that due to barriers to entry, regulation may be required to protect buyers. To the extent that entry is free and the market is contestable, it will be subsequently demonstrated that this form of regulation is unwarranted. In other words, a critical variable in determining the proper role of regulation in a given market is the extent to which there is free entry in that market. The remainder of this section will therefore examine more carefully the nature of barriers to entry, in order to characterize a contestable market.

Consider two models that have been used to describe entry behavior. The first depicts an asymmetric industry in which there is a single dominant firm and a competitive fringe, which consists of a large number of independent producers that are operating on a small scale compared to the dominant firm.[8] In this model no strategic interaction exists among firms in the industry. Each of the competitive fringe firms is assumed to be a price taker, and the aggregate behavior of this sector is completely described by means of a supply function, as in Figure 7.2. The dominant firm faces a residual demand given by the difference between market demand and fringe supply. Like any monopolist, the dominant firm monopolist is assumed to choose a price and quantity (shown as p_{dom} and q_{dom} in Figure 7.2) so as to maximize residual profits.

In this model it is not generally advantageous for the dominant firm to prevent all entry by competitive firms. Furthermore, the monopolist does not pursue a limit pricing strategy because a trade-off between present and future profits does not exist.[9] Rather, the

---

[8] A classic example of a dominant firm with a competitive fringe is the electric power industry. The dominant firm is a regulated public utility that generates power from a number of sources. The competitive fringe consists of a large number of very small-scale hydroelectric facilities. The supply of small-scale hydroelectric power depends on both geography (number of inches of rainfall, speed and vertical drop in water flows, etc.) and the availability of used or abandoned equipment to locate at the sites. In many cases the public utility is required by law to purchase power from the small-scale producer that at a price reflects the marginal cost of alternative fuels. More details may be found in McPhee (1981).

[9] Limit pricing will be discussed more completely in the model of large-scale entry, below, and in Section 7.6. It should be noted, however, that limit pricing behavior does arise in the dominant firm model if the rate of future competitive entry is a function of the dominant firm's current price. This model has been explored by Gaskins (1971).

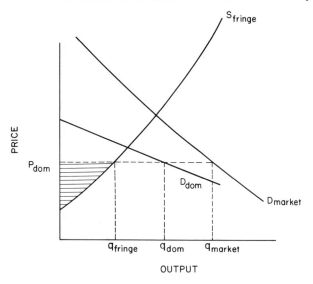

FIGURE 7.2

dominant firm accommodates the entry behavior or the competitive sector into the objective function that it seeks to maximize.

This model is based on a presumption that there are barriers to the entry of large-scale firms. Otherwise, the individual firms in the competitive fringe could be expected to grow over time, because they earn supernormal profits, as shown by the shaded area in Figure 7.2. The nature of the barriers to entry is not, however, described or in any way explained in the dominant firm model.

The second model of entry attempts to describe large-scale entry by firms that are potentially able to compete on the same basis as the incumbent firm.[10] The advantage of incumbency, however, turns out to be a substantial advantage in this type of model. As Scherer (1970; p. 225) states:

The problem in essence, is that a firm contemplating entry at a large scale has reason to fear that its incremental output contribution will be absorbed by the market only if the price is reduced. As a result, even though the entrant's costs will be just as low as those of firms presently in the industry, and even though the pre-entry price exceeds the entrant's full expected unit cost, the price after entry may fall below cost, and entry will prove to be unprofitable. If this is anticipated, entry will be deterred.

[10] The model of large-scale entry is due to Bain (1956), Sylos-Labini (1962), and Modigliani (1958).

Everything depends on what the potential entrant expects the incumbent firm to do after entry occurs. Bain (1956) and Sylos-Labini (1962) assume that potential entrants expect incumbent firms to continue to produce output at preentry levels. Consider Figure 7.3 in which the market demand and the average costs of the incumbent firm are shown as solid lines. Suppose that the monopoly price and output pair is given by p_m and q_m in Figure 7.3. Then if a potential entrant expects that q_m will be maintained after entry, it follows that the residual demand remaining to the entrant is given by $D_e = D_{market} - q_m$. It is as if the entrant expects the monopolist to adhere to the totally inelastic supply function S_m in Figure 7.3, even at prices below average cost. If the entrant has a similar cost function, clearly there is no price and output combination at which a profit could be made, and so entry is deterred. In fact, for the cost and demand functions as shown in Figure 7.3, the incumbent firm is able to deter entry by a significantly more efficient rival, even at the profit-maximizing price.

Now consider Figure 7.4 in which either average cost is lower or market demand is higher. Here, under the Bain-Sylos-Labini assumptions, a price equal to the monopoly price p_m would invite entry if a rival has the same average costs as the incumbent. However, by choosing a lower price p_l and an output q_l, the incumbent firm can drive the residual demand curve to a point of tangency with average cost, thereby deterring entry.

In this model p_l is a limit price, as opposed to a price that merely limits entry. By choosing a price other than p_m, and accepting less than maximum profits in the short run, the incumbent firm is able to prevent entry, and so presumably to maximize profits in the long run.

Given the assumption that incumbent firms maintain preentry outputs after entry occurs, the preceding argument demonstrates that economies of scale are themselves a barrier to entry. Therefore if this assumption is an accurate characterization of the behavior of real firms, then natural monopoly markets are never contestable markets. This view is perhaps the dominant view in the economics profession at present. However, there have been a few dissenting voices. Demsetz (1968) was one of the first to argue that there is no contradiction in the assertion that a natural monopoly market is also potentially competitive.[11] Although, indeed, economies of scale do prevent more than one firm from actively operating in the market at any given time, it is perfectly plausible to suppose that a large

[11] See Crain and Ekelund (1976) for further discussion of the Demsetz argument and related issues.

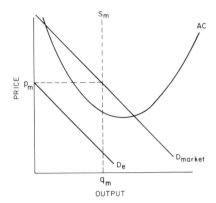

FIGURE 7.3

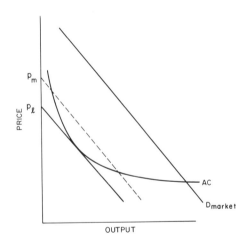

FIGURE 7.4

number of potential entrants would be willing to replace the natural monopolist. For example, franchise bidding schemes, which allow a regulatory body to choose a supplier on the basis of competitive bids, have received some attention in the regulatory literature.[12]

[12] See, for example, Williamson (1976).

The contestability of a natural monopoly market then depends on the efficacy of the process of potential competition. A priori there is no reason to expect competition among a given number of potential rivals to be any more or less intense than competition among the same number of active rivals. The main problem apparently is that in a natural monopoly market it is uncertain as to how many potential rivals really exist. It seems clear, however, that the logic of the Demsetz argument is correct, in that potential competition can conceivably work. If so, then it must also be concluded that, contrary to the Bain-Sylos-Labini argument, economies of scale do not of themselves constitute a barrier to entry. In this case a natural monopoly market could resemble in most respects a perfectly competitive market, in that profits would be forced to zero and regulation in which the sole objective is to set price equal to average cost would not be required.[13]

Thus far it has been demonstrated that a fixed cost may or may not be a barrier to entry. Consider now the effects of sunk costs on entry. Recall that in any given project or expenditure of funds, the sunk cost is the difference between the ex ante opportunity cost of the funds and the value that could be recovered, ex-post, if it is decided to terminate the project. A fixed cost may or may not be sunk, but every sunk cost is fixed, ex post.[14] Unlike a fixed cost, however, a sunk cost always acts as a barrier to entry.

Spence (1977) was one of the first to demonstrate formally that sunk costs deter entry.[15] In his model, firms were shown to gain an advantage by building plants of larger capacity than would be required in the absence of entry. The excess capacity acts as a signal to potential entrants that the incumbent firm is prepared to maintain, or even increase, output if entry should occur.

---

[13] There is one respect, however, in which a contestable market is unlike a competitive market. As Telser (1969) observes, in reply to Demsetz (1968), free entry can guarantee at most zero profits among the active firms in the market. A fully efficient outcome requires that price equal marginal cost, which in the case of a natural monopoly market requires either a two-part tariff or an outside subsidy. This section compares a market equilibrium under free entry to a regulated outcome, which may also fall short of the first best solution.

[14] A useful example from Chapter 3 is the cost of an airplane in a given market. There is clearly a fixed cost but not a sunk cost because the capital may without cost be transferred to a different market of almost equal value. Bailey and Panzar (1981) discuss the airline market in greater detail.

[15] See also Spence (1979), Dixit (1980), and Eaton and Lipsey (1980).

Of course, sunk costs may also act as barriers to entry in the absence of strategic behavior by incumbent firms. Because a sunk cost is a cost that would be incurred by a new entrant but not by the incumbent firm, every sunk cost is a barrier to entry. However, the two concepts are not identical. First, as Baumol, Panzar, and Willig (1982) observe, there may be barriers to entry that are not sunk costs, such as legal fees that an entering firm would have to incur but which the incumbent firm never had to pay. Second, entry in an oligopoly market is still, in fact, a complicated dynamic game. Sunk costs are a barrier to entry primarily because they make certain threats by the incumbent firm more credible. For example, the incumbent firm may threaten to price at variable cost and below the full cost of production. But for the same reason an aggressive rival could rely on the fact that costs are sunk to convince the incumbent firm that it intended to stay in the industry, once entry occurred. In other words, the degree of contestability of a market depends in part upon the relative abilities of the incumbent firm and its potential rivals to make credible threats about the behavior they would pursue if entry should occur. Chapter 8 will consider a relatively simple model that illustrates the potential contribution of noncooperative game theory to the theory of entry and exit.

7.3   Some complications in a dynamic natural monopoly market

In the previous section models of static market competition were used to demonstrate that, given a sufficient number of potential competitors, a contestable market equilibrium with zero profits for active firms may exist. In a dynamic market, however, a number of complications arise. Consider, for example, a market that is a natural monopoly at the current and all future outputs and in which demand is growing over time, as in Figure 7.5. At time t the price $p(t)$ is a sustainable natural monopoly price. If demand grows during period $t + 1$, however, $p(t)$ is clearly not sustainable in the new period.

Of course, if supply is sufficiently flexible, then a natural monopoly firm can price along its average cost curve at every moment in time. However, the production at a particular time generally involves a commitment to a plant of a particular scale. If a firm attempts to anticipate future demand growth by building a plant of larger scale than necessary for the current period, then in a contestable market it would be underpriced by a rival firm with a smaller plant. However, a plant that allows the minimum price at

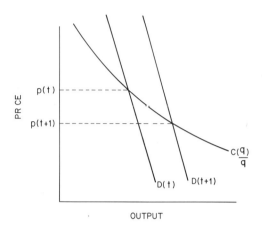

FIGURE 7.5

time t will be smaller than optimal in all future periods. Usually, it is not possible to take full advantage of economies of scale by expanding a plant in small increments. Furthermore, if there are sunk costs, the old plant cannot be exchanged without cost for a new one of optimal size in every period. Therefore it may be concluded that a dynamic market with sunk costs and growing demand is unlikely to be contestable.[16]

The same conclusion follows if technology rather than demand changes over time, as demonstrated in Figure 7.6. At time t the price $p(t)$ is a sustainable price. At a future period a rival firm in the market may have access to newer technology that has lower average costs, as represented by $AC(t + 1)$ in Figure 7.6. Thus at time $(t + 1)$ the price $p(t)$ is no longer sustainable.

In practice, firms can be expected to pursue a number of strategies that may serve to guarantee a stable demand for some interval of time. For example, as already suggested, one valid goal of regulation is to protect a natural monopoly firm from the opportunistic behavior of customers and other firms. This form of regulation can be justified more readily in the case of dynamic unsustainability, as previously described, than in the case of static unsustainability, because the latter requires more precise knowledge of the firm's cost function.

In the absence of regulation, firms can be expected to secure long-term contracts from their customers that guarantee a minimum

[16] The first example in Section 6.3 reaches the same conclusion from a somewhat different perspective.

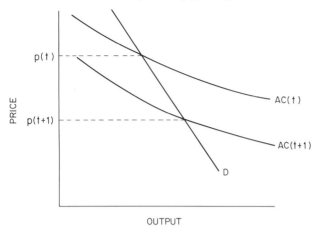

FIGURE 7.6

level of demand at some prespecified price. However, contracts of this form present a number of difficulties. If events other than the expected changes in demand or technology occur, either the customers or the firm may wish to renegotiate the contract, which may lead to prolonged and costly bargaining. In the case of changing technology, such contracts pose severe moral hazard problems, because the rate of technological change generally depends on the research activity of the firm. In any event, it must be recognized that analysis of a dynamic contestable market is considerably more complex than the analysis of the simple static model of the previous section. For further discussion of the dynamic aspects of competition the reader is referred to Knight (1921b) and to the more recent discussion of dynamic nonsustainability in Baumol, Panzar, and Willig (1982).

7.4   Limit and predatory pricing

The need for a theory of limit pricing and predatory pricing arises from the complex nature U.S. antitrust laws, particularly Section 2 of the Sherman Act of 1890. Section 2 prohibits any firm from monopolizing or conspiring to monopolize any part of trade or commerce. There are many actions by a firm that can be interpreted as monopolization, but the most important ones, and those that lend themselves to the most precise analysis, are the strategies that firms follow in setting price. This section will be concerned with an economic analysis of monopolization, through limit or predatory pricing.

There are no precise definitions of monopolization in either the legal or the economic literature. Generally speaking, a specific action may be deemed monopolizing if it either

1. tends to impair overall economic efficiency;

2. harms the process of competition;

3. has the effect of excluding an equally or more efficient rival;

4. tends to reduce the attractiveness of offers against which the firm must compete.

These criteria are by no means mutually exclusive, but they do reflect somewhat different points of view. Condition 1 was used by Scherer (1976) in his analyses of predatory pricing and by Posner (1976) throughout his discussion of exclusionary activities. Condition 3 was also suggested by Posner as an operational definition of predatory pricing. Finally, condition 4 is due to Markovits (1975).

The preceding criteria may now be applied to the pricing behavior of firms in a monopoly or oligopoly market. Limit pricing was introduced in Section 7.2 in describing barriers to entry. As before, a limit price is defined as a stationary price over time, which is used to maximize long-run profits, taking full account of the strategic interactions among firms. On the other hand, a predatory price is one in which short-term profits are sacrificed in order to attain a higher level of long-run profits by deterring entry. Any price by its very nature limits entry. In pursuing a limit pricing strategy, a firm is assumed to take recognition of the entry-limiting potential. In a predatory pricing strategy a firm is assumed to intimidate or threaten other firms by means of its pricing policy.

First, let us consider predatory pricing. A significant part of the economies literature on this topic has sought to argue that predatory pricing is an irrational policy for a monopolist to pursue, because it would always be more efficient (for the monopolist) to buy rather than punish the rival firm and simultaneously to punish itself.[17] Although this analysis alone is flawless it is largely irrelevant for the present discussion, because the act of predation may be monopolizing whether or not it is irrational and the option to buy a competing firm may be forbidden or otherwise impractical in the case of natural monopoly.

As the term suggests, predatory pricing is unambiguously a monopolizing action, according to the above-mentioned criteria. Predatory behavior is almost certain to be socially inefficient,

---

[17] See, for example, McGee (1958). Telser (1966) presents a related argument.

involving prices that are less than marginal cost in an initial period, and if successful, involving prices that are higher than average cost in the long run. By the remaining criteria, predatory pricing is even more obviously a monopolizing action.

However, although predation is easy to condemn it is not simple to define in practice. There is, for example, a lengthy debate between Areeda and Turner (1975) and Scherer (1976) concerning the exact definition of a predatory price for a single output monopolist. Areeda and Turner define a monopolist's price to be predatory if it is below both the average total cost and marginal cost. Because marginal cost is difficult to measure, the rule is relaxed in the end, so that only prices set below the average variable cost are called predatory. Scherer, stressing the standard of economic efficiency as the ultimate objective of the antitrust laws, points out a number of objections to the preceding rule. Among these is the fact that if the rule is enforced loosely, then an inefficiency results from a price less than marginal cost, whereas if it is enforced rigidly, it may result in passive and noncompetitive behavior on the part of the monopolist. The greatest flaw of the rule, according to Scherer, is predictability.

It should be noted that most of Scherer's objections apply to the case of a monopolist who is operating in the range of increasing average cost. In the case of declining costs, most economists would agree that pricing below marginal cost is evidence of predatory behavior. The Areeda-Turner rule specifically refers to short-run marginal cost, but because predatory behavior is a long-run phenomenon, it is argued by Posner (1976) that pricing below long-run marginal cost is also evidence of predation, if there is reasonable suspicion of intent to exclude rivals.

Next consider limit pricing behavior. Figure 7.4 and the accompanying discussion in Section 7.2 demonstrated that a price $p_l < p_m$ could always be found that would prevent the entry of a rival firm, having the same average cost function, if it is assumed that the rival expects the output q_l of the monopolist to be maintained after entry occurs. Although p_l is apparently a stationary price, this type of behavior is very close to predatory pricing. Indeed, by the four previous criteria, this form of limit pricing behavior is as clearly monopolizing as is predatory pricing.

It is, however, the expectation on the part of rival firms that q_l will be maintained, rather than the current price p_l, that deters entry. In general, such expectations depend on the willingness of the monopoly firm to price below average cost, which requires an actual demonstration from time to time.

The analysis of Section 7.2 indicates that in a contestable market a firm which is constrained to use a true stationary pricing policy can never set the price above the average cost in the long run. However, if there are barriers to entry, so that rival firms face a higher average cost than the incumbent firm at every output, then a true limit pricing strategy can deter entry. The question of whether such a limit pricing strategy is monopolizing necessarily depends on the nature of the entry barrier.

As a representative example, suppose that a single firm produces an output subject to declining average cost, and because some of the costs are sunk, is able to set the price above the average cost (See Figure 7.7). In this case the preceding criteria are somewhat ambiguous. A profit-maximizing monopolist would choose a price slightly less than p_e. Because the monopolist could find a price p such that $p_o < p < p_e$ at which total costs (including sunk costs) are covered in the long run, the limit pricing strategy is inefficient. However, it does not follow that measures designed to prevent this kind of limit pricing would improve efficiency overall, for they may discourage new or replacement investments. Also, a limit price in this instance has a "tendency to exclude an equally efficient rival"; but, of course, in a natural monopoly industry, in which only one firm can operate, any price that is a long-run equilibrium price will exclude equally efficient rivals. Thus whether or not limit pricing of this form is monopolizing under the law, the economic arguments against it are ambiguous.

A different model of limit pricing is the dominant firm-competitive fringe industry. In this form of industry a profit-maximizing monopolist would set a price such that marginal revenue of the residual demand (market demand minus competitive supply) is equal to marginal cost. A regulated monopolist would set a price equal to average cost. In either case the effect would be to limit entry of some portion of the competitive fringe. However, as pointed out in Section 7.2, this model assumes no strategic interaction between the dominant firm and the competitive sector. A higher price would bring about more entry, but only by firms that produce at higher average cost than the dominant firm. Therefore a limiting price of this form cannot in any reasonable interpretation of the model be considered a monopolizing action.

Notice in Figure 7.8 that an exogenous increase in supply leads to a decrease in residual demand and to a decrease in the profit-maximizing price of the dominant firm. (A regulated dominant firm, however, would set a higher price.) That is, the dominant firm model can lead to behavior that appears to be predatory in nature. However, as long as each competitive producer remains small, and no strategic interaction with the dominant firm exists, then the

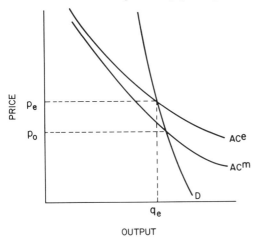

FIGURE 7.7

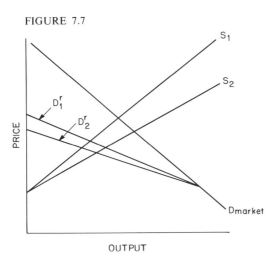

FIGURE 7.8

preceding conclusion remains valid. If growth in the competitive sector continues, however, there is a point at which the model of large-scale entry becomes appropriate. Then the nature of the price and output strategy of the incumbent firm determines whether its pricing behavior is monopolizing.

This concludes the brief discussion of both limit and predatory pricing. Additional references that the interested reader should consult are: Bork (1978), Joskow and Klevorick (1979), Kreps and Wilson (1980), McGee (1980), Milgrom and Roberts (1980), Selten (1974), Spence (1977), and Williamson (1977).

7.5   Concluding comments

This chapter has been concerned with a number of issues that are relevant to the regulation and market performance of industries that are natural monopolies or natural oligopolies. It has not attempted to describe the institutional details of the regulatory process, or to provide a comprehensive theory of regulation. Instead, the focal point has been the viability of competition as an alternative to regulation.

It was shown that free and unrestricted entry can in theory be a viable substitute for direct regulation in a natural monopoly or natural oligopoly market. A market in which barriers to entry are absent is called a contestable market, and Section 7.2 describes some of the conditions under which a market is contestable. In particular, a market can be contestable if there are fixed costs, or more generally, if there are economies of scale, in production. However, large sunk costs do act as a barrier to entry and their presence may indicate that the market is noncontestable.

The remaining sections of Chapter 7 were concerned with other circumstances in which a market is not fully contestable. Section 7.3 suggested some of the difficulties that may arise in a dynamic market. Section 7.4 contained a brief survey of results on both limit and predatory pricing that can occur only in the presence of barriers to entry. Although neither of these forms of strategic pricing is consistent with a contestable market, it was concluded that true limit pricing is a generally acceptable pricing policy, whereas predatory pricing is clearly anticompetitive.

The most important conclusion of this chapter is that competition is in some circumstances theoretically viable in both natural monopoly and natural oligopoly markets. However, there are also limits to the viability of competition in such markets. Both this and the preceding chapter have attempted to describe the conditions under which competition is most likely to be workable.

CHAPTER 8

Noncooperative equilibria in a contestable market

This chapter continues the analysis of a contestable market that was begun in Chapter 7 by developing a model that uses the theory of noncooperative games. The analysis of such a model will provide new insights into three separate but related areas: (1) The determination of conditions under which a contestable market equilibrium exists will be useful in assessing the proper role of regulation in natural monopoly and natural oligopoly markets. (2) The noncooperative game theoretic framework is one method by which the theory of sustainability, as described in Chapter 5, can be made more rigorous and complete.[1] (3) The noncooperative model will provide an alternative approach to the question of market stability, which was analyzed in a cooperative game theoretic framework in Chapter 6.

Section 8.1 contains a description of the economic structure of both the model and the basic concept of a noncooperative equilibrium. The market that will be studied consists of two or more firms that produce a single output and have identical U-shaped average cost functions. Firms are assumed to compete by simultaneously choosing prices. Outputs and profits to each firm are then determined as a function of the vector of prices chosen by each firm. A price vector is an equilibrium price if no firm can increase its profit by a unilateral change in its own price. One simple model of equilibrium is considered in Section 8.1 and rejected as unrealistic.

In Section 8.2 a more complex equilibrium is described and a number of results are established. First, it is shown in Proposition

---

[1] Recall from Chapter 5 that the result that natural monopoly may be unsustainable is unsatisfactory because it was not derived in an equilibrium context. Unsustainable monopoly invites entry, but there is nothing in the theory to determine what happens after entry occurs.

8.2 that at this type of equilibrium every firm must earn zero profits. In Propositions 8.3 through 8.6 the set of equilibria is completely characterized for both natural monopoly and natural oligopoly markets. The most important conclusion is that, given enough potential competition, an equilibrium necessarily exists.

8.1   Preliminary results

This chapter considers a model of a market based on a noncooperative game in which firms are the players. Each firm is assumed to produce a single homogeneous output q according to the cost function $C(q)$. It is also assumed that average cost has the familiar U-shape as in Figure 8.1a, reflecting fixed costs or scale economies at low levels of output, followed by diseconomies of scale at higher outputs. Assume that there is a unique output q_o at which average cost reaches a minimum and that marginal cost is strictly increasing for outputs greater than or equal to q_o. Therefore the total cost function C must be strictly convex beyond q_o, although it need only exhibit declining average cost up to q_o. Representative cost functions that satisfy these conditions are shown in Figure 8.1b and c.

Market demand will be given by the function $D(p)$, which is assumed to be downward sloping, so that the inverse function $D^{-1}(q)$ exists.[2] Let $p_o = D^{-1}(q_o)$.

In a noncooperative game it is necessary to specify a set of players, a set of strategies for each player, and a payoff function that shows the return to each player as a function of his or her own strategy choice and the strategies chosen by other players. Thus let the players be represented by the integers $1, \ldots, n$. Let S_i be the strategy set for player i and $h_i(s_1, \ldots, s_n)$ be the payoff to i if $s_j \in S_j$ for $j = 1, \ldots, n$.

For convenience in the remainder of this chapter upper case letters are used to represent vectors and lower case letters to represent scalar quantities. Let $S = (s_1, \ldots, s_n)$ be a particular strategy vector and let $S|\bar{s}_i$ represent the vector $(s_i, \ldots, s_{i-1}, \bar{s}_i, s_{i+1}, \ldots, s_n)$ in which $\bar{s}_i$ replaces s_i as the ith component of S. Then a Nash equilibrium in the game is a strategy vector S such that for every $i = 1, \ldots, n$

$$h_i(S) \geq h_i(S|\bar{s}_i) \text{ for all } \bar{s}_i \in S_i$$

[2]   In the cooperative game models of Chapter 6 the behavior of firms was subsumed in the structure of the model. Similarly, in the present model, buyers play no essential role other than to determine the aggregate demand function $D(p)$.

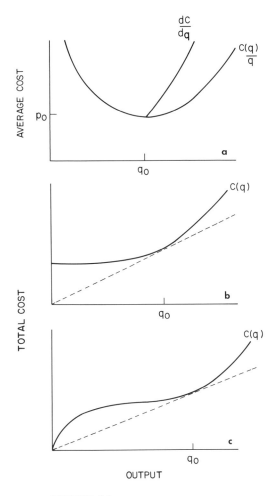

FIGURE 8.1

No player can improve his or her own payoff in a Nash equilibrium, assuming the strategies of other players remain fixed.[3]

In this model there will be n firms in a market and each firm will be assumed to use price as a strategic variable. Prices may be chosen from the set of nonnegative real numbers. A noncooperative game involving prices was first described by Bertrand

---

[3] This chapter will consider only Nash equilibria in pure strategies. A mixed strategy, in which a player specifies a probability distribution on two or more pure strategies, would not be appropriate in the present economic context.

(1883) in response to a quantity game defined by Cournot (1838). Later the Bertrand model was expanded upon by Edgeworth (1925) to include some of the results of the present model. More recently, a number of Cournot-Nash equilibrium models similar to this one have been analyzed.[4]

In order to complete the specification of the game, one must define the payoff functions h_i that give the return to each firm as a function of the vector $P = (p_1, \ldots, p_n)$ of prices of all firms. The most straightforward definition is:

$$h_i(P) = 0 \tag{8.1a}$$

if $p_i > p_j$ for some $j = 1, \ldots, n$, and

$$h_i(P) = p_i \frac{D(p_i)}{k} - C\left[\frac{D(p_i)}{k}\right] \tag{8.1b}$$

if $p_i \leq p_j$ for all $j = 1, \ldots, n$, where k is the number of firms choosing the lowest price.

In this game players simultaneously announce prices and the low price players divide the demand equally among themselves. However, although its definition is intuitively plausible, this game generally does not have a Nash equilibrium.

Consider first the case of natural monopoly in Figure 8.2. If market demand is given by $D_1(p)$, then the natural monopoly is sustainable. Let p_m be the lowest price at which $D^{-1}(q) = C(q)/q$, and suppose that the number of firms n is greater than one. Let $m(P)$ represent the minimum component of the price vector P. If $m(P) > p_m$, then clearly P cannot be an equilibrium. For if $p_i > m(P)$ for some i, then firm i could choose $\hat{p}_i = m(P) - \epsilon$, where ϵ is a small positive number, and could guarantee a positive profit. On the other hand, if $p_i = m(P)$ for all $i = 1, \ldots, n$, then any firm could choose $m(P) - \epsilon$ and increase its profit. If $m(P) = p_m$ and the minimum component of P is unique, then P cannot be an equilibrium, for the low price firm could gain by raising its price a small amount. Finally, if there are two or more firms that choose p_m, P cannot be an equilibrium because each firm would earn negative profits under the rule that divides market demand, and so each would prefer to raise its price and guarantee a zero profit. This argument applies even if market demand intersects average cost at its minimum point q_o.

Next consider the case of unsustainable natural monopoly, which occurs if demand is given by $D_2(p)$ in Figure 8.2. Let p_m be the

---

[4] See, for example, Novshek (1980), Novshek and Sonnenschein (1978), and Grossman (1981).

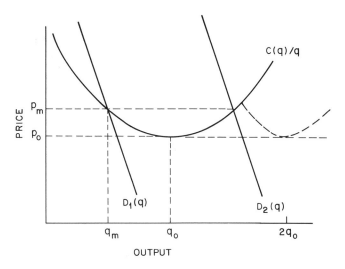

FIGURE 8.2

price at which D_2 crosses the average cost curve $C(q)/q$. Suppose first that $m(P) \leq p_m$. Because the industry is assumed to be a natural monopoly, it follows that the intersection of D_2 and $C(q)/q$ must lie below the average cost function for two active firms (shown as a broken curve in Figure 8.2). Therefore at $p \leq p_m$ two or more firms sharing the total market demand earn negative profits, and so P could not be an equilibrium. But if $m(P) > p_m$, then some firm could increase its profit by lowering its price to $m(P) - \epsilon$, so again, there can be no equilibrium.

The preceding arguments may be summarized as follows:

Proposition 8.1:
In the game defined by equations (8.1a) and (8.1b), if demand is such that the industry is a natural monopoly and there are at least two firms in the industry, then no Nash equilibrium exists.

If the preceding model is extended to the case of natural oligopoly there may be Nash equilibria and firms can even earn positive profits in equilibrium. Suppose, for example, that exactly k firms choose the minimum price $m(P) > p_o$ and that $kq_o = D[m(P)]$. Then it is possible, depending on the shape of the average cost, that no inactive firm would wish to lower its price to $m(P)$ because this might result in negative profits for all active firms. But also, no active firm would wish to lower its price if it is required to serve all the market demand at that price.

8.2   A Bertrand-Nash model of competition

The result of Section 8.1 is an artifact of the simplistic assumption, embodied in equation (8.1b), that the low price firms must equally share the total market demand. An alternative approach is the following.[5] A firm that announces a price p is in fact willing to supply only those outputs q such that $pq \geq C(q)$. Since $C(0) = 0$, a firm is willing to supply the zero output at any price. If $p \geq p_o$, then the firm is also willing to supply the set of outputs bounded by the average cost function as in Figure 8.3. Given that a firm has the opportunity to produce at a price p, one can reasonably suppose that it chooses the quantity q which gives the maximum return.

There is at this point some ambiguity in the definition of the return functions h_i. Suppose, however, that firms come into the game with a priority ranking based, for example, on the order in which they originally entered the market. Then it is reasonable to suppose that in the event of a tie for the lowest price, the highest ranking firm is allowed to choose any output less than or equal to the market demand at the minimum price. The second ranking firm may then choose from the residual demand, and so on.

If market demand is not exhausted by the low price firms, then the firm or firms having the next lowest price may choose from the remaining demand. Because, by assumption, every firm is willing to supply zero output, the preceding allocation of outputs is feasible.[6]

This discussion may be formalized in the following game. Given a set of firms $i = 1, \ldots, n$, I will say that i has a higher rank than j if $i < j$. Given a price vector $P = (p_1, \ldots, p_n)$, let $m_1(P)$ be the lowest price and $T_1 = \{i : p_i = m(P)\}$. Similarly, let $m_k(P)$ be the kth lowest price and $T_k = \{i : p_i = m_{k(P)}\}$ for $k = 2, 3, \ldots$. The return to each player is then given recursively as follows. If $i \in T_1$,

$$h_i(P) = \text{Max } \{p_i q_i - C(q_i)\} \tag{8.2a}$$

subject to

$$q_i \leq D[m_1(P)] - \sum_{\substack{j \in T_1 \\ j < i}} q_j \tag{8.2b}$$

---

[5]   The model of this section is based on a recent paper of Grossman (1981). However, in Grossman's model, firms choose supply functions rather than prices.

[6]   Because it will be shown that in equilibrium, firms will earn zero profits, each firm will in fact be indifferent between producing and not producing. Therefore the total production and its allocation among firms is indeterminate. This is to be expected in a model of a contestable market. However, the ambiguity could be removed by assuming that every firm prefers to produce at a positive level, if possible.

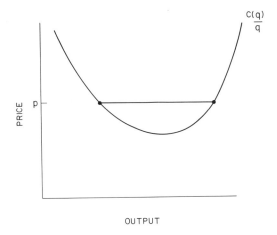

FIGURE 8.3

If $i \in T_k$, then

$$h_i(P) = \text{Max} \{p_i q_i - C(q_i)\} \qquad (8.2c)$$

subject to

$$q_i \leq D[m_k(P)] - \sum_{r=1}^{k-1} \sum_{j \in T_r} q_j - \sum_{\substack{j \in T_k \\ j < i}} q_j \qquad (8.2d)$$

In order to describe the nature of an equilibrium in this game consider Figure 8.4. Each firm is assumed to maximize profit with respect to the quantity q_i, subject to the constraint that demand is less than or equal to the residual demand. The residual demand $R(p_i)$ is equal to the market demand minus the quantities chosen by lower price firms, and by higher ranking firms with the same price. Thus demand facing a firm i is perfectly elastic at p_i, up to residual demand. Maximum profits are then determined by setting output $\bar{q}_i$ such that $p_i = dC/dq$ at $\bar{q}_i$, or by setting q_i equal to residual demand at p_i. In the former case it is necessarily true that $\bar{q}_i > q_o$, because marginal cost is greater than average cost only at outputs $q > q_o$.

Of course, the monopoly solution, given residual demand, would call for a higher price and lower output. Indeed, the firm is free to set any price that it wishes. However, if it sets a price higher than p_i, this will in general cause a discontinuous leftward shift in residual demand; similarly, a lower price will induce a rightward shift. Every firm must take these effects into account in its pricing strategy.

It is instructive to compare the game defined in expressions (8.2a) to (8.2d) to the theory of sustainability. In both formulations, firms are required to earn nonnegative profits. In addition, firms are assumed to be able to maintain their market share unless a rival firm

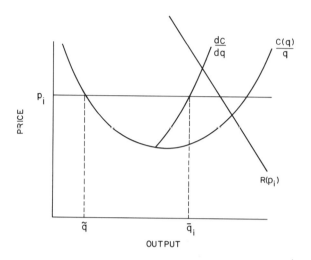

FIGURE 8.4

offers a lower price. Unlike the theory of sustainability and the previous game, however, firms are not in the present game required to satisfy the total market demand.

Before proceeding to investigate the existence of equilibrium in this model, some preliminary results will be established which will be useful in simplifying future proofs. Given a price vector P, let $\pi_i(P) = p_i q_i - C(q_i)$ be the profit earned by firm i, where q_i is chosen in accordance with expressions (8.2a) to (8.2d).

Lemma 8.1:

   If P is a price vector such that $p_i = p_j$ for some $i \neq j$, and either $\pi_i(P) > 0$ or $\pi_j(P) > 0$, then P cannot be an equilibrium.

Proof:

   Suppose that P is an equilibrium price that satisfies the previous conditions and that $i < j$. Then $\pi_i(P) > 0$, for $\pi_j(P) > 0$ and $\pi_i(P) = 0$ is impossible under expressions (8.2). Therefore, as in Figure 8.4, firm i must have chosen an output q_i such that $\tilde{q} < q_i \leq \bar{q}_i$, where $\tilde{q}$ is the smallest output such that $p_i \tilde{q} = C(\tilde{q})$ and $\bar{q}_i$ is the profit-maximizing output at p_i. Suppose that $\pi_j(P) = 0$, so that $q_j = 0$ or $q_j = \tilde{q}$. Then firm j could increase its profit by setting $\hat{p}_j = p_i - \epsilon$, because it could then gain all of firm i's customers. Next suppose that $\pi_j(P) > 0$, so that $q_j > \tilde{q}$. Then since i has a higher rank than j, expressions (8.2) imply that $q_i = \bar{q}_i$, which gives the maximum profit at p_i. But by the same logic, $q_j = \bar{q}_i$, because otherwise firm j could increase profits by lowering its price. Extending this argument one can demonstrate that it is necessary that $q_k = \bar{q}_i$ for all firms k such that $p_k = p_i$, if P is to be an equilibrium. Now consider the residual demand facing firm i at prices $p \geq p_i$, given by

$$R(p) = D(p) - \sum_{k:p_k \leq p_i} q_k(P)$$

where $D(p)$ is market demand and $q_k(P)$ is the quantity chosen by firm k, according to expressions (8.2), given the price vector P. By definition, $R(p_i) \geq \bar{q}_i$. Because every other firm k for which $p_k = p_i$ is already producing at the point of maximum profit, for fixed p_k, a small increase in p_i would not result in an increase in the output of any other firm, given that all other firms maintain their prices as in P. In other words, $R(p)$ represents the true residual demand for small increases in p_i. If $R(p_i) > \bar{q}_i$, firm i could clearly increase profits by increasing p_i a small amount (see Figure 8.4). But if $R(p_i) = \bar{q}_i$, firm i could still increase profits by a small increase in p_i, because the marginal revenue associated with $R(p_i)$ is necessarily less than p_i which is equal to marginal cost at $\bar{q}_i$. Therefore the profit-maximizing strategy for firm i unambiguously calls for an increase in p_i, and so P cannot be an equilibrium.

Lemma 8.2:

   If P is a price vector such that only one firm chooses the price p_i, $\pi_i(P) > 0$, and $p_j > p_i$ for some j, then P cannot be an equilibrium.

Proof:

   If $q_j = 0$, then $\pi_j(P) = 0$ and firm j could increase profits by setting $\hat{p}_j = p_i - \epsilon$. If $q_j > 0$, then since $p_j > p_i$, it must be true, by expressions (8.2), that $q_i = \bar{q}_i$, where $\bar{q}_i$ is the output at which marginal cost is equal to p_i, as in Figure 8.4. Because firm i is the only firm choosing p_i, the argument in the proof of Lemma 8.1 applies, and so P cannot be an equilibrium.

The preceding lemmas may be used to prove the following:

Proposition 8.2:

   If P is an equilibrium price vector, and $n \geq 2$, then $\pi_i(P) = 0$ for $i = 1, \ldots, n$.

Proof:

   Given the two lemmas, it follows that the only possible way for a firm i to make a profit in equilibrium is that it be the unique highest price firm, with price $p_i > p_0$. But any one of the lower price, zero profit firms could raise its price to $p_i - \epsilon$, thereby making a positive profit. Thus, there cannot be an equilibrium price vector in which any firm earns a positive profit.

Proposition 8.2 confirms that the game described by expressions (8.2) may be interpreted as a model of a contestable market. The remainder of this chapter will be devoted to the explicit characterization of the set of equilibrium price vectors.

Consider first the case of sustainable natural monopoly in which demand intersects average cost when average cost is falling, as in D_1 in Figure 8.2. If $n = 1$, then the equilibrium is the usual monopoly solution in which a profit-maximizing price is chosen. Suppose then that $n \geq 2$. Let p_m be the lowest price at which $D_1^{-1}(q) = C(q)/q$ as in Figure 8.2. Then the vector P^m, in which $p_i = p_m$ for $i = 1, \ldots, n$, is a Nash equilibrium.

At p_m the only feasible outputs are 0 or q_m and each firm is indifferent between production of the full market demand and nonproduction. There is at most only one active firm in the market and all firms earn zero profits. An individual firm can in no way earn positive profits by choosing a different price, because at $p < p_m$, there is no output less than or equal to demand at which average cost is less than price. But at $p > p_m$ the firm cannot attract any customers.

Suppose that $P^e \neq P^m$ is an equilibrium. Then $p_i^e = p_j^e = p_m$ for some $i \neq j$. By Proposition 8.2, any equilibrium must involve zero profits by all firms. If the minimum price $m(P^e) > p_m$, then some firm could earn a positive profit by changing its price to $m(P^e) - \epsilon$. But if only one firm chooses p_m, that firm could increase profits by raising its price a small amount.

The preceding discussion constitutes a proof of the following result:

Proposition 8.3:

  If demand is such that there is a sustainable natural monopoly and $n \geq 2$, then an equilibrium exists, and every such equilibrium must have $p_i^e = p_j^e = p_m$ for some $i \neq j$, where p_m is the lowest price at which $D^{-1}(q) = C(q)/q$.

Now consider the case of unsustainable natural monopoly. Again, if $n = 1$, the usual monopoly solution prevails. Therefore suppose $n \geq 2$. In Figure 8.5 the average cost function $C(q - q_o)/(q - q_o)$ represents the average cost of producing the residual output, if one firm produces at minimum average cost. Suppose that market demand is never greater than $C(q - q_o)/(q - q_o)$ as in D_1 of Figure 8.5. Then any price vector P^o in which $p_i^o = p_j^o = p_o$ for some $i \neq j$ is an equilibrium. If any firm k chooses $p_k < p_o$, then necessarily $q_k = 0$. Suppose that $i < j$ and that i is the highest ranking firm that chooses p_o. Then firm i is indifferent between setting $q_i = q_o$ and $q_i = 0$. By convention it will be assumed that $q_i = q_o$, and so necessarily $q_j = 0$. Given that $q_i = q_o$, it is not possible for any inactive firm to earn a positive profit. But if firm i attempts to set $p_i > p_o$, then firm j will increase production to q_o and so i cannot earn a positive profit. Therefore P^o is an equilibrium.

Next suppose P^e is a price vector for which it is not true that $p_i^e = p_j^e = p_o$ for some $i \neq j$. Then exactly as in the case of sustainable monopoly, P^e cannot be an equilibrium. If $m(P^e) > p_o$, some firm could increase its profit by setting $p = m(P^e) - \epsilon$. If only one firm sets $p_i = p_o$, that firm could increase its profit by raising its

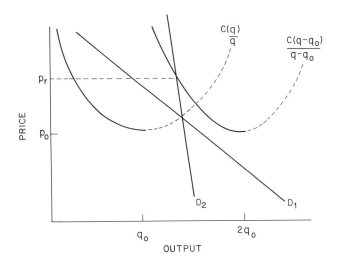

FIGURE 8.5

price. The following result has therefore been established:

Proposition 8.4:

 If demand is such that natural monopoly is unsustainable, $n \geq 2$, and the inverse market demand $D^{-1}(q)$ is never greater than the residual average cost, $C(q - q_o)/(q - q_o)$, then an equilibrium exists and all such equilibria must satisfy $p_i^e = p_j^e = p_o$ for some $i \neq j$, where p_o is the minimum average cost.

 A natural monopoly is unsustainable if the average cost of serving market demand, given a zero profit constraint and an obligation to serve, is greater than the minimum average cost. The result in Proposition 8.4 demonstrates that in a contestable market (which operates according to the rules embodied in expressions (8.2a) to (8.2d)) firms will reach a stable equilibrium by producing at the minimum average cost output q_o and allowing some demand to go unsatisfied. This solution is inefficient, because there are unsatisfied customers who would be willing to pay more than the marginal cost of production. (Of course, the natural monopoly solution is also inefficient in this sense, because price is equal to average cost, which is less than marginal cost.)

 There is, however, a different possible outcome in the case of unsustainable monopoly, which will now be described. Suppose that the inverse demand $D^{-1}(q)$ exceeds residual average cost for some outputs, as is the case for D_2 in Figure 8.5. Here, if $n = 2$, there is no equilibrium price vector. By the previous arguments, the only potential equilibrium is $P^o = (p_o, p_o)$. At P^o, both firms earn zero profit, but either firm could earn a positive profit by choosing the monopoly price, given the residual demand $D_2(p) - q_o$.

A similar argument applies if $n = 3$. However, if $n \geq 4$, then an equilibrium exists. Let p_r be the lowest price at which inverse market demand is equal to residual average cost. That is,

$$p_r = D_2^{-1}(q_r) = \frac{C(q_r - q_o)}{q_r - q_o}$$

and

$$D_2^{-1}(q) < \frac{C(q - q_o)}{q - q_o} \text{ for } q > q_r$$

Then the price vector P^e is an equilibrium if $p_1^e = p_2^e = p_o$; $p_3^e = p_4^e = p_r$; and p_j^e is arbitrary for $j > 4$. Each firm earns zero profits with P^e and by the usual arguments no firm can earn a positive profit by a unilateral change in its price. Similarly, the essential uniqueness of P^e follows directly. Therefore the following result has been established:

Proposition 8.5:

If demand is such that natural monopoly is unsustainable and the inverse market demand $D^{-1}(q)$ is greater than the residual average cost for some outputs, then

(i)   If $n = 2$ or $n = 3$, no equilibrium exists.

(ii) If $n \geq 4$, an equilibrium exists, and all such equilibria must satisfy $p_i^e = p_j^e = p_o$; $p_k^e = p_l^e = p_r$ for some $i \neq j \neq k \neq l$; where p_r is the lowest price such that

$$p_r = D^{-1}(q_r) = \frac{C(q_r - q_o)}{q_r - q_o}$$

and p_o is the minimum average cost.

One can now characterize the equilibria in the general case. Suppose that market demand is such that

$$k\, q_o < D(p_o) \leq (k + 1)q_o$$

In Figure 8.6 the average cost of residual demand $C(q - kq_o)/(q - kq_o)$ is shown, along with two possible demand functions. Suppose that demand is never greater than residual average cost, as in D_1, assuming that k firms produce q_o. Then if $n \geq k + 1$, an equilibrium exists, and is given by any P^e such that $p_i^e = p_o$, $i = 1, \ldots, k + 1$. The argument to demonstrate that P^e is an equilibrium is by now familiar. At p_o there can be at most k active firms. Therefore given P^e, there is at least one inactive firm at the price p_o so that no firm can successfully raise its price.

It can be demonstrated in fact that all equilibria must have at least $k + 1$ prices equal to p_o. Suppose this is not so. By Proposition 8.2, if P is an equilibrium, then $\pi_i(P) = 0$ for $i = 1, \ldots, n$. If P is such that k or fewer firms set $p = p_o$, then since $D(p_o) > kq_o$ the residual

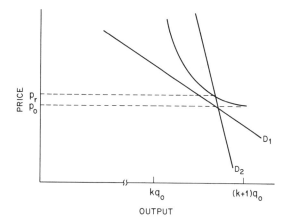

FIGURE 8.6

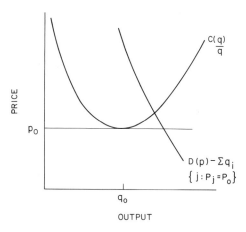

FIGURE 8.7

demand curve must cross average cost $C(q)/q$ at some output $q > q_o$, as in Figure 8.7. Therefore any zero profit firm could set $p = p_o + \epsilon$ and earn a positive profit, so P cannot be an equilibrium.

By the same argument, if $1 < n \leq k$, then no equilibrium exists.

Now suppose that $kq_o < D(p_o) \leq (k + 1)q_o$ and that the inverse demand $D^{-1}(q)$ lies above residual average cost $C(q - kq_o)/(q - kq_o)$, as is the case for D_2 in Figure 8.6. Then if $n \geq k + 3$, an equilibrium P^e exists and is given by

$$p_i^e = p_o \quad i = 1, \ldots, k + 1;$$

$$p_{k+2}^e = p_{k+3}^e = p_r;$$

where p_r is the lowest price such that

$$p_r = D^{-1}(q_r) = \frac{C(q_r - kq_o)}{q_r - kq_o}$$

It is a straightforward exercise to verify that all equilibria must have at least $k + 1$ prices equal to p_o and at least two prices equal to p_r. By the same argument it can be shown that no equilibrium exists if $1 < n \leq k + 2$.

This discussion is sufficient to prove the following:

Proposition 8.6:

If demand is such that $kq_o < D(p_o) \leq (k + 1)q_o$ and $D^{-1}(q)$ lies everywhere below residual average cost, $C(q - kq_o)/(q - kq_o)$, then

(i) If $n \geq k + 1$, an equilibrium exists and all such equilibria must have at least $(k + 1)$ prices equal to p_o.

(ii) If $1 < n \leq k$, no equilibrium exists.

If demand is such that $kq_o < D(p_o) \leq (k + 1)q_o$ and $D^{-1}(q)$ is greater than residual average cost for some outputs, then

(iii) If $n \geq k + 3$, an equilibrium exists and all such equilibria must have at least $k + 1$ prices equal to p_o and two prices equal to p_r, where

$$p_r = D^{-1}(q_r) = \frac{C(q_r - kq_o)}{q_r - kq_o}$$

(iv) If $1 < n \leq k + 2$, no equilibrium exists.

Proposition 8.6 and the special cases described in Propositions 8.3, 8.4, and 8.5 are interesting for a number of reasons. The most important implication is that given sufficient competition, an equilibrium involving zero profits for all active firms always exists. Competition is sufficient if there is at least one inactive (in equilibrium) firm for every type of active firm. In this model, because all firms have the same average cost function, a firm is characterized only by the price that it charges in equilibrium. For some configurations of demand there is only one possible price, the minimum average cost p_o, for an active firm in equilibrium. Hence only one type of firm exists. Roughly speaking, these equilibria occur when demand is sufficiently elastic, as seen in Figure 8.6. On the other hand, for inelastic demand, there can be two types of firm. All but one of the active firms must produce at p_o, and the remaining one must produce at the lowest possible price, which is equal to the average cost of the remaining demand.

As previously indicated, these equilibria are inefficient, despite the fact that most firms operate at the minimum average cost output. Unless $D(p_o) = kq_o$ for some integer k, there is either unsatisfied demand in equilibrium or demand is served at two different prices. However, the regulated natural monopoly outcome is also inefficient because the price is not equal to marginal cost. No obvious welfare comparison can be made between the regulated and the unregulated outcomes.

8.3   Concluding comments

Chapter 8 is the final purely theoretical chapter in this book. Here a simple model has been considered in which firms are assumed to compete according to the rules of a certain noncooperative game. It is useful to contrast the results of this model with those of earlier models in Chapters 5, 6, and 7. The first attempt to model competitive entry was the theory of sustainability, which was developed in Chapter 5. There it was shown that undesirable entry in a natural monopoly market may exist if the incumbent natural monopoly firm is required to choose a stationary price and an output that together guarantee nonnegative profits and satisfy all consumer demand. In this chapter a plausible model of noncooperative equilibrium has partially confirmed the theory of sustainability. In this model a stable equilibrium is reached if there is enough potential competition and if firms are unconstrained in their choice of price and output.[7]

In the case of sustainable natural monopoly the equilibria of Chapter 8 are exactly the same as the sustainable outcomes described in Chapter 5. That is, there is one active firm that satisfies the entire market demand at a price equal to average cost of production.

For unsustainable natural monopoly and sufficient potential competition, there are two possible outcomes. Only one active firm in the market may produce an output such that average cost is a minimum and some consumer demand is unsatisfied. Alternatively, two active firms may produce two different outputs at two different prices. If the customers of the low price firm are conceptually taken out of the market, then the remaining demand is entirely satisfied by the high price firm. However, there is no mechanism for determining which customers are served by the low price firm. Therefore the equilibria described in this chapter are not entirely satisfactory. The same forces that make the price of a single firm unsustainable in Chapter 5 may lead to conflicts among the buyers at the equilibria in Chapter 8.

A similar kind of instability was studied from the viewpoint of

---

[7] In particular, firms must be allowed to produce less than the market demand at their chosen price, even if no other active firms are in the market.

cooperative game theory in Chapter 6. In Section 6.2 it was shown that whenever demand is not exactly equal to supply, an unstable market in the form of an empty core results. In the noncooperative model of the present chapter the outcome is stable so that a noncooperative equilibrium exists. However, as pointed out in the preceding paragraph, these equilibria are fundamentally indeterminate, because the buyers are not explicitly treated as players in the game.

A final comparison can be made between the equilibria of this chapter in which firms use price as the strategic variable and the equilibria that would result if firms compete by setting quantities rather than prices. Section 7.2 of Chapter 7 contains an analysis that suggests the results that follow from a naive quantity-setting model. In such a model there are an abundance of equilibria, including equilibria in which firms earn positive profits and limit price in order to deter entry.

However, in a more sophisticated version of the quantity-setting model it would be reasonable to assume that firms are unwilling to supply a given output q at a price less than $C(q)/q$. Then one can define a rule similar to expressions (8.2a) to (8.2d) that describes each firm's profit as a function of the vector $Q = (q_1, \ldots, q_n)$ of quantities offered by each firm. The results of this kind of analysis are similar to the price-setting model of this chapter. If there is enough competition, then all equilibria involve zero profits and outputs equal to the minimum average cost output for all but one firm. However, if there is insufficient competition, then instead of the nonexistence of equilibrium, multiple equilibria exist and firms are able to make positive profits in equilibrium.

CHAPTER 9

Natural monopoly and the telecommunications industry

Chapters 4 through 8 have developed a theory of natural monopoly in highly abstract terms. In this concluding chapter some of that theory will be applied in an examination of both the institutional and technological structure of the telecommunications industry. The function of this chapter is not to determine whether or not the telecommunications industry is a natural monopoly. Instead, the chapter will satisfy three more modest objectives: (1) The major elements of the theory will be reviewed in the more concrete and structured setting of the telecommunications industry. (2) Existing empirical studies of the industry will be evaluated. (3) Issues relevant to the future theoretical and applied research will be discussed.

Section 9.1 will consider the nature of demand in telecommunications markets. There are a number of important characteristics, some of which are shared by other industries and some that are unique to telecommunications. The demand for communication is inherently a two-party interdependent process. Furthermore, the demand is time dependent but varies over time, and the output of the industry is nonstorable. Finally, demand in telecommunications is a demand for access to the network and potential use, as well as a demand for actual transmission of messages. Each of these characteristics will be shown to have a specific effect on telecommunications costs and in particular on the subadditivity of costs.

In Section 9.2 telecommunications technology for transmission, switching, network planning, and network operation will be discussed. It will be demonstrated that transmission is characterized

This chapter expresses only the author's personal viewpoint regarding policy issues in the telecommunications industry, and does not necessarily reflect the views and opinions of AT&T or Bell Laboratories.

by significant economies of scale. The costs of switching are most usefully illustrated in the context of aggregate network planning, and both network planning and network management will be shown to be subject to important subadditivity effects.

A discussion of econometric testing of telecommunications costs in Section 9.3 will first consider some basic issues involved in testing for scale economies in the industry and review some of the reasons that scale economies are not adequate for a test of natural monopoly. Then a large number of actual empirical studies of the industry will be reviewed.

Finally, Section 9.4 will describe the prospects for competition in telecommunications. Examples of potential nonsustainability will be considered as well as the potential for unstable or suboptimal competition. Unstable competition may result from overlapping communities of interest in various submarkets. Suboptimal competition will be approached from the point of view of the contractual costs in a competitive market.

9.1   The nature of demand in telecommunications

A reasonably broad definition of the telecommunications industry is that it provides for electronic, point-to-point communication needs among groups of people or machines. The largest portion of the industry output is currently the provision of voice telephone service for business and residential customers. Telecommunications is a part of a broader communications industry, which includes the postal service, express freight carriers, and portions of the transportation industry. Telecommunications may also be viewed as a part of the broader information-processing industry. However, the present chapter will not be concerned with the strict definition of industry boundaries, despite the obvious importance of that task. It will be assumed that the market boundaries among telecommunications, transportation, and information processing are well defined. Furthermore, this section will focus on the provision of basic telephone service to individuals and businesses and will not specifically address issues associated with the provision of private lines or private networks to business users.

The demand for telecommunications outputs has a number of distinguishing characteristics. Communication is inherently a two-party or multiparty process. Therefore the demand for telecommunications includes both the demand for incoming and outgoing messages. Communication is also time dependent — the desire to communicate occurs at a particular point in time and must be satisfied at or close to the time at which the demand is expressed. In addition, the output of a communications service is by nature nonstorable. Thus capacity in the telecommunications industry is necessarily related to peak demand rather than to average demand. Finally, and perhaps most importantly, the demand for telecommunications service includes the demand for potential communications with every other user of the service. Therefore a communications service is necessarily supplied by means of a network in which flows of messages may be directed in both directions between any two subscribers. Each of these demand characteristics has important implications for the supply of telecommunications outputs and in particular for the existence of subadditivity of the telecommunications cost function.

First, consider the time-dependent nature of demand. Demand for communication has both predictable and random variability within any given time period. Variability of demand is evident from the observed fact that the number of calls initiated depends on the time of day, day of the week, and season of the year. This form of variability can be predicted with great accuracy by statistical techniques. However, it gives rise to the familiar peak-load problem common to public utilities and other service industries. Because output cannot be stored and capacity cannot be rapidly expanded or contracted, there is a need to supply capacity that is adequate for peak levels of expected demand. Generally, this means that the telephone plant must be constructed in order to handle demand during the average busy hour during the average busy day of the busy season of the year. In other nonpeak periods, there is necessarily a level of excess capacity.[1]

Of course, time dependence and variability of demands are not unique to the telecommunications industry. Other public utilities, such as electricity and gas, as well as many unregulated industries, such as the restaurant and entertainment industries face a similar time profile of demand. However, in each of these industries it is technically possible to store output for short periods of time. Therefore the capacity in these industries is more flexible than in telecommunications, and supply can adjust more readily to meet demands. For example, day-to-day variations in the demand for

---

[1] Time-varying prices may be used to even out the time profile of demand, but there are practical limits to the ability of the pricing system to remove all such fluctuations.

electricity can be smoothed by the storage potential of hydroelectric or pump storage systems. Natural gas may also be centrally stored for short periods of time. Only in the long run is it necessary to have central integrated planning to ensure that supply is adequate to meet demands. In a telecommunications network such integrated planning is required to handle day-to-day fluctuations in traffic.

The need for integrated planning is one of the most complex and difficult issues to be addressed in an examination of natural monopoly in telecommunications. Much of Section 9.2 will discuss stylized examples that illustrate the need for planning in a network. At present the reader should recall the important interrelationship between demand variability and the relative advantage of planning over a competitive market solution. This issue was considered in a more formal context in the first example of Section 6.3.

Periodic demand also leads to a directly observable technological subadditivity. The capacity of each component of an optimal network for a single supplier is designed to handle the maximum demand expected for that component. During off-peak periods there is necessarily excess capacity. If demand is fragmented among multiple suppliers, however, it is unlikely that the periodic profile of each supplier would coincide with the original profile of demand. But if multiple suppliers face different peak periods, then it necessarily follows that the combined capacities of multiple suppliers must exceed the capacity of a single supplier. The extra capacity in the system is true excess capacity and is an economic waste. An extreme example of the noncoincidence of demand with multiple suppliers is illustrated in Figure 9.1. A single supplier is shown to have a demand profile with two peak periods — a business demand peak during the daytime and a residential peak in the early evening. If demand is fragmented so that business and residence demands are served by different suppliers, then the combined capacities substantially exceed the capacity of a single supplier.

In addition to its predictable variability, demand for telecommunications is a random variable. Although the average demand in a given period can be known, the actual demand cannot be known in advance. The capacity of a telephone system is engineered to satisfy demand with the expectation that some calls will be blocked during busy times. The amount of blocking is one aspect of the grade of service, and blocking is controlled by the amount of switching and transmission capacity installed in the network. More capacity implies fewer blocked calls and a higher grade of service.

The need for probabilistic engineering gives rise to an important subadditivity effect. Table 9.1 and Figure 9.2 illustrate this effect for

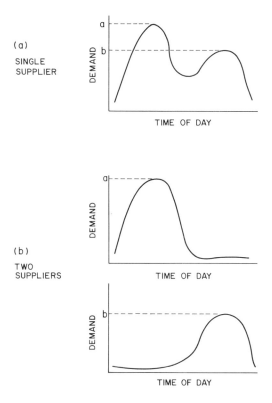

(a)

SINGLE
SUPPLIER

(b)

TWO
SUPPLIERS

FIGURE 9.1

a specific example, in which grade of service is summarized by a specific blocking probability and demand is characterized by Poisson arrival. It is clear from the table and the diagrams that economies of scale exist for both blocking probabilities and that for a given number of circuits the economies are more pronounced at higher grades of service (lower blocking probability). The economies of scale, however, decline substantially as the number of circuits increases. Therefore for small demands a fragmentation of the network could result in a significant cost penalty, because more circuits would be required to maintain the same grade of service. At larger demands the costs of fragmentation are less pronounced.

The next characteristic of demand, which distinguishes telecommunications from most other utilities, is the interdependent nature of demand. Communication is inherently a two-party or multiparty process. But only one party is typically charged. This results in an economic externality, which complicates somewhat the use of the prices in the industry.

TABLE 9.1. *Capacity of a communications system (100 call-seconds per hour) by number of circuits and grade of service*

Number of Circuits	Blocking Probability = .01		Blocking Probability = .10	
	Capacity	Number of Circuits ÷Capacity	Capacity	Number of Circuits ÷Capacity
1	0.4	2.5	3.8	.263
2	5.4	.370	19.1	.105
3	15.7	.191	39.6	.076
4	29.6	.135	63.0	.063
5	46.1	.108	88.0	.057
6	64.4	.093	113	.053
7	83.9	.083	140	.050
8	105	.076	168	.048
9	126	.071	195	.046
10	149	.067	224	.045
16	294	.054	401	.040
32	732	.044	900	.036
50	1261	.040	1482	.034
64	1687	.038	1943	.033
100	2816	.036	3149	.032
128	3713	.034	4094	.031
150	4427	.034	4843	.031

Source: Waverman [1975: 214]

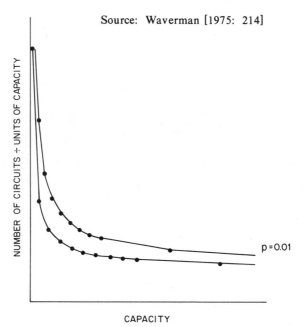

FIGURE 9.2

Interdependency of demand has two aspects. First is the externality associated with access to the system. A potential subscriber receives a benefit from joining the network that depends on both the number of other users, most of whom are unknown initially, and the identity of specific users who are already in the system. That is, a communications service is valuable in that it allows communication with a large number of people and because it allows more frequent contact with a smaller number of close friends. A circle of friends or business contacts may be described as a community of interest. Therefore one might say that demand for telecommunications is characterized by a large number of overlapping communities of interest.[2]

A second form of externality is associated with the use of a communication system. Each communication involves at least two parties, yet only the one initiating the call is charged. Evidence suggests that this form of externality is less significant than that associated with access. Generally, frequent users are able to internalize the problem by sharing in the placing of calls. It is also technically possible, although not necessarily desirable, to charge both parties in a call.

An alternative way to describe the basic externality in communication is to note the public good characteristics of a telephone network.[3] A telephone network benefits all those who subscribe by lowering the costs of communication among its members. In effect, all those who join a network are purchasing the economic good — improved communication. This good, however, is a public good because the level of improved communication is of course the same for all users of the system. Individuals who join a network need not place similar value on it. The optimal communications network will be one for which the sum of the marginal benefits from an additional subscriber equals the marginal cost of that subscriber.[4] In general, each subscriber should pay a different price for access in an optimal network.

An important aspect of the demand for telecommunications is quality of service. One aspect of service quality — the probability that an attempted call will be blocked — has already been mentioned

---

[2] Externalities in communications are discussed at greater length in Squire (1973), Rohlfs (1974), and Willig (1979a).

[3] See, for example, Artle and Averous (1973).

[4] This is the standard result for optimal production of public goods and is explained more fully in Chapter 3.

as a source of a basic economy of scale in telecommunications costs. In addition to blocking probability, there are other aspects of quality such as privacy (number of parties on a line) and the distortion of messages as they are transmitted. Usually high-quality service is more costly to provide than lower-quality service. In Section 9.4 it will be shown that competition in terms of service quality can in theory lead to unstable or suboptimal market outcomes.

A final comment on demand concerns the aggregation of output. As shown in Chapter 2 for the railroad industry, the measurement of output in the telecommunications industry is a difficult process. Actual output in the industry includes both the interconnection of all subscribers in a nationwide network and the transmission of messages between subscriber pairs. Due to the complexity of the network, each message transmission could be viewed as a distinct output in the industry. More plausibly, usage may be aggregated by either origin (business versus residential) or type (analog voice, analog data, hard copy, private line, digital service, etc.). Alternatively, a geographic aggregation is possible. In some cases it may be useful to consider revenue divided by a price index, which results in a totally aggregated, one-dimensional measure of output.

The level of aggregation to be considered depends on the question being addressed. In an investigation of scale economies in the industry a single aggregate measure of output is generally used, although some multiple output scale economy studies have been done. In any event, it is assumed in such studies that as output expands, all outputs expand together in the same proportion.

On the other hand, for a treatment of the subadditivity question, at least some level of disaggregation is required. A test for subadditivity is a comparison of the cost of a single firm with the cost of two or more firms; or alternatively, it is a comparison of the industry cost before and after entry in a market with a dominant firm and many small competitors. The type of disaggregation then depends on the likely avenues for competitive entry. If entry is expected primarily in business services, the business — residential split is relevant. If entry occurs in geographical submarkets, then a geographical disaggregation is necessary.

The interested reader may wish to consult Taylor (1980) and the references cited therein for additional information on both the theory and empirical measurement of telecommunications demand. We will next examine the characteristics of technology in the telecommunications industry, paying particular attention to the potential sources of both economies of scale and more general multiple output subadditivity in telecommunications cost functions.

9.2   Characteristics of telecommunications technology

The telecommunications industry is complex and multilayered, including research and development, manufacturing of supplies, provision of access to a network, and the transmission of messages. The discussion in this chapter — this section in particular — will primarily be confined to the provision of local access to business and residential users and to the transmission of intercity messages on the switched and private line networks. Questions concerning the vertical structure of the industry will be largely ignored.

This section will focus on telecommunications supply. Figure 9.3, which illustrates a conceptual view of the local and intercity telephone network, reveals a number of important characteristics of a modern telephone network. Individual access to the network is gained through each user's terminal hardware and a wire loop that connects it to a local office. The local office consists of a switch that is capable of interconnecting all possible pairs of terminal devices connected to it. After the local office, a typical intercity call is sent to a toll center switch. The toll switch determines the desired destination and selects a route from among the available open channels. Finally, at the receiving destination the process works in reverse order and the call is received at the desired location.

As Figure 9.3 suggests, there are several distinct components to telecommunications technology, although in fact all components are interrelated. Let us now turn to a more detailed look at these individual components, beginning with the costs of transmission. Originally, telephone messages were carried on open wires, and a pair of wires were required for each circuit. Local access to the network is still provided by wire pairs that are bundled in cables for the connection of individual subscribers to the local office. In order to connect local offices, however, and to make toll service feasible, one requires higher capacity transmission media. Coaxial cable systems and microwave radio systems have been developed since the 1940s to carry high-density traffic. Both frequency division and time division multiplexing are used to carry many individual communication channels on a single medium, thereby increasing the capacity of that medium. These developments have allowed for a dramatic reduction in the average cost (per circuit mile) of transmitting messages through the network.

More recent developments in long distance transmission include transmission by both extraterrestrial satellite and optical fibers. Satellite transmission is another form of microwave radio transmission in which some of the antennas and amplifiers are located thousands of miles above the surface of the earth. Optical fiber transmission consists of the transmission of light beams (either

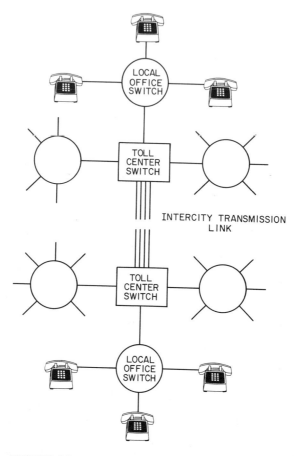

FIGURE 9.3

laser or light-emitting diode) in thin highly transparent glass fibers. Optical fibers allow high capacity transmission in a cable of relatively low cross-sectional area, and so are well suited for replacing existing cables in densely populated regions.

Transmission of telephone messages is subject to substantial economies of scale. However, it is important to specify carefully what is being held constant as economies of scale are measured. First, there is a short-run "economy of fill." Due to fixed costs associated with installation of a transmission medium it is desirable to install a given system in anticipation of future demand. Therefore transmission media frequently operate at less than full capacity. As demand grows the cost of activating circuits on a given system is relatively low, and so each transmission system experiences an economy of fill until full capacity operation is achieved.

Of more relevance to the question of subadditivity in

telecommunications cost functions is the comparison of the average cost at full capacity of different transmission systems. Figure 9.4 and Table 9.2 present these data for eleven different transmission systems. Although the data do not include all currently available systems, they illustrate the dramatic reduction in average cost per circuit-mile as total capacity of the system grows.

If all the transmission systems in Figure 9.4 were of the same vintage, then there would be unmistakable evidence of economies of scale in transmission. However, in addition to a pure economy of scale, an interdependence between technology and scale exists. Generally speaking, the major advances in transmission technology have brought forth systems of larger capacity and lower average cost at full capacity. Therefore it is difficult to separate the effects of scale and technology in a diagram such as Figure 9.4. The interaction of scale and technology is of great importance in the appraisal of econometric tests for scale economies in telecommunications. Section 9.3 will describe a number of attempts to deal with this issue.

The second component of telecommunications cost is the cost of switching. It will be seen that switching is substantially more complex than transmission. Although economies of scale are generally adequate to describe transmission systems, the economies associated with switching are more properly viewed in the context of overall network planning.

The purpose of switching is to interconnect transmission paths. A primitive telephone system without any switches whatsoever would require the direct connection of every terminal set to every other terminal set in the network. For example, in the eight-node network in Figure 9.5a, twenty-eight transmission links and fifty-six terminal sets are required in order to allow all possible interconnections without switching. If a switch is introduced at each node, in the form of a dial or push-button telephone, the number of terminal sets is reduced to eight. However, there is a cost associated with the introduction of switching, because each call must then be processed twice by a switch at the originating and receiving nodes.

A switch at each terminal does not reduce the costs of transmission, which can grow quite rapidly as the number of nodes grow. A one-hundred-node network requires 4,950 interconnecting links, and in general, an n node network requires $n(n-1)/2$ links. A central switch can drastically reduce the costs of transmission, as shown in Figure 9.5b. Here only eight links are required for interconnection, and n links are required in an n node network. Of course, the costs of switching have also increased, because with a central switch, every call must be switched three times instead of two.

The costs of transmission can in some circumstances be reduced even further by the introduction of additional switches, as shown in Figure 9.5c. The costs of transmission are lower after the

TABLE 9.2. *Approximate cost of two-way voice channels derived on various types of facilities*

Type of Facility	Average Cost per Route Mile	Voice Channel Capacity	Average Cost per Circuit Mile
Analog			
L1-8 Coax.	31,000	1,800	17.22
L3-12 Coax.	58,440	9,000	6.49
L4-20 Coax.	102,000	32,400	3.15
L5-22 Coax. (1973)	130,600	90,000	1.45
TD2 Radio (Unexpanded)	26,010	6,000	4.34
TH1 Over TD2 Radio	30,700	10,800	2.84
TH3 Radio	32,300	10,800	2.99
TD3 Under TH3	26,940	12,000	2.25
Digital			
T1 Carrier	64,760	3,600	17.99
T2 Carrier (1972)	68,000	9,200	7.39
T5-22 Coax. (1976)	126,020	81,000	1.56

Source: A.T.&T. [1970: 59 Chart 5]

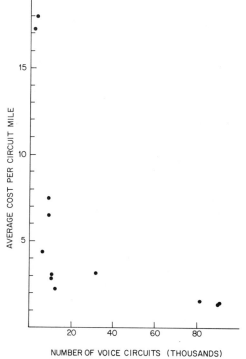

FIGURE 9.4

introduction of a second switch for two reasons: (1) Each terminal set is used only a small portion of time and so it is possible for one group of users to share the transmission capacity that connects it to another group of users. (2) Economies of scale in transmission, even without shared use, make it attractive to concentrate demand whenever possible. Of course, the savings in transmission cost must be compared to the increase in switching costs. In general, the greater the geographic dispersion of groups of customers is, the greater will be the savings in transmission relative to the increased cost of switching.

As Figure 9.5 illustrates, the costs of switching cannot be meaningfully described outside the context of optimal network design and management. Thus the final components of telecommunications technology to be addressed in this section are the optimal design of network facilities and the optimal routing of messages across a given network.

First, consider the optimal planning of network facilities — that is, switching machines and transmission media. As seen in Figure 9.5, a basic trade-off in the design of a telecommunications network involves the substitution of switching capacity for transmission capacity. In fact the same basic principles of network design may be used to construct a multileveled hierarchy of switching centers. A highly simplified portion of this hierarchy is shown in Figure 9.6. After reaching a local switching center, in which individual subscribers are directly interconnected through a central switch, demand may be further concentrated into a toll center and ultimately, into higher level sectional and regional centers. At each level of concentration, greater shared use of facilities is possible and the economies of scale in transmission can be exploited to best advantage.

To test for subadditivity of overall network costs, one must conceptually fragment the network in order to compare the cost of a single supplier network with the cost of one having two or more suppliers. If the single supplier is assumed to choose the cost-minimizing network, then it follows that costs in the fragmented network are higher. That is, in the conceptual experiment there is necessarily a network subadditivity effect. Recent simulation studies of network cost, and in particular, the study of Skoog (in press) have documented this effect in great detail.

Due to the complexity of the overall network, a simple demonstration of network subadditivity cannot be given. However, the basic nature of the subadditivity effect is revealed in an examination of a simple triangular network, as shown in Figure 9.7. Let x, y, and z represent the traffic demand among the pairs of nodes AC, AB, and BC, respectively. If x is small relative to y and z, and if the distance between A and C is large relative to the distances between AB and BC (i.e., if the triangle is flat), then it may be more efficient to carry the AC traffic along the AB and BC

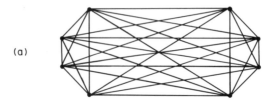

(a)

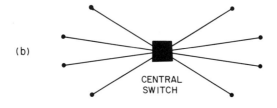

(b)

CENTRAL
SWITCH

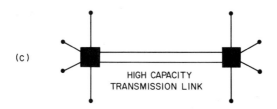

(c)

HIGH CAPACITY
TRANSMISSION LINK

FIGURE 9.5

REGIONAL
CENTER

SECTIONAL
CENTER

TOLL
CENTER

LOCAL
SWITCHING
CENTER

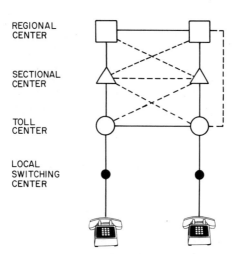

FIGURE 9.6

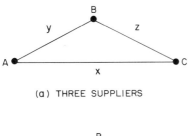

(a) THREE SUPPLIERS

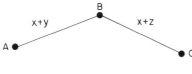

(b) ONE SUPPLIER

FIGURE 9.7

routes rather than construct a link for AC. If intercity transmission is provided by multiple suppliers, many similar arrangements would be ruled out, or at best could be made only after a contractual agreement among the suppliers. Fundamentally the subadditivity associated with network costs is an example of firm subadditivity rather than plant subadditivity.[5]

Once a set of network facilities is in place there is still a need to manage optimally the flow of messages in the network. Network management and design are interrelated because proper management through alternate routing of messages and other techniques can reduce the level of total capacity that is required. The basic tool of network management is automated alternative routing of messages over many possible paths through the network. In the triangular network shown in Figure 9.8 a direct route is typically constructed between every pair of nodes. Consider the traffic from A to C. Normally all the A to C traffic would be routed along a high usage transmission link that directly connects the nodes. However, in periods of unusually heavy traffic it is possible to overflow some of the A to C traffic onto an alternative route, such as A to B and B to C.

In actual practice there are many alternative nodes such as B that might be used to handle overflow traffic from A to C. Furthermore, alternate routing typically proceeds in a definite progression up the switching hierarchy, as shown in Figure 9.6. For example, the primary route between two terminal nodes may involve a path

5 The terms "plant subadditivity" and "firm subadditivity" are defined and discussed in Section 4.4 of Chapter 4.

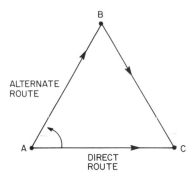

FIGURE 9.8

between the two toll centers, which are geographically closest to the terminal nodes. If this path is blocked, then alternative paths are searched for in a preplanned sequence that involves higher level sectional centers and regional centers, as shown by the dotted lines in Figure 9.6. Each time the path moves to a higher level center the distance that the message travels generally increases and the probability of completing the call increases because of the higher capacity transmission links.

A simple numerical example of the potential cost savings due to alternate routing is shown in Figure 9.9. In a triangular network the *AC* route experiences a peak nighttime demand, which can be overflowed onto the *AB* and *BC* portion of the network. Therefore total capacity on the *AC* link is lower in a network in which alternate routing is possible. When intercity transmission is handled by two or more suppliers, the possibilities for alternate routing are diminished. Therefore alternate routing is a source of network subadditivity.

This concludes the discussion of telecommunications cost characteristics. The reader who is interested in further details may consult a number of sources. Ellis (1975), Yaged (1975), and Hall (1975) discuss economies of scale in transmission, switching, and network planning based on engineering cost simulations. A concise review of telecommunications technology is contained in AT&T (1980). Both the technical and economic characteristics of telecommunications networks are surveyed in Littlechild (1979). An ambitious and comprehensive study of network costs may be found in Skoog (in press). Skoog describes in great detail the specific subadditivity characteristics of individual network components and those in a model of the overall network. This study captures many of the essential multiple output effects that cannot be measured as a simple economy of scale. Other sources concerning subadditivity in telecommunications are the exhibits in FCC Docket 20003, which contain simulation studies of costs in the

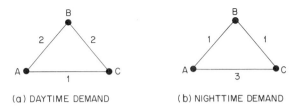

(a) DAYTIME DEMAND   (b) NIGHTTIME DEMAND

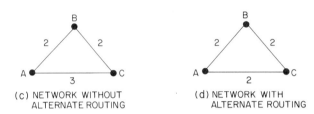

(c) NETWORK WITHOUT   (d) NETWORK WITH
    ALTERNATE ROUTING   ALTERNATE ROUTING

FIGURE 9.9

Bell System.[6] Finally, there have been several recent reports of independent consulting firms in which a model of the telecommunication system is presented and studied.[7]

9.3   Econometric studies of the telecommunications industry

When studies, which rely on measurements of inputs and outputs that have been generated in a real production process, are conducted in the telecommunications industry, aggregated output measures are generally used and an estimate of systemwide economies of scale is made. In principle, these studies capture diseconomies of scale that may be present in the industry, such as organizational diseconomies, not generally accounted for in simulation studies of network cost. However, an econometric study cannot approach the detailed measurement of cost functions, and in particular, multiproduct cost functions, of which a simulation study is capable.

Let us begin with a discussion of some of the methodological issues shared by most econometric studies. In estimating telecommunications cost functions, one is faced with a common

[6]   See, for example, AT&T (1976a; 1976b; 1976c; 1976d).
[7]   See Stone, Schankerman, and Fenton (1976) and Meyer, et al. (1979).

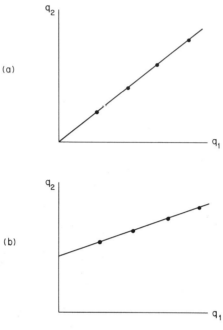

FIGURE 9.10

problem — the aggregation of output. As described in Section 9.1, output in the industry is inherently multidimensional. In practice, however, aggregate revenue is generally used as a proxy for total output. Assuming constant output prices, a change in revenue measures a change in an average output in the same way that a price index measures the change in an average price. Several elementary observations are possible concerning tests for economies of scale.

First, it is necessary that all outputs change in roughly the same proportion when revenues change, as in Figure 9.10a, in order to have a valid measure of economies of scale. If some outputs grow more rapidly than others, as in Figure 9.10b, then the resulting measure of aggregate output will not reflect economies of scale.

In order to measure economies of scale, one must also determine what should be held constant in a comparison of the total costs of producing different outputs. For example, in the very short run most factors of production are fixed. That is, they cannot be adjusted when there are small changes in output. With fixed factors of production the shape of the average cost function can be easily predicted. With a fixed plant and a low level of output, output can be expanded by increasing only the variable factors of production. Because the cost of fixed factors is divided among more units of output, the average total cost necessarily falls. At some point, output reaches the capacity at which the fixed plant was designed. Further increases in output then require more costly adjustments in the variable factors (such as overtime pay for labor) and so average costs begin to rise. In the short run there are nearly always economies of scale at low levels of output, followed by diseconomies of scale at larger outputs.

Telecommunications technology offers an example of a short-run economy of scale in the optimal solution to the dynamic capacity expansion problem. Both transmission and switching systems are typically installed in anticipation of future demand growth. The cost of activating circuits on a given system is small relative to total costs, and so the average total costs (per circuit-mile) of a given system inevitably fall until full capacity is reached. Suppose, for example, that demand is growing linearly over time. An optimal solution to the capacity expansion problem, shown in Figure 9.11a involves the installation of a fixed-sized plant at regular intervals of time. In the short run there are economies of fill as shown in Figure 9.11b, but in the longer run the observed average costs are constant.

Constant average costs suggest that there must be long-run constant returns to scale. However, an econometric study of long-run telecommunications costs should account for the possible existence of firm subadditivity, as well as of plant subadditivity. In Section 4.4 the capacity expansion problem was used as an example of potential firm subadditivity that may exist in the absence of plant subadditivity. In order to produce at minimum cost in the long run, the firm needs to install each unit of plant at the proper time. Long-run cost minimization in a growing industry is necessarily dynamic in character. If in an optimal capacity expansion sequence the planned additions to capacity are sufficiently large relative to total capacity, then two or more firms serving the same market could attain the cost-minimizing expansion sequence only through coordinated investment planning. Therefore measured constant returns to scale in the intermediate run may give way to increasing returns to scale in the very long run, when the firm costs as well as plant costs are taken into account.

The measurement of long-run total costs requires that all factors of production be variable. However, in the long run an additional complication arises if outputs are measured at different points in time and if technology changes. Conceptually, one could measure long-run economies of scale by estimating the costs at a single point in time of producing many different outputs when all factors of production are allowed to vary. That is, one would conceptually design, from the ground up, plants for producing small, intermediate, and large outputs and then compare the average total

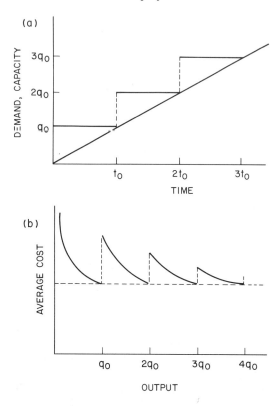

FIGURE 9.11

costs of each. This would measure a pure long-run economy of scale.

In the real world one is rarely able to perform such a clear-cut test. Generally, outputs are measured at different points in time, because in order to hold all the relevant variables constant, one must use time-series data for a single firm or industry. (Using cross-section data at one point in time would be feasible only if both small and large firms are identical in all relevant aspects except scale of operation.) After doing this, one may need to separate the effects of larger scale and changing technology on the average total costs of production.

When technological change is exogenous to the industry, a correction for it should be made before measuring scale economies. The effect of exogenous technological change is to shift the true average cost function. Actual measurements of average costs at different outputs will therefore not reflect in any way the true degree of scale economies in the industry. For example, the invention of photocopy machines has lowered the average cost of administrative functions in all industries but without reflecting an economy of scale

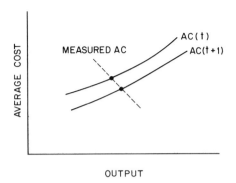

FIGURE 9.12

in management. Figure 9.12 illustrates a situation in which true long-run diseconomies of scale are consistent with measured "economies of scale" if technological change is not taken into account. The lower average cost at higher output results entirely from the shift in the average cost function due to technological change. However, average costs with constant technology are uniformly increasing.

Endogenous technological change is more complex. In an industry such as telecommunications, which serves a growing market, it is possible that technology and scale of operation are interdependent. That is, a physical plant may be designed at one point in time to satisfy the current market demand at the lowest total cost. Later when demand has grown, a new higher-capacity plant may be designed. Let us suppose that the new plant has lower average costs than the old one. The new plant may embody new technology that was not known or available at the time the first plant was constructed. However, as long as the new technology is a direct result of the larger scale for which it was designed and is not applicable for a smaller scale of the plant, clearly the lower average costs of the new plant reflect a pure long-run economy of scale.

There is a semantic issue as to whether one should refer to the preceding economy as an economy of scale or an economy of endogenous technological change. In either case the final conclusion is the same. Larger outputs mean lower average costs and the lower average costs cannot be attained until the larger scale is achieved. The only real issue is that of distinguishing between the endogenous technological change and the exogenous technological change that may have occurred simultaneously.

When econometricians measure scale economies they generally correct for exogenous technological change. But at the same time, they correct for — i.e. attempt to cancel out the effects of — endogenous technological change. In an industry such as telecommunications, in which a growing market has been served by a technologically active firm, this procedure may result in a misrepresentation of the true underlying long-run economies of scale.

A final comment should be made concerning the role of research and development in producing technological change. In order to produce endogenous technological change, one should devote resources to basic and applied research. Thus in the very long run it would be desirable to measure economies of scale so as to reflect the economies associated with producing new technologies. However, neither economic theory nor econometric practice can adequately deal with research and development at the present time.

Even if economies of scale are measured correctly, they are neither necessary nor sufficient for subadditivity, as clarified in Chapter 4. In particular, if a diseconomy of scope in a multi-output industry exists, then there cannot be subadditivity whatever the level of scale economies. On the other hand, if there are economies of scope, then it is reasonably certain that the cost function is subadditive if there are also scale economies.[8] Because a test for economies of scope is feasible using current econometric technique, such a test would be an appropriate extension of studies of scale economies in the telecommunications industry. A better test would be one for trans-ray convexity or quasiconvexity, which were shown in Chapter 4 to be sufficient for subadditivity when combined with industry economies of scale.

A number of studies of the telecommunications industry will now be discussed in chronological order, based upon their publication date.[9] Most of the reports state their findings in terms of the scale elasticity E, which may be interpreted as follows. Let

$$q = f(x)$$

represent a production function, where q is a single homogeneous output and x is a single homogeneous input. Then there are economies of scale if and only if

$$E = \frac{\% \text{ change in output}}{\% \text{ change in input}} = \frac{df}{dx} \cdot \frac{x}{f(x)} > 1$$

If there are both multiple inputs and outputs, production is characterized by a transformation function F such that for all feasible input-output pairs (q, x),

$$F(q_1, \ldots, q_n ; x_1, \ldots, x_m) \geq 0$$

Then there are economies of scale at (q, x) if

$$F(\lambda^E q_1, \ldots, \lambda^E q_n ; \lambda x_1, \ldots, \lambda x_m) \geq 0$$

---

[8] However, recall that there is a counterexample in Chapter 4.

[9] In addition to the studies discussed here, one may also wish to consult Christensen, Cummings, and Schoech (1980); Davis, Caccoppolo, and Chaudry (1973); and Fishelson (1977).

for some $E > 1$ and all λ such that $1 \leq \lambda \leq 1 + \epsilon$ for some $\epsilon > 0$. The most familiar form of production function is the Cobb-Douglas form

$$q = k \; x_1^\alpha \; x_2^\beta$$

for which the scale elasticity $E = \alpha + \beta$.

One of the first studies of telecommunications production functions was conducted by Dobell, Taylor, Waverman, Lin, and Copeland (1972), for the Canadian government. The authors estimated a Cobb-Douglas production function using time-series data. Technological change was included in the specification via the proxy variable of percentage of direct-dialed toll calls. For Bell of Canada, their model generated a scale elasticity of 1.11, which was significantly greater than one at a 97.6 percent confidence level. However, for a combined cross section — time-series estimate, using data for the Trans-Canada Telephone System (an informal association of smaller companies) — the production function results were indicative of constant returns to scale. The authors attributed the latter result to inferior data. They also investigated returns to scale indirectly through an input requirement function that measures the minimum input required for a given level of output. These findings also confirmed the presence of increasing returns to scale in the industry.

Two different functional forms, a multiplicative nonhomogeneous and an additive nonhomogeneous production function, were estimated separately by Vinod (1972) and Sudit (1973). Both studies gave results that are consistent with economies of scale. Vinod used Bell System data from 1947 to 1970 and Sudit used the same Bell System data plus data from Bell Canada for 1952 to 1967. Scale elasticities varied from less than one in the post-World War II years to more than two in the late 1960s. However, neither author corrected for the effects of technological change in their data. Although this is not necessarily inappropriate, as already suggested, the failure to correct means that these results are not comparable with other studies of the industry.

Mantell (1974; 1975) has conducted studies of the telecommunications industry by using both Cobb-Douglas and nonhomogeneous production functions. Technological change was accounted for in two ways — through the percentage of direct-dialed calls and the percentage of the telephones serviced by cross bar exchanges. Time-series data on the Bell System for the period 1946-70 were provided by the Federal Communications Commission. For the Cobb-Douglas form, scale elasticities of 1.16 and 1.04 were reported when the proxies for technology were, respectively, the percentage of direct-dialed calls and the percentage of cross bar exchanges. For the nonhomogeneous production function comparable estimates were 1.17 and 1.00.

By computing scale elasticities for input requirements functions and by attempting to fit a number of cost functions, Mantell obtained results that were consistent with those previously quoted. His findings tended to confirm the presence of aggregate economies of scale in the industry but showed that the magnitude of the scale economy is sensitive to the particular form of estimation.

Vinod (1976a) commented on the earlier study of Mantell and reestimated one of his models by using ridge regression techniques. Vinod's results indicated that use of ridge regression tended to increase the estimate of scale economies — from 1.04 to 1.20. Vinod (1976b) also used ridge regression techniques in an estimation of a joint production function for telecommunications. Value-added measures for both toll and local services were taken as output variables in an additively separable translog production function. Technological change was assumed to be Hicks neutral. Bell System data for the period 1947 through 1973 were used. The principal findings were that systemwide scale elasticity varied between 1.19 and 1.23 from 1947-73; partial scale elasticity for toll service, holding local service constant varied between 2.95 and 2.98; and partial scale elasticity for local service, holding toll service constant, varied between 1.99 and 2.09. Thus toll service was found to exhibit stronger scale economies during the period studied.

Although the use of a multiple output production function is a significant advance over earlier studies, it is not sufficient for a definitive test of subadditivity in the industry. For this purpose, some measure of trans-ray convexity or similar condition, as outlined in Chapter 4, would be necessary. Vinod recognized this fact but suggested that such a test is not feasible.

Fuss and Waverman (1977) have developed an ambitious multiple output, multiple input model, from which they derived a translog cost function. This cost function was estimated by using Bell Canada data from 1952 to 1975. Estimates of scale elasticity were ambiguous, but rose from less than one in the early years to greater than one in the later years. The authors also rejected the hypothesis of separability (into inputs and outputs) of the transformation function and found weak evidence of cost complementarity between local and toll services and between the toll service and private line. The authors commented on the implication of these findings for subadditivity (there was no strong evidence to support subadditivity) but admitted that their test was not a suitable one.

Two papers by Nadiri and Schankerman (1980; 1981) attempted to explain the role of technological change and its relationship to scale economies in the Bell System. In one paper (1981) the authors estimated a translog total cost function by using Bell System data for the period 1947-76. Output was measured by the sum of deflated revenue in local and toll services. Inputs included labor, materials, capital, and research and development expenditures. Their estimates of the scale elasticity, including the effects of internal technological change, ranged from 1.81 to 2.35 for three different versions of the basic model. In addition, the authors found that the optimal mix of inputs depended on the scale of output and the degree of external time-related technical change.

In another paper, Nadiri and Schankerman (1980) treated research and development as a quasifixed factor. That is, research and development, and also capital in another version of the model, were assumed to be costly to adjust and were not assumed to be equal to their long-run cost-minimizing values at every point in time. A variable cost function of other inputs could then be estimated and an optimal value of the quasifixed input computed. The authors applied this procedure to Bell System data for 1947-76 using a translog cost function. Scale elasticities of 1.61 to 2.0 were found when research and development was assumed to be quasifixed. With capital quasifixed, the comparable estimates were 1.49 to 1.69. The hypotheses that Bell System use of capital and research and development was cost minimizing could not be rejected, but the power of that test was low. Finally, the net rate of return to research and development was estimated to be in the range of 25 to 40 percent, which is higher than comparable estimates for general manufacturing industries.

To summarize the empirical studies of telecommunications costs, one may say that there is a general consensus regarding the degree of scale economies in the industry, which most writers found to be in the range 1.04 to 1.16, when technical changes were corrected for by proxy variables and considerably higher when the effects of endogenous technical change were included. Some authors have tested for scale economies in a multiple output production function. One paper by Fuss and Waverman (1977) addressed the issue of cost complementarity, although the test is by no means definitive. Future empirical work should concentrate on multiple output production, and if possible, on cost functions that reflect in some way the network aspects of telecommunications costs.

9.4 Competition in telecommunications and the changing structure of the industry

It was shown in Chapter 2 that "destructive competition" has been linked historically with the concept of natural monopoly. In fact, as a motivating force for regulation of railroads, the fear of destructive competition may have been more persuasive than arguments that the industry was a natural monopoly.

The history of the telecommunications industry in the United States is similar in this respect to the history of railroads. After the Bell patents expired in 1893, there was substantial competitive entry into the industry. By 1907, AT&T's share of the market was approximately 50 percent.

This era was also a period of rapid growth in the industry. In

1893 there were 266,431 telephones in the country; by 1907, there were over six million.[10] Part of the entry then consisted of independent companies that provided service to communities that previously had none. Part of the entry, however, occurred in markets already served by Bell. It was this duplication of facilities that was most prominent in the public debate as a symptom of destructive competition.

Evidence from the competitive era of telecommunications, however, is not proof of destructive competition. During this period the industry was in fundamental disequilibrium because supply could not keep pace with the rapidly growing demand. Intuition suggests, and evidence supports, the argument that duplication of facilities at the local level is costly. Therefore much of the instability of the industry during the competitive era may be interpreted as the gradual consolidation of local natural monopolies within the industry.

Ultimately, the industry became dominated by AT&T, which served the major population centers and provided all long distance toll services. Beginning in the 1960s, however, a number of regulatory decisions by the Federal Communications Commission (FCC) opened the industry to competition, first in terminal equipment, later in private line services, and finally in switched toll service.

The purpose of this section will be to consider, primarily as an application of some results on market stability and competitive behavior from Chapters 5 through 8, the prospects for competition in the current telecommunications industry.[11] There are several possible forms that competition in an industry such as telecommunications may take. Two generic forms that can be described as symmetric and asymmetric competition will be described in the remainder of this section.

Competition is "asymmetric" if one firm is overwhelmingly larger than each of its potential competitors and if the rules of competitive conduct differ between the large and small firms.[12] An example of

---

[10] See Gabel (1969, p. 344).

[11] More extensive discussions of competition in the telecommunications industry may be found in Korek et al. (1977); Meyer et al. (1979); or Stone, Schankerman, and Fenton (1976). Also, see Jones (1977) and Waverman (1975).

[12] The largest firm must also have a dominant market share. That is, it must be larger, although perhaps not overwhelmingly larger, than all potential competitors together.

asymmetric competition is the dominant firm with competitive fringe model, which was discussed in Chapter 7. Here the asymmetry results from the fact that the dominant firm is a price setter, whereas the competitive fringe firms are price takers. Another example of asymmetric competition is natural monopoly in a contestable market. Here again, the dominant firm is a price setter, but in addition, the monopolist is not allowed to respond to entry if it should occur.

"Symmetric" competition is best defined as competition that is not asymmetric. Firms need not be of equal size; but generally speaking, there should be at least one other firm of comparable size to any given firm in the market. More importantly, all firms in the market must be able to compete on a free and equal basis.

In the telecommunications industry, competition at present is clearly asymmetric due to the dominance of the Bell System and the pervasive regulations that govern competitive conduct. There are indications, however, that as the industry grows it is evolving toward more symmetric competition.[13]

I do not wish to assert here that symmetric competition is necessarily superior to asymmetric competition. Instead I wish to point out potential difficulties that may be associated with both forms of competition. In any case the form of competition is ultimately dictated by technology. It is not possible to impose symmetric competition on a pure natural monopoly industry. And in a classical competitive industry competition is necessarily symmetric.

First, consider the potential difficulties with asymmetric competition in telecommunications. One difficulty that has received considerable attention is the issue of cream-skimming,[14] which has been alleged to occur because the Bell System has set prices for long-distance service on an average cost basis per unit of distance. Because of the economies of scale in transmission, the total cost to a

---

[13] As this book goes to press an important antitrust case (U.S. vs. AT&T, Civil Action No. 74-1698) is near to a conclusion that will largely determine the future role of competition in the industry. A preliminary agreement between the Department of Justice and AT&T has been reached which calls for the divestiture by AT&T of its local operating companies. In return AT&T would retain control of the Western Electric Company and Bell Laboratories and would be allowed substantial freedom to compete in information processing and other markets related to telecommunications.

[14] See, for example, Kahn (1971, pp. 221-46).

competing firm of serving a high-density route between two major metropolitan areas can be lower than the average systemwide cost to the Bell System. After entry was allowed by the FCC in 1960 actual entry by new firms did occur.[15]

There are a number of arguments that can be made against entry that can be characterized as cream-skimming. One is the mandate for universal service expressed in the Communications Act of 1934, according to which rates for basic telephone service were intended to be affordable to the largest possible user group. On purely economic grounds, it can be argued that prices less than marginal costs can in some circumstances be justified by the externalities associated with access and usage of the telephone system.

On the other hand, there are persuasive and well-known economic arguments in favor of prices that reflect costs of production.[16] The cream-skimming argument by itself does not justify restrictions on competitive entry in a market. However, a more persuasive argument against cream-skimming results from the asymmetric form of competition that often accompanies it. If entry is attractive in high-density intercity markets because the Bell System long-distance rates are set on an average cost basis, then ultimately those rates must be allowed to change to reflect actual cost on each route rather than systemwide average costs. If prices are not allowed to adjust, then the entry that does occur is inefficient and ultimately destabilizing. If allowed to continue over a long period of time, the Bell System, as a regulated common carrier, would be left with only low-density routes that it could serve only at a price reflecting the higher costs of serving such markets.

Closely related to cream-skimming is the question of sustainability and the possible nonsustainability of a natural monopolist's prices. In Chapter 7 it was argued that the most likely occurrence of a nonsustainable price is in a dynamic market with large sunk costs. One straightforward example is provided by the dynamic capacity expansion problem. In a growing telecommunications market, capacity for both switching and transmission must be installed in anticipation of future demand due to the fixed costs associated with installation. In Figure 9.13 demand is assumed to grow linearly with

[15] There were actually two decisions in 1959 and 1960, known as the "above-890" decisions. The number 890 refers to the portion of the microwave radio spectrum used by common carriers and potential entrants. See Kahn (1971, pp. 129-36) for further institutional details.

[16] These arguments are based on the discussion in Chapter 3 of the optimality properties of competitive prices. In markets that are not competitive, Ramsey optimal prices are related both to marginal cost of production and elasticity of demand.

time according to the function $D(t)$. One hypothetical expansion sequence that satisfies this demand is illustrated by the horizontal bars above the demand function in Figure 9.13. At time 0 capacity of q_1 is installed. At time t_1 the capacity q_1 is exhausted and a larger capacity q_2 is installed, either by replacement of q_1 or by an increment of capacity equal to $q_2 - q_1$. At each point of time there is some excess capacity and so prices over time must reflect the costs of this excess capacity.

If competition is asymmetric there is an alternative expansion sequence that can result in lower costs and therefore in lower prices. At time t_1 a firm without the obligation to serve all demand could install a capacity of q_1 and by setting the price slightly larger than the average cost of a fully utilized plant could earn a positive profit. At time t_2 such a firm could install capacity q_2 and again set the price so as to operate at full capacity. Therefore the market is dynamically nonsustainable.

A similar issue arises due to the variability of demand for telecommunications. Given a time profile of total market demand, the Bell System as a regulated common carrier must construct capacity sufficient to serve all market demand, subject to a given level of service quality. A competing firm, however, is not constrained to serve all, or any portion of total demand. During periods of peak demand, the competitive firm can turn away customers, who then must overflow into the dominant firm network. The effect of this strategy is to generate a more uniform time profile of demand for the competitive firm, and also to accentuate the peak-load problem faced by the dominant firm.

Let us now turn to an analysis of symmetric competition in which all firms in the market have the same obligations and ability to compete. The discussion of Chapters 7 and 8 suggested that competition of this form might be highly effective as long as the market is contestable and there are enough potential competitors. The first and most important question therefore is whether or not telecommunications markets are contestable.

A definitive response to the question of contestability of telecommunications markets cannot be given without a more extensive study. However, a number of brief comments can be made. First, entry into certain portions of the market appears to be relatively free. After the FCC restrictions on competition in intercity transmission were removed, a large number of small but apparently viable firms have entered into competition with the Bell System in providing private line services and regular switched toll service to businesses and individuals. In addition, several large firms are currently seen as potential competitors.

On the other hand, entry is not equally free in all sectors of the

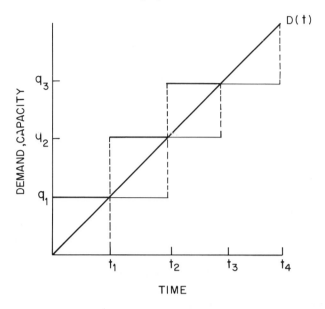

FIGURE 9.13

market. For example, intercity transmission by coaxial cable
involves significant sunk costs, which are in many ways similar to
the sunk costs in the railroad industry. The provision of local access
to individual subscribers is similarly characterized by significant sunk
costs. Furthermore, the provision of local access is almost without
question a pure natural monopoly, due to the duplication of facilities
that would result from competition for access.[17] Therefore
competition for local access must be between one active monopolist
and one or more potential, but never active, competitors. Besides
franchise bidding schemes there is no direct evidence that this form
of competition is viable.

Even if telecommunications markets are judged to be contestable,
there is no guarantee that they will be stable. Communication by its
very nature involves the formation of communities of interest. But
as shown in Chapter 6, when overlapping communities of interest
exist, there is a potential for market instability.[18] An example of the
potential for instability is suggested by the growth of private

---

[17] That is, if two or more competing companies offer local service, then a
given user must subscribe to both systems in order to communicate with
all other subscribers.

[18] In particular, see Proposition 6.4 and Examples 6.2 and 6.3. In addition,
the example in Section 5.3 is relevant.

business switched networks. It may be more efficient for an individual business to construct or lease its own communications network for its internal use, rather than to share in the cost of the common intercity network. As such networks grow, they divert resources from the common one. Because all users, including the users of private line networks, ultimately depend on the nationwide switched network, there is a potential for a misallocation of resources.

Another aspect of the possible conflict of interest is the different types of networks that are required for both business and residential use. For example, large and small businesses may demand data transmission services that require high speed and high quality transmission. At the same time, small businesses and residential users may desire a network with low access charges. Finally, large businesses and residential users may want low intercity toll charges. Thus there is the potential for the triangular instability that was discussed in Section 5.3.

Certain public good aspects of the telecommunications network also create a potential for conflict. At a very basic level there is a trade-off to be made between the costs of both terminal and common control equipment in the network. For example, an individual can purchase a telephone answering device that plays a recorded message and receives incoming messages. An identical service can also be provided by a central switching machine. It may or may not be more efficient to have centralized information processing in the network. If centralized services are more efficient, however, it does not automatically follow that they could survive in a competitive market.

Logically distinct from the potential for instability is the fact that a symmetrically competitive market may be more costly to manage than either asymmetric competition or regulated natural monopoly. One such example is the penalty resulting from nonstandardization of equipment. For instance, in a technologically dynamic industry such as consumer electronics there is often a period of uncertainty as rival firms compete for the right to set the industry standard. Where the compatibility of equipment is required, as is currently true, for example, with video disk players, both consumers and producers suffer from the uncertainty.

Another cost of a competitive market is that of contracting if two or more firms are required to act in concert.[19] Suppose, as an

---

[19] This argument is also made by Waverman (1975).

extreme case, that intercity telephone transmission is provided in a competitive market and that there is exactly one supplier along each link in the network connecting major local service areas (or nodes). If there are n nodes in the total network, then there are $n(n-1)/2$ potential suppliers of intercity toll service. In order to complete a particular internodal call, the local service company would have to make a contractual agreement with enough competitive internodal carriers to establish a connected path between nodes. The number of possible paths, however, is incredibly large. A relatively small twelve-node network has approximately ten million possible paths.[20] Therefore effective competition for intercity transmission requires that each local service company engage in a large number of bilateral negotiations.

If competition in intercity transmission is less extreme — for example, if there are only two competing carriers — contractual costs are still incurred. It was argued in Section 9.2 that a major component of firm subadditivity for telecommunications costs consists of the optimal planning of the aggregate network. In general, an optimal plan for the entire network does not coincide with one for a subportion of the network. For example, a switching machine that primarily serves the needs of one portion of the network may be most suitably located in another portion.

Some examples of potential transactions costs in a competitive market are suggested by the separations procedures by which toll revenues are divided between Bell and non-Bell operating companies. Typically, the division is based on the ownership of equipment that is used to make the toll call. Thus when it is time to modernize or expand the plant, the location of new equipment is constrained by the fact that neither side wishes to lose any portion of its toll revenue.

A final aspect of the costs of symmetric competition is the public good nature of the telephone network. For example, the most favorable microwave sites are determined by the topography of the landscape, and in most parts of the country the number of these locations is limited. If competition is to be totally symmetric, then the sites themselves must be shared. But a sharing of sites requires

[20] The number of paths containing i links between any two nodes is given by $(n-2)!/(n-i-1)!$. The total number of paths is found by summing over i from 1 to $n-1$. Then the approximation $e \approx 1 + 1/1! + 1/2! + \ldots + 1/(n-2)!$ gives the total number of paths as approximately 2.71 $[(n-1)!]$.

a sharing of the costs associated with them. Because the costs involved are largely fixed, there is no obvious or uniquely efficient way to allocate the costs. Inevitably the competing firms must bargain over their share of the cost.

In conclusion, the comments of this section should not be taken to imply that competition in telecommunications is inherently unworkable. The arguments do suggest, however, that competition in the industry is not a costless process. In particular, if the institutional structure of the industry continues to change, as the industry is transformed from regulated monopoly to a more competitive industry, then new institutions must arise. Inevitably the interim period will involve some instability and economic waste.

9.5   Concluding comments

This concludes the examination of natural monopoly characteristics in the telecommunications industry. A definitive answer to the question of whether or not the industry is a natural monopoly has not been given. Indeed, there can be no simple answer to this question. Quite clearly, the industry has many of the characteristics of a natural monopoly. At the same time, changing technology is expanding the boundaries of the industry and blurring the distinctions between communications and information processing. Certainly under the broadest definition this evolving industry is not a natural monopoly. Future policy decisions that will influence the course of development of telecommunications must ultimately be based on detailed analyses of the technology and demand characteristics of the industry. The purpose of this chapter has been to suggest a number of issues that are highly relevant in such a public policy debate. In addition, it is hoped that the student of industrial organization has gained some additional insight on the nature of both cost subadditivity and competition in natural monopoly or natural oligopoly markets.

The primary conclusion to be drawn is that the abstract concepts discussed in previous chapters can, with some effort, be identified in the context of a specific technology and competitive environment. However, empirical studies of industrial organization are only beginning to incorporate the proper methodology for the study of multiple output natural monopoly. It is hoped that this book will be helpful in the development of both future theories and future empirical work on the subject of natural monopoly.

References

Abraham, L. G. 1960. "The Complexity of the Transmission Network" *Bell Laboratories Record, 38*, 43-8.

Alchian, A. A. and Demsetz, H. 1972. "Production, Information Costs, and Economic Organization" *American Economic Review, 62*, 777-95.

American Telephone and Telegraph Company. 1970. "Comments of American Telephone and Telegraph Company, Part III," FCC Docket 18920, Washington, D.C.

    1976a. "Multiple Supplier Network Study" Exhibit 57, FCC Docket 20003, Washington, D.C.

    1976b. "Principles of Network Engineering" Exhibit 58, FCC Docket 20003, Washington, D.C.

    1976c. "Comparison of the Costs of Common and Specialized Networks" (Prepared by Systems Applications, Inc.) Exhibit 61, FCC Docket 20003, Washington, D.C.

    1976d. "An Evaluation of A.T.T.'s Multiple Supplier Network Study" (Prepared by Systems Applications, Inc.) Exhibit 66, FCC Docket 20003, Washington, D.C.

    1980. *United States v. American Telephone and Telegraph Company, Civil Action No. 74-1698, Defendants' Third Statement of Contentions and Proof.* U.S. District Court for the District of Columbia.

Areeda, P. and Turner, D. F. 1975. "Predatory Pricing and Related Practices Under Section 2 of the Sherman Act" *Harvard Law Review, 88*, 697.

Arrow, K. J. 1971. "Political and Economic Evaluation of Social Effects and Externalities" In *Frontiers of Quantative Economics*, M. Intriligator, ed. Amsterdam: North Holland, pp. 3-25.

Arrow, K. J. and Hahn, F. H. 1971. *General Competitive Analysis.* San Francisco: Holden-Day.

Artle, R. and Averous, C. 1973. "The Telephone System as a Public Good: Static and Dynamic Aspects" *Bell Journal of Economics, 4*, 89-100.

Aumann, R. J. 1967. "A Survey of Cooperative Games Without Side Payments" In *Essays in Mathematical Economics in Honor of Oskar Morgenstern,* M. Shubik, ed. Princeton, NJ: Princeton University Press, 3-28.

Averch, H. and Johnson, L. L. 1962. "Behavior of the Firm under Regulatory Constraint" *American Economic Review, 52*, 1053-69.

Bailey, E. E. 1973. *Economic Theory of Regulatory Constraint.* Lexington, MA: Lexington Books.

    1981. "Contestability and the Design of Regulatory and Antitrust Policy" *American Economic Review, 71*, 178-83.

Bailey, E. E. and Panzar, J. C. 1981. "The Contestability of Airline Markets During the Transition to Deregulation" *Law and Contemporary Problems, 44*, 125-46.

References 215

Bain, J. S. 1956. *Barriers to New Competition*. Cambridge, MA: Harvard University Press.

Baumol, W. J. 1952. "The Transactions Demand for Cash: An Inventory Theoretic Approach," *Quarterly Journal of Economics, 66*, 545-56.

— 1975. "Scale Economies, Average Cost and the Profitability of Marginal Cost Pricing" In *Essays in Urban Economics and Public Finance in Honor of William S. Vickrey*, R. E. Griesson, ed. Lexington, MA: Heath.

— 1977. "On the Proper Cost Tests for Natural Monopoly in a Multiproduct Industry" *American Economic Review, 67*, 809-22.

Baumol, W. J., Bailey, E. E., and Willig, R. D. 1977. "Weak Invisible Hand Theorems on the Sustainability of Prices in a Multiproduct Monopoly" *American Economic Review, 67*, 350-65.

Baumol, W. J. and Bradford, D. F. 1970. "Optimal Departures from Marginal Cost Pricing" *American Economic Review, 60*, 265-83.

Baumol, W. J. and Braunstein, Y. M. 1977. "Empirical Study of Scale Economies and Production Complementarity: The Case of Journal Publication," *Journal of Political Economy, 85,* 1037-48.

Baumol, W. J., Eckstein, O., and Kahn, A. E. 1970. "Competition and Monopoly in Telecommunications Services" Unpublished manuscript.

Baumol, W. J., Panzar, J. C., and Willig, R. D. 1982. *Contestable Markets and the Theory of Industry Structure*. New York: Harcourt Brace Jovanovich.

Baumol, W. J. and Willig, R. D. 1981. "Fixed Cost, Sunk Cost, Entry Barriers and Sustainability of Monopoly" *Quarterly Journal of Economics, 96*, 405-32.

Beckenstein, A. R. 1975. "Scale Economies in the Multiplant Firm: Theory and Empirical Evidence" *Bell Journal of Economics*, *6*, 644-57.

Bertrand, J. 1883. Review of "Théorie mathématique de la richesse sociale" and "Recherches sur less principes mathématiques de la théorie des richesses" *Journal des Savants*, 499-508.

Boies, D. 1968. "Experiment in Mercantilism: Minimum Rate Regulation by the Interstate Commerce Commission" *Columbia Law Review, 68*, 599-663.

Boiteux, M. 1971. "On the Management of Public Monopolies Subject to Budgetary Constraints" *Journal of Economic Theory, 3*, 219-40.

Bonbright, J. C. 1961. *Principles of Public Utility Rates*. New York: Columbia University Press.

Bondareva, O. 1962. "The Core of an n-person Game" *Vestnik Leningrad University, 17*, 141-2.

Borch, K. 1962. "Application of Game Theory to Some Problems in Automobile Insurance" *Astin Bulletin, 2*, 208-21.

Bork, R. H. 1978. *The Antitrust Paradox: A Policy at War with Itself*. New York: Basic Books.

Braeutigam, R. R. 1979. "Optimal Pricing with Intermodal Competition" *American Economic Review, 69*, 38-49.

Brown, R., Caves, D., and Christensen, L. 1979. "Modelling the Structure of Costs and Production for Multiproduct Firms" *Southern Economic Journal 46*, 256-73.

Burns, A. F. 1936. *The Decline of Competition: A Study of the Evolution of American Industry*. New York: McGraw-Hill.

Chamberlain, E. H. 1936. *Theory of Monopolistic Competition*. Cambridge, MA: Harvard University Press.

Champsaur, P. 1975. "How to Share the Cost of a Public Good" *International Journal of Game Theory*, *4*, 113-29.

Chandler, A. D. Jr. 1977. *The Visible Hand: The Managerial Revolution in American Business*. Cambridge, MA: Harvard University Press.

Chenery, H. B. 1952. "Overcapacity and the Acceleration Principle" *Econometrica*, *20*, 1-28.

Cheung, S. 1973. "The Fable of the Bees: An Economic Investigation" *Journal of Law and Economics*, *16*, 11-33.

Christensen, L., Cummings, D., and Schoech, P. 1980. "Econometric Estimation of Scale Economies in Telecommunications" Social Systems Research Institute, Discussion Paper No. 8013, University of Wisconsin.

Clark, J. M. 1923. *The Economics of Overhead Costs*. Chicago: University of Chicago Press.

1939. *The Social Control of Business*. New York: McGraw-Hill.

1940. "Towards a Concept of Workable Competition" *American Economic Review*, *30*, 241-56.

Coase, R. H. 1937. "The Nature of the Firm" *Economica*, *4*, 386-405.

1970. "The Theory of Public Utility Pricing and Its Application" *Bell Journal of Economics*, *1*, 113-28.

Cournot, A. 1838. *Recherches sur les principes mathématiques de la théorie des richesses*. Paris: Hachette. (English ed: *Researches into the Mathematical Principles of the Theory of Wealth*, N. T. Bacon, transl. New York: Augustus M. Kelly, 1960.)

Crain, W. M. and Ekelund, R. B., Jr. 1976. "Chadwick and Demsetz on Competition and Regulation" *Journal of Law and Economics*, *19*, 149-62.

Davis, B. E., Caccoppolo, G. J., and Chaudry, M. A. 1973. "An Econometric Planning Model for American Telephone and Telegraph Company" *Bell Journal of Economics*, *4*, 29-56.

Debreu, G. 1959. *Theory of Value*. New York: Wiley.

Demsetz, H. 1968. "Why Regulate Utilities?" *Journal of Law and Economics*, *11*, 55-65.

Dixit, A. 1980. "The Role of Investment in Entry-Deterrence" *Economic Journal*, *90*, 95-106.

Dobell, A. R., Taylor, L. D., Waverman, L. L., Lin, T. H., and Copeland, M. D. G. 1972. "Telephone Communications in Canada: Demand, Production and Investment Decisions" *Bell Journal of Economics*, *3*, 175-219.

Dorfman, J. 1969. *Two Essays by Henry Carter Adams*. New York: Augustus M. Kelly.

Dupuit, J. 1844. "De la Mesure de l'Utilité des Travaux Publics" *Annales des Ponts et Chausses*, *8*. Reprinted in *Readings in Welfare Economics*, K. Arrow and T. Scitovsky, eds. Homewood, IL: Irwin, 1969, (255-83).

Eaton, B. C. and Lipsey, R. G. 1980. "Exit Barriers Are Entry Barriers: The Durability of Capital as a Barrier to Entry" *Bell Journal of Economics*, *11*, 721-29.

Edgeworth, F. Y. 1925. *Papers Relating to Political Economy*, vol. 1. London: Macmillan.

Eldor, D., Sudit, E. F., and Vinod, H. D. 1979. "Telecommunications, CES Production Function: A Reply" *Applied Economics*, *11*, 133-38.

Ellis, L. W. 1975. "The Law of the Economics of Scale Applied to Telecommunications System Design" *Electrical Communication*, *50*, 1-19.

Ely, R. T. 1937. *Outlines of Economics*. New York: Macmillan.

Farrer, T. H. 1902. *The State in Its Relation to Trade*. London: Macmillan.

Faulhaber, G. R. 1971. "Competition and the Dynamics of Growth in Telecommunications" Unpublished manuscript.

1972. "On Subsidization: Some Observations and Tentative Conclusions" Proceedings of a Conference on Communication Policy Research, Washington, D.C.

1975. "Cross-Subsidization: Pricing in Public Enterprises" *American Economic Review*, *65*, 966-77.

Faulhaber, G. and Levinson, S. 1981. "Subsidy Free Prices and Anonymous Equity," *American Economic Review*, *71*, 1083-91.

Feller, W. 1957. *An Introduction to Probability Theory and Its Applications*, 2nd ed., vol. 1. New York: Wiley.

Fishelson, G. 1977. "Telecommunications, CES Production Function" *Applied Economics*, *9*, 9-18.

Friedlaender, A. F. 1969. *The Dilemma of Freight Transport Regulation*. Washington, D.C.: Brookings Institution.

Friedlaender, A. F. and Spady, R. H. 1981. *Freight Transport Regulation: Equity, Efficiency, and Competition in the Rail and Trucking Industries*. Cambridge, MA: MIT Press.

Friedman, M. 1962. Price Theory: A Provisional Text. Chicago: Aldine.

Fuss, M. and Waverman, L. 1977. "Multi-Product, Multi-Input Cost Functions for a Regulated Utility: The Case of Telecommunications in Canada" Presented at NBER Conference on Public Regulation, Washington, D.C., December 1977.

Gabel, R. 1971. "The Early Competitive Era in Telephone Communications, 1893-1920," *Law and Contemporary Problems, 34*, 340-59.

Gaskins, D. W. 1971. "Dynamic Limit Pricing: Optimal Pricing Under Threat of Entry" *Journal of Economic Theory*, *3*, 306-22.

Ginsberg, W. 1974. "The Multiplant Firm with Increasing Returns to Scale" *Journal of Economic Theory*, *9*, 283-92.

Gold, B. 1981. "Changing Perspectives on Size, Scale, and Returns: An Interpretative Survey" *Journal of Economic Literature*, *19*, 5-33.

Goldberg, V. P. 1976. "Regulation and Administered Contracts" *Bell Journal of Economics*, *7*, 426-48.

Griliches, Z. 1972. "Cost Allocation in Railroad Regulation" *Bell Journal of Economics*, *3*, 26-41.

Grossman, S. J. 1981. "Nash Equilibrium and the Industrial Organization of Markets with Large Fixed Costs" *Econometrica*, *49*, 1149-72.

Groves, T. and Ledyard, J. 1977. "Optimal Allocation of Public Goods: A Solution to the Free Rider Problem" *Econometrica, 45*, 783-809.

Hall, A. D. 1975. "An Overview of Economics of Scale in Existing Communications Systems" *IEEE Transactions on Systems, Man, and Cybernetics*, *5*, 1-14.

Harris, R. G. 1977. "Economics of Traffic Density in the Rail Freight Industry" *Bell Journal of Economics*, *8*, 556-64.

Hasenkamp, G. 1976a. *Specification and Estimation of Multiple Output Production Functions*. New York: Springer-Verlag.

1976b. "A Study of Multiple-Output Production Functions: Klein's Railroad Study Revisited" *Journal of Econometrics*, *4*, 253-62.

Hilton, G. 1966. "The Consistency of the Interstate Commerce Act" *Journal of Law and Economics*, *9*, 87-113.

Hotelling, H. 1929. "Stability in Competition" *Economic Journal, 39*, 41-57.

——— 1938. "The General Welfare in Relation to Problems of Taxation and of Railway and Utility Rates" *Econometrica, 6,* 242-69.

Ichiishi, T. 1980. "A Note on Existence of a Core in a Production Economy with Increasing Returns" Unpublished.

Jones, W. K. 1977. "Deregulation and Regulatory Reform in Natural-Monopoly Markets" In *Deregulating American Industry*, D. L. Martin and W. F. Schwartz, eds. Lexington, MA: Lexington Books.

Joskow, P. L. and Klevorick, A. K. 1979. "A Framework for Analyzing Predatory Pricing Policy" *Yale Law Journal, 89*, 213.

Kahn, A. E. 1971 *The Economics of Regulation: Principles and Institutions,* vol. II. New York: Wiley.

Kalai, E. and Zemel, E. 1980. "On Totally Balanced Games and Games of Flow" Discussion Paper No. 413, Department of Managerial Economics and Decision Sciences, Northwestern University.

——— 1981. "Generalized Network Problems Yielding Totally Balanced Games" Unpublished manuscript.

Kaysen, C. and Turner, D. 1959. *Antitrust Policy: An Economic and Legal Analysis.* Cambridge, MA: Harvard University Press.

Klein, B., Crawford, R. G., and Alchian, A. A. 1978. "Vertical Integration, Appropriable Rents, and the Competitive Contracting Process" *Journal of Law and Economics, 21,* 297-326.

Klein, L. R. [1953] *A Textbook of Econometrics.* Evanston, IL: Row Peterson.

Knight, F. H. 1921a. *Risk, Uncertainty and Profit.* Boston: Houghton Mifflin.

——— 1921b. "Cost of Production and Price" *Journal of Political Economy, 29*, 304-35. Reprinted in F. H. Knight, *The Ethics of Competition and Other Essays*, New York: Harper & Row, 1935.

Koopmans, T. C. 1957. *Three Essays on the State of Economic Science.* New York: McGraw-Hill.

Koopmans, T. C. and Beckmann, M. J. 1957. "Assignment Problems and the Location of Economic Activities" *Econometrica, 25*, 53-76.

Korek, M., Allan, D. S., Brandes, E. M., Fletcher, M. W., Jones, F. J., Kent, W. A., Krausz, L. I., Olszewski, R., Rojahn, L. R., and Rosse, J. N. 1977. *Analysis of Issues and Findings in FCC Docket 20003.* Menlo Park, CA: Stanford Research Institute.

Kreps, D. and Wilson, R. 1980. "On the Chain-Store Paradox and Predation: Reputation for Toughness" Technical Report No. 317, IMSSS, Stanford University.

Lindahl, E. 1958. "Just Taxation-A Positive Solution" In *Classics in the Theory of Public Finance*, Musgrave and Peacock, eds. London: Macmillan, 168-76.

Lipsey, R. G. and Lancaster, K. 1956. "The General Theory of the Second Best" *Review of Economic Studies, 24*, 11-32.

Little, I. M. D. 1951. "Direct Versus Indirect Taxes" *The Economic Journal, 61*, 577-84.

Littlechild, S. C. 1975. "Common Costs, Fixed Charges, Clubs, and Games" *Review of Economic Studies, 42*, 117-24.

——— 1979. *Elements of Telecommunications Economics.* Stevenage, Peter Peregrinus.

Loeb, M. and Magat, W. A. 1979. "A Decentralized Method for Utility Regulation" *Journal of Law and Economics, 22*, 399-404.

Lowry, E. D. 1973. "Justification for Regulation: The Case for Natural Monopoly" *Public Utilities Fortnightly*, November 8, 1973, 1-7.

McGee, J. S. 1958. "Predatory Price Cutting: The Standard Oil (N.J.) Case" *Journal of Law and Economics, 1*, 137.

1980. "Predatory Pricing Revisited" *Journal of Law and Economics, 23*, 289-330.

McPhee, J. 1981. "Small Scale Hydroelectric Power" *The New Yorker*, February 23, 1981, 44-87.

Manne, A. S. 1961. "Capacity Expansion and Probabilistic Growth" *Econometrica, 29*, 632-49.

Mantell, L. H. 1974. "An Econometric Study of Returns to Scale in the Bell System" Staff Research Paper, Office of Telecommunications Policy, Washington, D.C.

1975. "Some Estimates of Returns to Scale in the Telephone Industry" *IEEE Transactions on Systems, Man, and Cybernetics, 5*, 23-30.

Markovits, R. 1975. "Some Preliminary Notes on the American Antitrust Law: Economic Tests of Legality" *Stanford Law Review, 27*, 841.

Marschak, J. and Radner, R. 1972. *Economic Theory of Teams*. New Haven: Yale ⟵ University Press.

Marshall, A. 1927. *Principles of Economics*, 8th ed. London: Macmillan.

Meyer, J. R., Wilson, R. W., Baughcum, M. A., Burton, E., and Caovette, L. 1979. *The Economics of Competition in the Telecommunications Industry*. Boston, MA: Charles River.

Milgrom, P. and Roberts, J. 1980. "Equilibrium Limit Pricing Doesn't Limit Entry" Discussion Paper 399R, Center for Mathematical Studies in Economics and Management Science, Northwestern University.

Mill, J. S. 1926. *Principles of Political Economy*. London: Longmans.

Mitchell, B. M. 1978. "Specifying and Estimating Multi-Product Cost Functions for a Regulated Telephone Company" Unpublished manuscript.

Modigliani, F. 1958. "New Developments on the Oligopoly Front" *Journal of Political Economy, 66*, 213-32.

Nadiri, M. I., and Schankerman, M. A. 1980. "Variable Cost Functions and the Rate of Return to Quasi-Fixed Factors: An Application to R&D in the Bell System" National Bureau of Economic Research Working Paper, No. 597.

1981. "The Structure of Production, Technological Change and the Rate of Growth of Total Factor Productivity in the Bell System" In *Productivity Measurement in Regulated Industries*, T. Cowing and R. Stevenson, eds. New York: Academic Press.

Novshek, W. 1980. "Cournot Equilibrium with Free Entry" *Review of Economic Studies, 47*, 473-86.

Novshek, W. and Sonnenschein, H. 1979. "Cournot and Walras Equilibrium" *Journal of Economic Theory, 19*, 223-66.

Panzar, J. C. 1980. "Sustainability, Efficiency, and Vertical Integration" In *Regulated Industries and Public Enterprise*, P. Kleindorfer and B. M. Mitchell eds. Lexington, MA: Heath.

Panzar, J. C. and Willig, R. D. 1977a. "Economics of Scale in Multi-Output Production" *Quarterly Journal of Economics, 91*, 481-93.

1977b. "Free Entry and the Sustainability of Natural Monopoly" *Bell Journal of Economics, 8*, 1-22.

1981. "Economics of Scope" *American Economic Review, 71*, 268-72. ⌡

Posner, R. A. 1969. "Natural Monopoly and Its Regulation" *Stanford Law Review, 21*,

220 References

548-643.

1976. *Antitrust Law: An Economic Perspective.* Chicago: University of Chicago Press.

Quinzii, M. 1980. "An Existence Theorem for the Core of a Productive Economy with Increasing Returns" Unpublished manuscript.

Radner, R. 1980a. "Optimal Equilibria in a Class of Repeated Games with Imperfect Montoring" Unpublished manuscript.

1980b. "Monitoring Cooperative Agreements in a Repeated Principal-Agent Relationship" Bell Laboratories Discussion Paper, No. 184.

Ramsey, F. 1927. "A Contribution to the Theory of Taxation" *Economic Journal, 37,* 47-61.

Ripley, W. Z. 1912. *Railroads: Rates and Regulation.* London: Longmans.

Robinson, J. 1934. *The Economics of Imperfect Competition.* London: Macmillan.

Rohlfs, J. 1974. "A Theory of Interdependent Demand for a Communications Service" *Bell Journal of Economics, 5,* 16-37.

Rosenbaum, R. A. 1950. "Sub-Additive Functions" *Duke Mathematical Journal, 17,* 227-47.

Samuelson, P. A. 1980. *Economics,* 11th ed. New York: McGraw-Hill.

Sandberg, I. W. 1975. "Two Theorems on a Justification of the Multiservice Regulated Company" *Bell Journal of Economics, 6,* 346-56.

1979. "On Competition, Regulation, and Market Structures" *IEEE Transactions on Systems, Man, and Cybernetics, 9,* 824-8.

Scarf, H. 1967. "The Core of an N Person Game" *Econometrica, 35,* 50-69.

Scarf, H. and Hansen, T. 1973. *The Computation of Economic Equilibria.* New Haven: Yale University Press.

Scherer, F. M. 1970. *Industrial Market Structure and Economic Performance.* Chicago: Rand McNally College.

1976. "Predatory Pricing and the Sherman Act: A Comment" *Harvard Law Review, 89,* 868.

Scherer, F. M., Beckenstein, A. R., Kaufer, E., and Murphey, R. D. 1975. *The Economics of Multiplant Operation: An International Comparisons Study.* Cambridge, MA: Harvard University Press.

Schmalensee, R. 1979. *The Control of Natural Monopolies.* Lexington, MA: Lexington Books.

Schumpeter, J. A. 1954. *History of Economic Analysis.* New York: Oxford University Press.

Selten, R. 1974. "The Chain store Paradox" Working Paper No. 18, Institute of Mathematical Economics, University of Bielfield, West Germany.

Shapley, L. S. 1967. "On Balanced Sets and Cores" *Naval Research Logistics Quarterly, 14,* 453-60.

1971. "Cores of Convex Games" *International Journal of Game Theory, 1,* 11-26.

Sharkey, W. W. 1977. "Efficient Production When Demand is Uncertain" *Journal of Public Economics, 8,* 369-84.

1979. "Existence of a Core When There Are Increasing Returns" *Econometrica, 47,* 869-76.

1981. "Existence of Sustainable Prices for Natural Monopoly Outputs" *Bell Journal of Economics, 12,* 144-54.

1982. "Suggestions for a Game Theoretic Approach for Public Utility Pricing and Cost Allocation" *Bell Journal of Economics, 13,* 57-68.

Sharkey, W. W. and Telser, L. G. 1978. "Supportable Cost Functions for the Multiproduct Firm" *Journal of Economic Theory, 18*, 23-37.

Simon, H. A. 1957. *Models of Man*. New York: Macmillan.

1976. *Administrative Behavior*, 3rd ed. New York: Macmillan.

Skoog, R. A. in press. *Telecommunications Networks: Design and Cost Characteristics*. Englewood Cliffs, NJ: Prentice-Hall.

Spady, R. H. 1979. *Econometric Estimation for the Regulated Transportation Industries*. New York: Garland.

Spence, A. M. 1974. *Market Signaling: Informational Transfer in Hiring and Related Screening Processes*. Cambridge, MA: Harvard University Press.

1977. "Entry, Capacity, Investment, and Oligopolistic Pricing" *Bell Journal of Economics, 8*, 534-44.

1979. "Investment Strategy and Growth in a New Market" *Bell Journal of Economics, 10*, 1-19.

Squire, L. 1973. "Some Aspects of Optimal Pricing for Telecommunications" *Bell Journal of Economics, 4*, 515-25.

Stigler, G. J. 1968. *The Organization of Industry*. Homewood, IL: Irwin.

Stone, R. F., Schankerman, M. A., and Fenton, C. G. 1976. *Selective Competition in the Telephone Industry: An Independent Appraisal Based on Responses to FCC Docket 20003*. Cambridge, MA: T&E.

Sudit, E. F. 1973. "Additive Non-Homogeneous Production Functions in Telecommunications" *Bell Journal of Economics, 4*, 499-514.

Sylos-Labini, P. 1962. *Oligopoly and Technical Progress* (translated from Italian by E. Henderson). Cambridge, MA: Harvard University Press.

Taylor, L. D. 1980. *Telecommunications Demand: A Survey and Critique*. Cambridge, MA: Ballinger.

Teece, D. in press. "Economies of Scope and the Scope of the enterprise" *Journal of Economic Behavior and Organization*.

Telser, L. G. 1966. "Cutthroat Competition and the Long Purse" *Journal of Law and Economics, 9*, 259-77.

1969. "On the Regulation of Industry: A Note" *Journal of Political Economy, 77*, 937-52.

1972. *Competition, Collusion, and Game Theory*. Chicago: Aldine-Atherton.

1978. *Economic Theory and the Core*. Chicago: University of Chicago Press.

1979. "Voting and Paying for Public Goods: An Application of the Theory of the Core" Unpublished manuscript.

ten Raa, T. 1981. "Supportability and Anonymous Equity" Unpublished manuscript.

Topkis, D. M. 1981. "Supermodular Optimization Games" Unpublished manuscript.

Vickrey, W. 1961. "Counterspeculation, Auctions, and Competitive Sealed Tenders" *Journal of Finance, 16*, 8-37.

Vinod, H. D. 1972. "Non-Homogeneous Production Functions and Applications to Telecommunications" *Bell Journal of Economics, 3*, 531-43.

1976a. "Application of New Ridge Regression Methods to a Study of Bell System Scale Economics" *Journal of the American Statistical Association, 71*, 835-41.

1976b. "Bell System Scale Economics and Estimation of Joint Production Functions" Exhibit 59, F.C.C. Docket 20003, Washington, D.C.

Vogelsang, I. and Finsinger, J. 1979. "A Regulatory Adjustment Process for Optimal Pricing by Multiproduct Monopoly Firms" *Bell Journal of Economics, 10*, 157-71.

von Weizsäcker, C. C. 1980a. "A Welfare Analysis of Barriers to Entry" *Bell Journal of Economics*, *11*, 399-420.

1980b. *Barriers to Entry: A Theoretical Treatment*. Berlin: Springer-Verlag.

Waverman, L. 1975. "The Regulation of Intercity Telecommunications" In *Promoting Competition in Regulated Markets*, A. Phillips, ed. Washington, D.C.: Brookings Institution, 201-40.

Williamson, O. E. 1975. *Markets and Hierarchies: Analysis and Antitrust Implications*. New York: Free Press.

1976 "Franchise Bidding for Natural Monopolies - In General and with Respect to CATV" *Bell Journal of Economics*, *7*, 73-104.

1977. "Predatory Pricing: A Strategic and Welfare Analysis" *Yale Law Journal*, *87*, 284.

1979. "Transaction-Cost Economics: The Governance of Contractual Relations" *Journal of Law and Economics*, *22*, 233-62.

Willig, R. D. 1979a. "The Theory of Network Access Pricing" In *Issues in Public Utility Regulation*, H. Trebing, ed. East Lansing, MI: Michigan State University, 109-152.

1979b. "Multi-Product Technology and Market Structure" *American Economic Review*, *69*, 346-51.

1980. "What Can Markets Control?" in *Perspectives on Postal Service Issues*, R. Sherman ed. Washington, D.C.: American Enterprise Institute.

Wilson, R. 1975. "Informational Economics of Scale" *Bell Journal of Economics*, *6*, 184-95.

Yaged, B. 1975. "Economics of Scale, Networks, and Network Cost Elasticity" *IEEE Transactions on Systems, Man, and Cybernetics*, *5*, 30-40.

Zajac, E. E. 1972. "Some Preliminary Thoughts on Subsidization" Proceedings of a Conference on Communication Policy Research, Washington, D.C.

1978. *Fairness or Efficiency: An Introduction to Public Utility Pricing*. Cambridge, MA: Ballinger.

Index

Date Due

JAN 3 1 2007			